Praise for

LEADING IN THE LAW WITH EMOTIONAL INTELLIGENCE

Leading in the Law with Emotional Intelligence is the cutting-edge collaboration of a law professor (and former associate dean) and a psychologist who has established numerous emotional intelligence-based leadership programs (across health systems, government agencies, engineer programs, and law schools). This is a superb book for lawyers, law students, and other professionals on how to build trust, manage conflict, and lead with humility, courage, and emotional intelligence. Emotional intelligence is tied to academic and career success, and EI skills can be taught and learned. The book is interactive, with self-discovery and reflection exercises to cultivate self-awareness, empathy, techniques to manage emotions, and abilities to connect with others. *Leading in the Law with Emotional Intelligence* is a remarkable manual of leadership skills that emphasize collaboration, listening to various perspectives, and developing healthy emotional habits to lead, as Durr and Zimmerman say, "from the inside out."

NANCY LEVIT
Associate Dean for Faculty and Curators' Distinguished Professor
and Edward D. Ellison Professor of Law,
University of Missouri—Kansas City School of Law
Co-author of *The Happy Lawyer: How to Build a Meaningful Life in the Law*

Far from being just another lawyer "self-help" book, this work presents the case for lawyer emotional intelligence based upon rigorous review of academic literature and empirical studies. Written in a straightforward style, the authors draw upon their years of experience teaching and counseling both law students and practitioners to show why emotional intelligence is a critical component of leadership in the law.

DAN BOWLING
Distinguished Fellow at Duke Law School
Former Senior Vice-President of Human Resources,
Coca-Cola Enterprises

In the decade since I took Cliff and Rob's inaugural course, I've consistently reflected on the many ways their teaching has shaped me as a law student, practicing lawyer, husband (to a psychologist, by sheer coincidence), father, and person. I'm very pleased that their crucial lessons and message will be reaching a wider audience. This book should be mandatory reading for law students, lawyers, and for anyone else who wishes to gain a greater understanding of leadership, the many ways that success can be defined, and, most importantly, themselves.

PETER MAYER
Former student and General Counsel, Mustang Litigation Funding

A practical guide that forces lawyers to look inward and practice self-awareness and empathy. Leading in the Law addresses an important topic missing from most legal education: emotional intelligence. A must-read for any lawyer who wants to develop the emotional intelligence necessary to effectively interact with clients, colleagues, witnesses, and judges.

KATHERINE E. RHOADES
Former student and Partner at Bartlit Beck LLP

Lawyers are leaders, and *Leading in the Law with Emotional Intelligence: The Path to Becoming a Twenty-First-Century Leader* is the definitive leadership guide for law students and lawyers alike. The authors clearly and engagingly explain what emotional intelligence is and why it matters more than ever in providing legal services as well as in a lawyer's role as a leader in any capacity—be it in their law firm, on a school board, or in a corporate boardroom. Equally important, the authors provide innumerable insightful examples and potent exercises that guide the reader to build the essential skills of empathic leadership.

MICHAEL T. COLATRELLA JR.
Inaugural Tracy A. Eglet Chair in Alternative Dispute Resolution & Professor of Law; Co-Director, Institute for Law Teaching & Learning, University of the Pacific, McGeorge School of Law

LEADING IN THE LAW → → → → → → → →
→ → → → WITH EMOTIONAL INTELLIGENCE

LEADING IN THE **LAW**

↓

WITH → → →

EMOTIONAL INTELLIGENCE

The Path to Becoming a Twenty-First-Century Leader

ROB DURR, PHD
CLIFF ZIMMERMAN

CAROLINA ACADEMIC PRESS
Durham, North Carolina

LIBRARY OF CONGRESS CATALOGING-IN-PUBLICATION DATA

Names: Durr, Rob, author. | Zimmerman, Cliff, author.
Title: Leading in the law with emotional intelligence : the path to becoming a 21st century leader / Rob Durr & Cliff Zimmerman.
Description: Durham, North Carolina : Carolina Academic Press, 2025. | Includes bibliographical references and index.
Identifiers: LCCN 2024050052 | ISBN 9781531029654 (paperback) | ISBN 9781531029661 (ebook)
Subjects: LCSH: Practice of law--Psychological aspects. | Lawyers--Psychological aspects. | Emotional intelligence.
Classification: LCC K346 .D87 2025 | DDC 340/.19--dc23/eng/20241022
LC record available at https://lccn.loc.gov/2024050052

Carolina Academic Press
700 Kent Street
Durham, North Carolina 27701
(919) 489-7486
www.cap-press.com

Printed in the United States of America

To Dea, for her constant support, reading, and conversations while walking, running, and everywhere else.

—CZ

For Ellie, Claire, and Maisie, who show me how to
feel and lead with love every day,
Lauren, for keeping me grounded and laughing,
And our future leaders, who will lead with heart and curiosity.

—ROB

Contents

Figures and Exercises **xi**

Acknowledgments **xv**

Preface **xvii**
Cliff: The Rocky Road to EI-Based Leadership xvii
Rob: In the EI Carpooling Lane with Cliff xx
Rob and Cliff: Creating an EI Leadership Driver's Manual xxii

Introduction **xxvii**
Research about Law Students, Lawyers, and Success xxix
A Balance in Values xxxi
From Values to Leadership xxxiii

Chapter I → Why Emotional Intelligence Matters for Lawyers **3**
A. Importance of Emotional Intelligence: Research and Academic Curricula 3
B. Legal Education Failing in Emotional Intelligence Nurturing 4
C. Problem—Connection—Solution 5
D. Emotional Intelligence and Leadership 10
E. A Tough Way to Start Law School 13

Chapter II → Understanding Emotional Intelligence: What It Is **19**
A. A Brief Historical Foundation 20
B. Current State of Emotional Intelligence Science: The Top Frameworks 21

C. The Emotional Intelligence Competencies That Matter for Lawyers 22
1. Self-Awareness 23
2. Self-Management 27
3. Social Awareness and Relationship Management 30
D. Strong Emotional Intelligence: Achievement, Performance, and Leadership 35

Chapter III → Know Thyself: Self-Awareness in Legal Practice 39
A. The Two-Branch Model of Self-Awareness 40
1. Deep Insight: Understanding Your Personal Narrative 42
2. Mindfulness: Developing Greater Current-Moment Self-Awareness 58
B. The Power of Psychological Assessment in Gaining Greater Self-Awareness 66

Chapter IV → Self-Management for Lawyers 75
A. Learning When to Brake 78
B. Learning How to Brake 80
C. Regulating Attention, Psychologically Speaking 83
D. Strengthening Self-Management 92
1. Explanatory Style 92
2. Resilience 94
3. Cognitive Interaction 95
4. Do You Have a Mantra? 105
5. Adaptability 106
6. Achievement Orientation 108
7. Positive Outlook 110
E. Finding Happiness 113
1. Lawyer (Un)happiness 113
2. Happiness Advantage 114
3. Boosting Your Mood 116

Chapter V → The Empathic Lawyer 121
A. Moving to Empathy 121
1. Visualizing How Emotional Intelligence Leads to Empathy 121
2. Overcoming Mental Heuristics 124

3. Embracing Social Awareness 126
B. Clarifying Empathy 128
1. Empathy versus Sympathy 128
2. Empathy and Lawyers 130
3. Empathy and Relationship Management 133
C. Building Empathy 134
1. Hurdles to Building Empathy That Are Unique to the Legal Field 135
2. Steps to Building Empathy 136
3. Five Practices of Empathy Empowerment 137
D. Applying Empathy 160
1. From the Content to the Dynamic 161
2. From Empathy to Loving-Kindness 162

Chapter VI → Relationship Management 171
A. The Social Nature of Humans and Loneliness 174
1. Social Capital and the American Deficit 174
2. Social Isolation and the Pandemic 176
3. Link Between Relationships and Happiness/ Health/Success 179
B. From Emotional Intelligence to Social Intelligence 180
1. Self-Awareness of Your Beliefs about Relationships 180
2. Self-Awareness of Your Personality Traits 184
C. The Four-Stage Model of Relationship Management 188
1. Identifying Stage 188
2. Initiating Stage 190
3. Developing Stage 193
4. Collaborating Stage 194
5. Recap of the Stages 196
D. Building Trust 197
1. Trust Models 199
2. Multicultural Leadership 201
3. Trust and Virtual Teams 212
4. Building Community and Relationships Post-Pandemic 215
E. Working on Teams 216
1. Benefits of Working in Groups 217
2. Concerns about Teamwork—Debunked 219
3. MBTI® and Team Relationships 224

F. Managing Conflict 226
1. Positive Contribution of Conflict 226
2. Conflict Management and EI Skills 227
3. Application of EI Skills as Conflict Management 228
G. Conclusion: The Two Faces of Empathy in Relationship Management 230

Chapter VII → Emotionally Intelligent Leadership: Filling the Gap in Twenty-First-Century Leadership 233
A. Clarifying What We Mean by *Leadership* 238
1. Emotional Intelligence and Organizational Culture 238
2. The Ubiquity of Leadership 241
3. Varied and Authentic Leadership Styles 244
B. The State of Leadership Theory: Lessons from One Hundred Years of Research 247
1. Authentic Leadership Theory 247
2. Resonant Leadership Theory 249
3. Combination of Theories 249
C. Leading in the Law with Emotional Intelligence: The Twenty-First-Century Leadership Profile 249
1. Humility 251
2. Integrity 258
3. Values 260
4. Professional Identity 262
5. Vulnerability (Comfort with Discomfort) 262
6. Courage 264
7. Trust 265
D. The Path Forward as a Twenty-First-Century Leader 268

Endnotes 271

Index 293

About the Authors 297

Figures and Exercises

FIGURES

FIGURE 1 The Emotional and Social Competency Framework 23
FIGURE 2 Self-Awareness Balance 61
FIGURE 3 Personality Type Self-Assessment 71
FIGURE 4 The Emotional and Social Competency Framework 78
FIGURE 5 Modal Model of Emotion 86
FIGURE 6 Five Families of Emotion-Regulation Strategies 89
FIGURE 7 ABCs of Human Functioning 98
FIGURE 8 The Emotional and Social Competency Framework 127
FIGURE 9 The Emotional and Social Competency Framework 158
FIGURE 10 Cyclical Nature of EI Domain Interactions 187
FIGURE 11 Four Stages of Relationship Development 189
FIGURE 12 The Five Dysfunctions of a Team 200
FIGURE 13 Twenty-First-Century Leadership Profile 237
FIGURE 14 Twenty-First-Century Leadership Profile 250

SELF-DISCOVERY EXERCISES

SELF-DISCOVERY EXERCISE 1 Best Boss xxxv
Reflection on Self-Discovery Exercise 1 xxxvi
SELF-DISCOVERY EXERCISE 2 On Stressors 14
Reflection on Self-Discovery Exercise 2 15
SELF-DISCOVERY EXERCISE 3 Goals for Improvement 37
SELF-DISCOVERY EXERCISE 4 Passion Mapping 53

SELF-DISCOVERY EXERCISE 5 Your MBTI® Personality Type 72
SELF-DISCOVERY EXERCISE 6 I Tend to . . . 85
Reflection on Self-Discovery Exercise 6 86
Review of Self-Discovery Exercise 6 and Subsequent Reflection 88
SELF-DISCOVERY EXERCISE 7 Explanatory Style Self-Test 94
SELF-DISCOVERY EXERCISE 8 Self-Management 97
SELF-DISCOVERY EXERCISE 9 Doing the ABCs 99
SELF-DISCOVERY EXERCISE 10 Creating a Thought Record 103
SELF-DISCOVERY EXERCISE 11 What's Your Mantra? 106
SELF-DISCOVERY EXERCISE 12 What Makes You Happy? 116
SELF-DISCOVERY EXERCISE 13 Happiness at Work 118
SELF-DISCOVERY EXERCISE 14 Thinking about Empathy 134
SELF-DISCOVERY EXERCISE 15 Being Curious 143
Reflection on Self-Discovery Exercise 15 143
SELF-DISCOVERY EXERCISE 16 Just Like Me and Loving-Kindness Mindfulness 163
SELF-DISCOVERY EXERCISE 17 What's Their Problem? 163
Reflection on Self-Discovery Exercise 18 181
SELF-DISCOVERY EXERCISE 18 Your Relationship with Relationships 181
SELF-DISCOVERY EXERCISE 19 Self-Awareness of Social Savvy 183
Reflection on Self-Discovery Exercise 19 183
SELF-DISCOVERY EXERCISE 20 Self-Awareness of Personality Traits 185
SELF-DISCOVERY EXERCISE 21 Exploring the Four Stages 197
SELF-DISCOVERY EXERCISE 22 Rating Self-Awareness 204
SELF-DISCOVERY EXERCISE 23 Know Your Biases 208
SELF-DISCOVERY EXERCISE 24 Knowledge of Others 210
SELF-DISCOVERY EXERCISE 25 Your Team Experience 223
SELF-DISCOVERY EXERCISE 26 Your Personality Type and Teams 225
SELF-DISCOVERY EXERCISE 27 Cultural Identifiers 241
SELF-DISCOVERY EXERCISE 28 Firm Values 254
SELF-DISCOVERY EXERCISE 29 Finding Humility 257
SELF-DISCOVERY EXERCISE 30 Find Your Ideal Self 261
SELF-DISCOVERY EXERCISE 31 My Legacy 261
SELF-DISCOVERY EXERCISE 32 Writing a Growth Contract for Yourself 269

REFLECTIVE WRITING

REFLECTIVE WRITING 1 xxxvi
REFLECTIVE WRITING 2 17
REFLECTIVE WRITING 3 38
REFLECTIVE WRITING 4 57
REFLECTIVE WRITING 5 65
REFLECTIVE WRITING 6 72
REFLECTIVE WRITING 7 84
REFLECTIVE WRITING 8 91
REFLECTIVE WRITING 9 105
REFLECTIVE WRITING 10 110
REFLECTIVE WRITING 11 114
REFLECTIVE WRITING 12 118
REFLECTIVE WRITING 13 146
REFLECTIVE WRITING 14 149
REFLECTIVE WRITING 15 152
REFLECTIVE WRITING 16 164
REFLECTIVE WRITING 17 168
REFLECTIVE WRITING 18 168
REFLECTIVE WRITING 19 209
REFLECTIVE WRITING 20 211
REFLECTIVE WRITING 21 224
REFLECTIVE WRITING 22 245

Acknowledgments

All books are the product of teamwork and we have had an incredible team who shared ideas, gave critical feedback, did great research, edited our words to sound better, worked on graphics, and pulled it all together in the end to produce this book. We want to acknowledge all (hopefully leaving no one out), particularly given the length of this project. We are deeply aware that we could not have done this without you and hope that we can add at least as much support to your ventures.

Hundreds of Northwestern Law students have taken the leadership course, in which they read predecessors of these chapters and completed early variations of these exercises. Thanks to all of the students we have taught and interacted with over the years. Your engagement and responses to the materials have been both inspiring and critical to the adaptations over time. During her first year of law school, Deidra McCall (JD '23) stepped forward to contribute the first student research to the project. Subsequently, Gabriella Goldstein (JD '25), Sarah Norise (JD '24), Michael Pranger (JD '23), Scott Shimizu (JD '24), and Elise Wu (JD '23) provided excellent research as we changed and updated the chapters. Aly Hiller (JD '25) took the research to a higher level and helped us get the project across the finish line. We are deeply grateful to all of you.

The work of several individuals has been inspirational to us in the project. Specifically, the research and thinking of Ken Sheldon, Larry Krieger, Richard Boyatzis, Annie McKee, Bill George, Dan Goleman, and Len Riskin have kept us grounded while opening doors for us to move forward. Thank you for your pathbreaking work, a level of achievement that we aspire to here.

We have greatly benefited from the administrative support of Shona Bonds and Jazzma Pryor at Northwestern. Sheila Sybrant's editing has made this manuscript more readable than we ever could have done on our own. Meg Mitchell at CAP loved the book idea from our very first conversation on the topic and shepherded us through the publication process where Scott Sipe provided key support to us as well. Surely many others, unknown to us, at CAP made it all work right as well. We are deeply grateful to all of you.

Many other Northwestern University colleagues supported the development of a for-credit course in higher education on emotional intelligence that laid the groundwork for this book and the course it is based on. Specifically, Wei-Jen Huang's passion for emotional intelligence and insights helped Rob's initial thinking on the topic, and Joe Holtgrieve, Assistant Dean for Undergraduate Engineering, and David Shor, Staff Psychologist at Northwestern in Counseling and Psychological Services (CAPS), both opened doors for what became the Leading in the Law course in the law school. Any and all errors are our own.

Preface

This book grew out of our work together in the Dean of Students' office at a Top 10 law school. As the dean of students (Cliff) and a licensed psychologist (Rob), we were charged with the mission of helping to equip law students with the essential life skills necessary to make it through law school and sustain a balanced and ethical legal career—to achieve success and thrive in the profession.

The origins of our collective experiences, which aided our work, go back a bit further than our time at Northwestern Pritzker School of Law. Our journey, apart and together, has been one of adventure and discovery. And in this book we share the road map with you to guide you on the path to leading in the law with emotional intelligence (EI) in the twenty-first century.

CLIFF:
THE ROCKY ROAD TO EI-BASED LEADERSHIP

In 2004, I became the associate dean and dean of students at Northwestern Law, a top law school with an accomplished faculty and alumni. Prior to that role, which is unmistakably one of leadership, I had little awareness of having any particular leadership skills or holding a meaningful leadership role. I had been a civil litigator in a small private practice, then a law teacher. I had received some training in the Myers-Briggs Type Indicator® (MBTI®), a personality assessment of unconscious preferences. I had briefly held the position of academic counselor in the law school. But none of these positions or trainings included substantive training or experience in leadership.

While problem-solving and strategic and analytical thinking skills from law school were beneficial, these planning and implementation skills and experiences have their limits. Thus, at the start of my time as associate dean and dean of students at Northwestern Law, I managed the job not necessarily spectacularly but certainly well enough. I welcomed the responsibility, perhaps taking on matters that were beyond my legal training. Legal training, as I understood it, meant that I could handle pretty much anything that came through the door. In private practice, however, I learned limits, sending the tax matters to a tax lawyer and the cases that were beyond my expertise to an expert in that area. In contrast, student problem-solving in an academic institution is the responsibility of the people in charge of the institution, and I was the one with direct responsibility for them. Not surprisingly, then, in the first few years, I made some mistakes and sometimes focused in the wrong places. But all in all, I competently did the job—lots of perspiration, some inspiration, and a decent scorecard for the job.

This felt right and comfortable until the tide of students struggling with law school and self-care reached a point where I recognized that my legal training and problem-solving skills no longer helped me or the students. Whether this was a change in the students or greater recognition on my part and the profession's awareness of the importance of psychological health, I could not say; but the trends became clearer, and my acuity for what I could and could not do in this realm became greater. In particular, more and more students with weakening or compromised mental health were coming into the office, and there was a simultaneous push for "practice-ready" graduates at the conclusion of law school. To be sure, most high-performing, highly successful, highly motivated students work past the basic anxiety and lowered self-esteem that comes with the first year of law school and are loath to attribute failings (lowercase *f*) to anything or anyone but themselves. I had been able to distinguish the serious (sent to counseling services) from the manageable (dealt with by me or my staff), but the balance was shifting fast under my feet. Part of the problem was my lack of training and expertise in psychology and counseling, and part was in the institutional counseling services being spread across a variety of schools within the university, each with very different needs and challenges. Top students were struggling with the impact of legal education on their ability to learn, and I needed help.

This challenge has been widely recognized in legal academia. Researchers have identified how legal education replaces students' intrinsic values (such as honesty, integrity, humility, self-care, family and other relations) with extrinsic values (such as money, prestige, and achievements)—with the result being reduced self-esteem, poor mental health (and increased anxiety and depression), and a decline in performance. But the concern is not just that some students have mental health concerns that are exacerbated in law school. Many students go to law school with strong mental and physical health and then become susceptible to the same mental health concerns either due to the rigor and demands of law school or because the displacement of their intrinsic values with extrinsic ones has a significant and detrimental impact on their self-worth, identity, and purpose.

My own journey through law school was marked by some of the struggles I was seeing in the students. No one in my family had gone to law school, so I knew little of what I was getting into or how and what to get out of it. I had no family financial support, so the cost of the venture, the debt incurred, and the pressures of those weights were on me alone. I also felt so alienated in the first year (1L) that I seriously considered leaving after the year was done. I only decided to stay after sage friends suggested that I take it one step at a time. That first step I took was working in a law school clinic during my first summer. What I did not realize then but know now is that the experiential learning brought out and developed key EI skills in me—validating the need for self-awareness and recognizing and building my empathy in particular. (These are two of four key domains in emotional intelligence, all of which will be explained in the chapters that follow.) Those 1L feelings and experiences were so strong that they remain with me to this day.

If I was going to be able to do the dean of students job that I had been hired to do, then I had to get help in this realm. I understood exactly what the research said and needed someone who understood what happens in the law school and in legal education to address the issues of law students. That person could work with the university's counseling and psychological services in the health center, but that person also had to work very closely with me to understand what they were dealing with and how to present a unified approach. That person would have to be physically in the law school to see students individually, in groups, and in larger gatherings, as well as at critical times like the start of the semester and during exams and on-campus interviewing—all of which would go a long way toward bringing balance to the students and helping them through law school.

Northwestern Law needed a dedicated psychologist, someone who would understand the students for who they are: a unique group of high-achieving individuals who were now in an ultra-intense and competitive environment; a diverse group hoping to enter what is still a very homogenous profession; and a young, idealistic, equity-driven group entering a world defined by events that most of us see as changes. It would take a team to address those students who were reeling under the pressures. Little did I know, at that time, that the team would then also ensure that everyone could understand the interconnected impact of legal education, debt, and mental health and well-being in the positive framework of leadership.

With this general research and after gathering specific data and trends on Northwestern Law students, I negotiated and lobbied for and then got the green light to hire a staff psychologist who would be both a member of the university's Counseling and Psychological Services (CAPS) team and dedicated to learning about and serving the law school population. From the hiring process, my team identified Rob as the best candidate, and our working relationship began.

ROB: IN THE EI CARPOOLING LANE WITH CLIFF

Being Northwestern Law's dedicated psychologist was a dream job for me. To have the opportunity to help hundreds of law students overcome psychological hurdles on an individual level while developing broader wellness programming in such an important profession was truly one of the greatest honors in my career. While I always valued the individual work, I entered the role with an eye toward expanding the notion of wellness services to include leadership, career development, and success.

My path to becoming a psychologist was defined by a life-changing experience of my own. I had participated in a semester-long National Outdoor Leadership School (NOLS) wilderness expedition during my sophomore year of college that entailed spending roughly one hundred days straight in the wilderness. I have always been introspective and questioned deep existential realities, such as the meaning of life and purpose. As a freshman in college, I recognized the gravity of career decision-making and the importance of finding a calling as I navigated the multitude of career paths and choices and recognized the weight of everyone in my life asking me, "What do you want to do with your life?" (i.e., "What are you going to major in?"). During that time period, I came to recognize the significance of finding a calling, a career path, that would provide meaning and a sense of purpose. I recognized that so much of a person's life and identity is determined by what they do for work, and as I grappled with that decision myself, felt the weight of it, and worked through it on the NOLS course, I found psychology and a love for helping others grow as leaders—a passion for helping others find a meaningful and balanced career of their own.

I spent the next decade earning a doctorate in psychology and learning the essential skills and practices that it takes not only to help others find a meaningful career path but also to help them thrive as leaders in all parts of their lives and attain success. I also grew passionate about helping specific professions identify and overcome the inherent challenges in their vocations. My research on career development, psychology, and leadership revealed that the same essential psychological and behavioral habits underlie mental health, career advancement and success, and exceptional leadership; that they ultimately fall under the EI umbrella; and that they can be developed in school simultaneously as students learn the intellectual and technical skills that they need to succeed.

My background in leadership and psychological health led to the realization that these two key differentiating factors of success in the legal profession share the same underlying mental and behavioral habits: in other words, wellness and leadership are intricately connected. By developing emotional intelligence during law school, graduates would be practice-ready to lead and find a balanced, sustainable approach to their legal careers. So when the Northwestern Law psychologist position was posted, I leaped at the opportunity to extend my work to another profession.

Even before joining Northwestern Law, I recognized the pioneering potential in this work. My private leadership consulting practice was already flourishing in business and medicine, and I knew that the legal profession was years if not decades behind these professions in incorporating psychological science and leadership development into training. I had successfully established mindfulness, EI-based leadership programs in a large health system, a state department of transportation, and the school of engineering at Northwestern. (The EI course for Northwestern's engineering school, a version of which is still offered to this day for all incoming Northwestern undergraduate students, was developed in collaboration with a dean in engineering and another psychologist at Northwestern.) I witnessed the power of emotional intelligence for physicians and engineers in rounding out their professional skills. These proactive methods to reach students who were not coming in of their own volition was a clear need and I thought that Cliff and I could build on those ideas in the law school setting. Initially, the course idea seemed nebulous to Cliff, and he pushed me to focus on more immediate needs.

Once in the role, I saw firsthand that many high-achieving students (and lawyers for that matter) were not seeking out mental health services for myriad reasons, and I recognized that various factors both in an individual's culture and within the culture of legal education often prevent lawyers from seeking help. Like all professional groups, law students and lawyers are interested in leadership and success, and if the skills needed to stay psychologically healthy could be incorporated into programs targeting these outcomes, I knew that I could reach far more students. I quickly realized that the answer was a for-credit "leadership course"—not waiting around in the clinic for students to find me once they were struggling.

ROB AND CLIFF: CREATING AN EI LEADERSHIP DRIVER'S MANUAL

Rob had built his programming and continually raised the prospect of developing a course that would be preventative, business-savvy, and grounded in empirical research from diverse fields including business, psychology, and neuroscience. We talked more and more specifically about what such a course would look like in the law school. Over time, the idea began to clarify and crystallize.

Through our conversations about the course and its components, Cliff came to realize (and make sense of) much about himself, his path, and his choices. For example, Rob's affinity for mindfulness gave Cliff a name for something that he had practiced, most intensely as a runner. Our conversations about planning, programming, and teaching brought to light the key aspects of personal values—something that also had been at the heart of Cliff's work but without a framework. For example, Cliff's decision that he could not manage the evolving student issues at Northwestern Law was tied to humility. His earlier decisions to go to and then stay in law school despite the alienation and mounting debt were driven by independence. And his caring ethic was pure empathy, and it defined not only his current work but also many of his job changes preceding his current role. Above all else, our conversations made Cliff more aware, or self-aware, of what he was thinking and feeling both in the moment and deeply—respectively, mindfulness and personal narrative or identity. This resonated deeply within Cliff as he began to see connections that he had not understood. He wondered, "What if I had understood those powerful aspects of self-awareness when I was in law school?"

At the same time that we were developing the course, we worked with thousands of students, addressing individual student issues, creating individualized plans for students, and developing community-wide programs presented at key points (orientation, exams, grade distribution, and on-campus interviewing). While attending to all students, we saw that the students who struggled more through law school lacked in areas that came naturally to outstanding students. However, it was not about their IQ or LSAT scores. This struggle was not with the cognitive skills that the legal field regards so highly. Instead, it had to do with well-being and being "well-rounded." Time and again, the students who ended up in our offices lacked emotional and social skills. (These experiences and others provide the basis for some of the anonymized vignettes that appear throughout this book.) Rob provided Cliff with the connection between psychological health and leadership, as well as the research in psychology, business, leadership, and organizational behavior identifying the distinguishing factor for these professionals as the lack of EI skills.[1]

As we discussed the leadership course, Cliff came to realize that what made him an effective leader (as reported to him by others) in the office and in the law school community was living and working his values: honesty, integrity, humility, empathy, a willingness to be vulnerable about his own experiences, and, above all else, the moment-to-moment and deep self-awareness of these values so that he could act on them. He also came to realize that he had taken the next step as well in creating time and space to understand his own emotions and act in an intentional way with that understanding. His leadership ability was almost completely attributable to a growing or high level of emotional intelligence—the core of the course that we were constructing.

With the understanding that these skills and competencies are visible, tangible, trainable, and measurable—and with Rob's clarity that the course had to be based on emotional intelligence—we developed one of the first EI-based leadership courses for law students: called "Leading in the Law;" it has been offered for credit since 2014. The course elevates students' ability to see themselves as leaders—of the legal community and of themselves—and to see the importance and value in having a high degree of self-awareness to get there. Growing their self-awareness is integral to students' avoiding and addressing the inherent pressures in legal education and properly assessing and addressing the wave of extrinsic values placed before them—which enables them to make the right decisions for themselves. Countless students have benefited in their law school careers and beyond. Luckily for them, the key habits and skills needed to achieve success (however it is defined) also lead to psychological health.

We have taught the course consistently since then and in a variety of formats, even as our lives and careers changed. Rob left his full-time position at Northwestern Law to develop a wide-ranging practice with a focus on leadership consulting and psychological assessment while maintaining his adjunct faculty role to teach the course. His methods use and build on the content of the course. In 2017, Cliff returned to teaching full-time and expanded the range of his courses, all the while bringing many of the methods here into his pedagogy. Through all of these changes, our focus on how EI competencies lead to strong leadership in both the law and life has remained constant.

↑ ↓ ↑

As we taught the course, we found that others' materials did not match our needs, so we used our course materials to create this book. In this book, we draw on our research and experiences to share how you can incorporate emotional intelligence into your personal and professional life and be a strong and effective leader in the twenty-first century.

We anticipate that you are investing in this book either to gain or hone your leadership skills or to explore the benefits of emotional intelligence in your life and career, or because you understand the importance of intrinsic values and recognize that your happiness and success require something more. We are with you for any of these reasons, as well as others that may apply.

One of our guiding values is generativity—the willingness to open doors for others, to make their journey smoother, and to inspire positive change. Thus, this book is about trying to make the profession better through the addition of each new generation of lawyers by assisting global efforts in making the law more humanistic and collaborative, as these virtues will always win over the traditional adversarial approach. This book and its individualized exploration through self-discovery and reflection exercises will help you, whether you are a law student or a lawyer, to develop a high(er) degree of self-awareness, to manage your emotions in making difficult decisions, and to understand (empathize) and resonate with others—thus finding your leadership skills to address the challenges of the twenty-first century.

Other core values for us are love and family. They have driven our respective career decisions: Cliff left the regular practice of law and shifted into teaching, and Rob focused his practice and leadership in Asheville, North Carolina, where his family is centered. Our core values underlie and connect to just about every decision we make in our lives. We hope that is clear in our actions and aids today's lawyers in deciding their paths as well.

ROB & CLIFF
JANUARY 2025

Introduction

What makes an effective leader? And what will make you an effective leader? While we mean *leader* in the traditional sense (the head of an organization or group of individuals) and in the lateral sense (people who step into guiding or directing roles in groups or teams), we also aim to expand your notion of leadership to include *leading in your life* to self-actualize and attain your goals. We came to answer these questions indirectly when we sought to answer a different one: "What do law students and lawyers need to succeed?" In discovering the answer to this latter question, we uncovered a strategy to enable you to develop your leadership skills for the professional and personal challenges of the twenty-first century.

Our purpose in writing this book is to aid you in achieving success and well-being—in law school, in the traditional practice of law, or in roles and organizations beyond—by helping you to develop and strengthen a clear set of skills best defined as emotional intelligence, or EI. By *emotional intelligence*, we mean a deep self-awareness and empathy, a strong resonance with others, and a self-understanding that drives one's purpose. Through learning about emotional intelligence and its component domains of self-awareness, self-management, social awareness, and relationship management, you will improve client service, personal well-being, and your relationships within organizations and institutions. Thus, the EI skills* described in the following chapters hold the

* We use the terms *skills* and *competencies* interchangeably to describe the parts of emotional intelligence that are teachable, learnable, and growable within you.

power to make a tremendous impact in your life as a law student, a practicing attorney, and a human being.

Over the years, we came to see this happen in real time during our leadership course and in consulting with legal professionals. First, a student leader responsible for enforcing the rules shared how she applied her newly developed self-awareness and self-management skills in dealing with a member who was not fulfilling their obligations; she used these skills to pause and find out what was really going on before deciding whether to discipline or give grace in this particular situation (rather than just deciding to punish, which is what she would have done prior to taking the course). This student leader learned vital information that helped her to frame a solution that got the work done and preserved a good relationship. A couple of years later, when we taught the course over winter break, several students came to our final class session with stories about how their self-awareness and empathy had allowed them to have better conversations with friends and family over the holidays (a time when conversations can sour quickly). Then we saw our students come to view each other in new ways: in one case, after participating in in-class sharing sessions that provided the opportunity to watch each other develop relationship-building abilities, one outgoing journal leader saw how a class member would be very capable of stepping into that same position the following year. And, finally, a practicing lawyer/client shared how, after talking with his spouse about empathic curiosity, the couple elevated their end-of-the-day conversations to better understand what the other was dealing with, which inherently deepened their relationship.

Thus, because of our personal experiences with law students and lawyers and a century's worth of research in the field of leadership, we now know that these central leadership skills and practices can be developed. We have found that law students and lawyers who are able to do this exhibit a different kind of leadership—one based in self-leadership with emotional intelligence at the core.

Learning this type of leadership is particularly important for you as law students and lawyers because life in our post-pandemic world can feel isolated and factionalized. Ultimately, leadership is about your ability to build connections with others—seeing others, finding their true potential, and helping them to see it as well—and how you make them feel in the process. Leadership requires seeing others' strengths and virtues, developing relationships that allow them to see their best selves, and inspiring them to become leaders in their own ways. The best leaders provide a mirror for others to see their own potential, to start to believe in themselves, and to find the motivation and courage to self-actualize—that is, to become their best selves and reach their greatest potential, both professionally and personally.

On your journey so far, you have probably encountered one or more of these leaders—people who inspired you, who really saw your gifts and virtues, who helped you believe in that version of yourself, and whose experiences influenced your own skills and values. This book outlines your next journey: one of self-discovery as a leader. The exercises, information, and legal application of material from fields as diverse as business, psychology, and medicine will equip you with the skills necessary to sustain happiness, develop rich relationships, and lead in the law in the twenty-first century.

RESEARCH ABOUT LAW STUDENTS, LAWYERS, AND SUCCESS

At this point, we need to unpack some paradoxes in legal education and the legal profession. Everyone enters law school with strong cognitive skills. Most admissions processes focus to a great degree on the measures of those skills as found in LSAT (or GRE) scores and GPA numbers, and to a lesser degree as reflected in interviews and essays. However, although the American Bar Association[1] has suggested that law schools assess emotional intelligence in the admissions process, an extensive law school search reveals that few, if any, currently do so.[2] This is so despite employers and clients expecting lawyers to have, in addition to critical cognitive skills, the skills to remain poised under immense pressure: they want lawyers who listen to their clients' needs, who strongly empathize to help meet those needs, who resonate with others, and who are aware of and able to regulate their own emotions so that when clients pay for the lawyer's services, they receive 100 percent of their lawyer's time and effort. These EI-related expectations make sense because, as confirmed by a meta-analysis (a summary of the research on a given topic), emotionally intelligent people perform better in their jobs.[3] Although all of these expectations implicate strong EI skills (and strong cognitive skills), these EI skills are only partially captured in high LSATs and GPAs.

While superior cognitive or intellectual abilities, legal knowledge, and hard work are necessary just to get in the game, key ingredients of success and performance are often left to fate to develop. Indeed, research shows that, roughly, only 15 percent of success is determined by intellectual abilities or technical skills and knowledge.[4] This suggests that 85 percent of what determines your happiness and success is outside of what you learned in law school. And chances are you feel this and know it to be true. So, what makes up over three-quarters of your success and happiness? Research suggests that much of it falls into the *how* and *why* of living. It's about how you approach and respond to the work that matters. Research suggests quite clearly that success and happiness for lawyers, and for people generally, has as much (if not more) to do with social and emotional intelligence as it does with legal knowledge and cognitive intelligence.

What happens, then, in law school is far from surprising and quite troubling. Legal education includes an approach that wears down individuality, undermines self-esteem, increases stress and anxiety, and escalates mental health concerns—and yet lawyers shaped by this approach are regularly promoted into leadership positions not only in the profession but also in business and government. Those who successfully navigate (and survive) both the education and profession are examples for all, but they represent only a fraction of those with the potential to bring their problem-solving and analytical skills to bear on the challenges of society and the world. If the process has worn them down and stripped them of their values, and if their primary motivation is personal gain, then they will bring little or no authenticity or resonance to their work as leaders.

Studies by Larry Krieger and Ken Sheldon, and by Jerome Organ, David Jaffe, and Katherine Bender, show that shortly after starting law school, a large portion of students experience diminished social, mental, and emotional well-being, and the incidence of depression and substance abuse rises dramatically.[5] Other studies show that depression and substance abuse continue into practice.[6] These studies identify as particular causes of these changes the replacement of law students' and lawyers' intrinsic motivations and values, which are healthy and sustaining, by extrinsic motivators that can be difficult to quantify and meet, particularly when amplified by the perfectionistic tendencies of many law students and lawyers. This research is supported by self-determination theory, one of the oldest theories on motivation in psychology, which posits that one will be far more motivated when driven by intrinsic as opposed to extrinsic factors.[7] As a limited example, law students' intrinsic values, such as a passion and drive for justice and fairness, are displaced by extrinsic values, such as economic gain, career achievement, and other rewards (journal editorial roles, leadership positions, and awards) along the way.[8] These extrinsic values are moving goalposts that students can easily and continually push further and further away as they achieve their goals, a process that amplifies mental health issues because it makes success seem tenuous.

A BALANCE IN VALUES

These extrinsic values are not inherently bad. It is OK to want to earn money, achieve promotions, and attain select positions in law school and life. But if extrinsic values come to replace your cherished intrinsic values and cannot be met or fully satisfied (for example, 90 percent of the students cannot be in the top 10 percent of the class), then you may feel personally challenged in ways that you have never been before. If not handled well, such challenges can negatively impact your physical and emotional well-being and, ultimately, your performance and success throughout your legal career. The door is then open to the development of negative personal habits and characteristics that could lead to divisive relationships, mental health concerns, or substance abuse.

The shift from intrinsic to extrinsic motivators occurs inherently in legal education. Students are encouraged to begin thinking about extrinsic motivators during their first semester: the first-year law student faces pressure to think about potential leads on summer associate positions for the next summer, their class rank, and which legal journal to serve on. All of these are presented as being dependent upon first-semester grades, and all are a means to receiving accolades and more. These established traditions in legal education are like dangling succulent fruit, enticing achievement-oriented law students to switch their focus away from the passionate intrinsic motivators that brought them to law school and toward an external and often shallower focus. In contrast, in the same time frame, doctoral and medical students become deeply engaged not only in learning and reading but also in pursuing their interests while developing a course of study based almost entirely on their intrinsic passions, interests, and values.

The replacement of intrinsic values with extrinsic ones also has broader implications. By instilling and elevating the importance of extrinsic gains in a zero-sum space, legal education displaces strong, preexisting skills and values, such as empathy, diversity and inclusion, equity, cultural competence, and social justice. It takes great personal will to maintain empathy (a capacity that can wax and wane) when first-year grades are on a rigid curve. The purity of learning, which flourishes in sharing ideas and solutions, can be clouded by a selfish desire to not want to help others to succeed—and surely you have heard stories of law students' trying to figure out who should be marginalized so that they get the low grades. To be blunt, these are not intellectually, socially, or emotionally healthy approaches to living, learning, lawyering, or leadership. Thus, we join you in search of the alternative: leading yourself and others with strong emotional intelligence.

Success requires personal dedication to a cause greater than yourself and relentless adherence to your core values in life and work; it comes when you passionately follow your interests and live your values. This can be more difficult than it sounds, especially when you grew up in an educational system and larger ecosystem that perpetually rewarded extrinsic accomplishments. The difficulty increases when you know what you are interested in, care about, find meaningful, and value and yet are continuously bombarded with complex and competing social, emotional, and career data. Answering the age-old question "Who are you?" can be quite challenging indeed, but doing so is nevertheless a prerequisite for developing strong, sustainable emotional intelligence. When you follow your authentic interests and abide by your values, happiness and success ensue. The key differentiating questions then become "How do you develop your interests and find your calling or purpose?" and "How do you become the leader of others and yourself?"

Specifically, the key skills necessary to strike a healthy balance between intrinsic and extrinsic values lie in self-awareness and self-management, two cornerstones of emotional intelligence and of benefit to all law students and lawyers. Emotionally intelligent lawyers are keenly aware of what is driving them and of the complex interplay between their emotional reactions, cognitions (internal narratives), and actions. Emotional intelligence provides the tools necessary for law students and lawyers to retain their deeply held intrinsic values while simultaneously (and healthily) pursuing extrinsic add-ons.

Fortunately, even if law schools do not screen for emotional intelligence in the law school admissions process, law students and lawyers can still build and develop their EI skills no matter where they are in their academic or professional careers. The key is that both the individual and the organization must value developing and enhancing the individual's EI skills.

FROM VALUES TO LEADERSHIP

Let's reframe the paradox described above as you transition into the heart of this book. Law students today bring with them a world of difference from almost every lawyer who is teaching or practicing. Today's students grew up against the backdrop of wars in Iraq and Afghanistan and view them as formative life events; have only ever known the ubiquity of technology; have always had a wealth of information (and its overwhelming nature) at their fingertips; have witnessed the normalization of incivility in American politics and lives; keenly feel the existential nature of the climate crisis; have been disproportionately impacted in certain ways by the COVID-19 pandemic; are accustomed to there being dissonance between what is true and what is fake; and are now having to contend with the growth of artificial intelligence (which can exacerbate a number of the other issues on this list). Lawyers who are even just a bit older view these events as *changes* from the past and not necessarily how the world works. This gap is both generational (in the typical sense) and stark (atypical if one thinks about the dramatic difference between the role of technology and information in the early twenty-first century versus the latter part of the twentieth century).[9] The stark nature of this gap means that current leaders in the legal community need to be aware of and responsive to the changes in who is entering law school and, in turn, entering the legal profession.[10] If the legal profession and its members are to grow and progress, its leaders need to be compassionate, empathetic, and self-aware—what we call *twenty-first century leaders.*

"Exercise" Your Leadership Potential

With that framing, let's talk about your self-discovery journey and exercises (not the kind that make you sweat—we promise!). This introduction and the chapters that follow each contain self-discovery exercises (followed by reflections on those exercises) and/or reflective writing exercises. These exercises include thought-provoking questions and journal prompts to help you develop emotional and social intelligence.

For these exercises, take out a piece of paper or open a new Word document and answer the prompts. Make sure to write out your responses. There is something irreplaceable about putting pen to paper (or fingers to keyboard). We recommend that you invest in an EI leadership development journal or notebook—a dedicated space to write your thoughts and responses. We know what you are thinking: "Really? A journal." But trust us, research is clear that if you really want to evolve as a leader, you must start with deep self-reflection, which is best achieved through thinking and writing so you can flex the brain regions necessary for insight. Having it all in one place can be a great way to grow and reflect on that growth!

We include reflective writing exercises in particular because reflection is a key aspect of learning. These exercises require taking time and space to consider what you are thinking about as you learn and recording those thoughts in a written format. Once you start to write, do not worry about "answering" the questions or about the length of your responses. In other words, you do not necessarily have to address every question directly, particularly if your answers to the questions coalesce into an otherwise thoughtful essay. Note that reflective writing is not concerned with characteristics found in typical written projects, such as structure, word or page limits, themes, and grammatical perfection. You know that phrase "Dance like no one is watching"? Well, just write and don't overthink it.

The following are tips for writing a reflective paper:

→ Choose a quiet space.
→ Clear and focus your mind on the prompt(s).
→ Write the first things that come to your mind.
→ Keep writing until you have emptied your mind of your thoughts.
→ Do not think.
→ Do not judge.
→ If you get stuck, write "I feel stuck." Keep writing.
→ You will know when you are done.

So we'll begin here with exercises related to leadership. These exercises will ask you to think about great leaders you have been privileged to know, to help illuminate the characteristics and skills necessary for success as a lawyer. You will then be asked to reflect on yourself and your leadership goals. To illuminate the essential characteristics and skills necessary for success as a lawyer, really spend time thinking about who have been the most influential people in your life. They will become your *representative heuristic*!

↑ ↓ ↑

SELF-DISCOVERY EXERCISE 1: BEST BOSS

1. List a few people you have known or worked for who epitomize great leadership, brought out the best in you, and inspired and motivated you.
2. Write some notes about what these people said or did that moved you.
3. Write about how each of these people affected you. What was the impact? How did they make you and others feel?
4. What characteristics come to mind when you think of them? Try to make a list of the characteristics that really capture their leadership.
5. Share one example with a friend, including why you thought of that person and the lessons that you can incorporate about leading.

[**STOP and COMPLETE before reading further.**]

↑ ↓ ↑

REFLECTION ON SELF-DISCOVERY EXERCISE 1

What conclusions can you draw from your notes about the most influential leaders in your life? What leadership traits, characteristics, and qualities come to mind? Try to write those out, if you haven't already. After making a list of the characteristics that define the leader you chose, what do you notice?

We have done this exercise with various professional groups across industries, and we always find the same result. Participants usually do not list technical competencies or specific knowledge about a particular industry. While those are important and obviously threshold competencies for the work, what differentiates typical from outstanding leaders (or lawyers) are social and emotional skills—that is, emotional intelligence (EI). The difference is about how those people make you feel and the way they influence you, not where their degree is from, where they previously worked, their status in the organization, or how much money they make. Most likely, the leader you chose saw you as a person and recognized and supported your strengths. You not only felt "seen" but also felt that they helped you to see your strengths. This style of leadership required self-awareness on their part in order to stay focused on you and your strengths—a value in bringing out the best in those around you—and deep empathy to understand who you are and where you are in your development. This highlights how emotional intelligence forms the foundation for several of the core leadership practices we hear executives wanting to develop (i.e., coaching, mentoring, succession planning). In the coming pages, we will explain how to develop many of the characteristics that you likely listed.

↑↓↑

REFLECTIVE WRITING 1

This is a good opportunity to start reflective writing and begin the process of clarifying who you are and what values drive your leadership. Knowing your values (work-life motivators) and from where they originate will allow you to stay on course throughout your personal and professional life as well as provide you with a roadmap for your decision-making. To really start to get in touch with what matters most to you, write a response to each prompt below. Remember: just start writing and try not to overthink it!

- → Who are you?
- → How did you get here?
- → Where are you going?
- → What brought you to read this book?
- → What do you hope to gain from this book and your journey?
- → What drives you now? What is your passion?
- → What was your passion when you started law school?

□ □ □

We will return to these questions throughout the book, so your reflection here is designed partly to set a baseline in your thinking as you start reading and partly to help you experience the rethinking and reconsideration of your answers as your thinking progresses. In other words, your answers may change and develop over a relatively brief period of time as your thinking about the meaning of the phrases changes or as new considerations make you rethink the pieces in your answers and how they fit together. But finding new meaning and reconsideration of previously held views or beliefs are key aspects of growth and problem-solving skills—and growth and problem-solving skills are both critical elements of becoming a better lawyer and a great leader.

LEADING IN THE LAW → → → → → → → → → → → → WITH EMOTIONAL INTELLIGENCE

CHAPTER 1

Why Emotional Intelligence Matters for Lawyers

THE TRADITIONAL FOCUS OF LEGAL EDUCATION is on thinking like a lawyer, as opposed to feeling like a lawyer. Thus, the inclusion of EI training in the law school curriculum has historically been viewed as oppositional to traditional legal education—so much so that even mentioning *emotion* in law circles will silence the conversation or provoke critique. But this is an uninformed reaction. Our work with law students and lawyers has highlighted that helping them develop emotional intelligence begins with clarifying why emotional intelligence matters, which we will do in this chapter.

A. Importance of Emotional Intelligence: Research and Academic Curricula

Gold-standard research in disciplines outside of the law, particularly in the social and biological sciences, is yielding evidence of the critical role that emotions play in the areas of performance, health, and overall success.[1] Additional research shows the potent role that emotions play in key aspects of law practice, for example, in negotiation.[2] And modern psychology teaches that being able to understand, use, and regulate emotions helps professionals in several key areas: focus, decision-making, memory, reading vital social cues, and embracing change.[3]

Other areas of professional education, including business and medical education, have expanded both their admissions criteria and their curricula to include emotional and social competencies. For many years, business schools have been assessing emotional intelligence in the admissions process. As early as 2013, Northwestern Kellogg School of Management's "How have you grown?" essay, for example, asked candidates to share how they had grown from setbacks as a means to assess their self-awareness. In 2000, the MIT Sloan School of Management started screening for emotional intelligence by using a four-zone grid competency model in its application process. Emory's Goizueta Business School offers a second-year course titled "Leading with Emotional Intelligence," teaching students the core competencies of emotional intelligence.[4] And medical students at the University of South Florida's Morsani College of Medicine participate in SELECT, an EI-based leadership development program.[5]

Just as business schools and the medical profession recognize the advantage of having graduates attuned to emotional intelligence, law firms also want practice-ready graduates.[6] In response, some law schools have started to consider emotional intelligence in their curricula.[7] This trend has surely been accentuated by the pandemic and will continue with post-pandemic changes in law firm infrastructure. But despite the unprecedented growth of practical-skills courses in law schools across the country and a robust body of literature highlighting the predictive validity of emotional intelligence for several key outcomes such as health and performance, an alarming deficit in focus on emotional intelligence in legal education and scholarship persists.[8]

B. Legal Education Failing in Emotional Intelligence Nurturing

Critical studies have shown that legal education changes individuals in ways that are deleterious to their emotional well-being. Initially, law school imposes a social and cultural change on students, some of whom adapt and conform and some of whom struggle. Law school creates a "culture of ... conformity" as it presses students to "think like a lawyer" and causes students to "think[] in terms of one-size-fits all metrics of success."[9] To a great extent, this law school culture has been the same for decades and has been described as "remarkably static, non-adaptive, and resistant to change."[10]

In addition, the law school learning process quickly defines success and the path to success in a very public and uniform way:

> Everyone has the same classes and exam schedule in the first year. Students are evaluated in most of their classes in relation to each other on a uniform metric. They find themselves going to the same meetings, applying through the same on-campus interview process for jobs, and competing for the same law reviews and clerkships. The most visible and easily accessible measures of success come from the results of these public competitions.[11]

Inherent in this process can be a loss of sense of self, a recalibration of success, and a manufacturing of personal pressure as the law school atmospheric pressure builds.

C. Problem—Connection—Solution

The point that we want to make is not that the entire legal education system and profession are tainted by emotional and professional instability (although some parts inherently foster it). Rather, the point that we want to make is that the numbers related to stress (the dissonance) are unacceptably high, the connection between the stressors and the resulting health conditions is very clear, and the solutions are at hand.[12]

The numbers are too high. Upon admission, law students have similar rates of depression, suicide, anxiety, etc., as those in the general public. Within the first year of law school, these numbers climb well beyond what is found in the general public. And among lawyers, the rates of depression, suicide, and anxiety far exceed those of the general public.[13]

The connection is ultra clear. The culture of the legal profession, as it starts in law school and extends into the practice of law, includes an array of elements that are ripe for the growth of mental health issues if the necessary EI competencies are not present. Consider the following circumstances related to legal education and entering the practice of law, and their contribution to the numbers reported above:

- Law school is incredibly expensive.
- Loans are typically more available than grants or scholarships.

- The better the law school you get into, the better your chances of a high-paying job.[14]
- A high-paying job will allow you to pay off your law school debt in a reasonable amount of time so that the debt does not burden the rest of your life and life choices.
- Law firms that offer the highest pay first hire law students as summer associates following their second year of law school.
- Law firms that offer the highest pay first interview law students for those summer associate positions during the summer following the first year of law school.
- Law firms use first-year law school grades as a key element in those hiring decisions.
- Law schools typically use a rigid curve to grade required first-year courses.
- The curve aims to control grade inflation.

Thus, most law students who are concerned about the cost of their legal education and/or who have ambitions for a top-paying job are concerned about their performance (and the performance of their peers) from the very first day of law school.

CARL'S STORY → To illustrate the potentially severe impact of this law school trajectory, let us share Carl's story. Carl had excelled in undergrad at a top liberal arts college, had worked in finance for several years and advanced quickly, and really wanted to be a lawyer. But when Carl was almost halfway through law school, he became paralyzed with fear, doubt, and debt. For reasons beyond his control, law firms were not looking for people like him (he still did not know what that meant, but that was what many told him). He had no 2L summer associate position, which meant that his ability to find a high-paying job after graduation was in serious doubt. He had already paid his third semester of tuition, so he was 50 percent in on his bet for a good-paying job to be able to pay off his debt. And now all he could think about was folding his hand and leaving law school. In his mind, he was a failure by every measure. He did not talk with others about his situation and fears. He had long forgotten the key reasons that led him to law school to begin with. He was embarrassed to find himself in this position. His law school friends had good jobs, his parents thought everything was going great (because he lied to maintain the relationship), and his non-law school friends just did not understand—they thought his mood was a natural by-product of being in law school.

As time went on, Carl was not sleeping at night and would sleep just a couple of hours during the day. Anyone standing within ten feet of him knew that he was struggling. He had a glazed look about his face that told you that even if he was going to class, he was not getting much out of it. Carl was depressed, beyond anxious, and at risk of derailing his career and burning out.

Carl's low emotional intelligence—specifically, his lack of self-awareness of his emotional overdrive and his inability to manage those emotions—led his friends to contact the dean of students, a flurry of failed attempts to communicate, and a wellness check at his home.

↔

Carl's story could just as easily be about a young associate struggling in a law firm.[15] The law-student or young-associate "Carls" (or "Carlas") who get into this situation are at home, paralyzed with fear, depressed, and unable to break out of their dim vision for the future. Concerns similar to the ones described in the bulleted list above can arise in practice as well:

- Once a law graduate lands a good-paying and prestigious job (commonly referred to as *Big Law*), the graduate's concern shifts to keeping it.
- The law graduate now has to pass the bar exam—a two- to three-day multifaceted test of knowledge, analytical ability, and endurance—to keep the job.
- Large law firms are built on a business model driven by the ability of partners to bring in clients, personally and collectively bill hours, and collect the fees.
- The model relies on young lawyers being the workers who generate the hours (to warrant their high pay), which in turn are billed at a higher rate to clients (to give even higher pay to partners).
- Producing billable hours drives the business model.

- Producing billable hours creates pressure to perform in quantity and quality.
- Producing billable hours places strain on relationships both within and outside the firm.

To be sure, we are not unveiling some unknown concerns in this section but rather are saying what many are thinking and few verbalize. While we spend a little time focused on what is not going well in the legal profession, no one really wants to sit in this thinking for too long. We also know that your experience may not reach a noticeable level to others, but the point is that the pressure and stress inherent in a profession of such high responsibility is widespread and touches everyone. Thus, we strongly believe that airing and talking through these matters are essential to their prevention in the first place and to their management if they occur.

The solution is quite obvious. Law students and lawyers, through their personal efforts and those of their teachers, mentors, and employers, need to utilize all potential resources to build protection against the detrimental side of stress. Some stress is healthy; it motivates us. But it is important to know where the line is between the healthy and unhealthy, and that takes self-awareness and self-management—the first steps in engaging emotional intelligence.

Emotional intelligence is key for lawyers because of the critical function that self-awareness plays in well-being and performance, which are intricately linked. Lawyers and law students necessarily work on a variety of professional demands every single day. Balancing this diverse work with different and often conflicting deadlines, demanding supervisors, and needy clients is stressful. Often, these workplace stressors are compounded by personal ones as well. Lawyers who are emotionally intelligent are self-aware, first and foremost. They recognize their emotional reactions, pay attention to the interpersonal dynamics as well as the content of any conversation, monitor their moods, and stay grounded in their values. In Carl's case, with higher emotional intelligence, he would have been able to recognize the lure of those extrinsic motivators, such as finding a high-paying job, and continued to stay focused on intrinsic motivators, such as learning, seeking knowledge, and improving the world in some passionate way—which were likely what drove him into law in the first place. Without self-awareness, it is virtually impossible for law students and lawyers to shift their behaviors and thinking throughout their day to achieve the outcomes they desire. Self-awareness is the core of emotional intelligence because with conscious awareness of one's cognitive and emotional reactions comes the power to choose how to proceed in any situation.

ROB TAKING THE LEAD* → In my work as a psychologist, I have counseled thousands of law students and practicing lawyers in both clinical and organizational consulting roles. Several themes have emerged from this work that illuminate the need for emotional intelligence in lawyers. One of the primary trends that has emerged is lawyer burnout and dissatisfaction, despite gains in financial and material wealth. It is not uncommon for practicing lawyers in the mid-stage of their career, when they have achieved partner (or even equity partner), bought the car of their dreams, and own a seven-figure house in the most desirable neighborhood and school system, to reach out to me because they continue to feel that something is missing from their life. If you are a leader in the legal field already, you likely realize how burnout and happiness relate to leadership, both in keeping yourself motivated and healthy and in addressing these matters across your organization.

I recently worked with a lawyer who had achieved equity partner by his mid-thirties, securing a strong financial position for himself and his family. He was a rock star by all professional measures but reported feeling unhappy, irritable, and overwhelmed most days with self-described monotonous routines and "meaningless work." Only through EI-based coaching was he able to recognize that his narrative (i.e., beliefs) on his professional work (and life) had become pessimistic and cynical. With increased emotional intelligence, he was able to identify his triggers, his automatic thoughts about those triggers, and how his thoughts, interpretations, and storylines were contributing to his mood. (We will define triggers and the role they play in Chapter IV.) As he became more emotionally intelligent, particularly with increased self-awareness of his unconscious responses (automatic cognitive, behavioral, and interpersonal responses, or default modes of responding), he was able to choose more adaptive ways to respond. Emotional intelligence is a set of habits and skills that, when developed, can have a profound impact on well-being.

* We use "Rob Taking the Lead" and "Cliff Taking the Lead" as a way to let you know which author is sharing an experience.

As my lawyer-client gained greater awareness of his mental outlook about his work, he was able to reframe his thinking, which improved his mood and boosted his performance in the following years.

↔

D. Emotional Intelligence and Leadership

Lawyers constantly work with clients and others, whether the core of that work is in litigation, transactions, regulation, or academia. They are often asked to lead from day one, not only in the traditional sense, like leading a team, but also in the more holistic, day-to-day sense of leading in their life, that is, being mindful and emotionally intelligent throughout all aspects of their life. Luckily, as we will say again and again, the same underlying characteristics that differentiate psychologically healthy lawyers from unhealthy ones also distinguish exceptional leaders from mediocre ones.

Emotionally intelligent leaders also have what it takes to lead in the twenty-first century. To tackle the complex issues we face as a global community today, we need to lead with curiosity, focus on collaboration, be able to hear various perspectives, and lead with our hearts in addition to our minds. While we tend to think of leadership as primarily involving interpersonal transactions, such as coaching and mentoring others, guiding them, and keeping them motivated, the research is clear that great leadership begins within the individual—what we refer to as *leadership from the inside out.* We cannot effectively manage or lead others without first knowing how to lead ourselves. Indeed, leadership is about healthy mental and emotional habits. Lawyers high in emotional intelligence build healthy relationships with other legal professionals through keen self-awareness of their thoughts and feelings and a strong focus on empathy. Working with others requires building and maintaining strong relationships, yet we have noticed a significant gap in students' relationship-management skills necessary to effectively lead oneself or teams in law school. This book is about filling that void with enhanced emotional intelligence.

Strong relationship skills are also needed in leading your clients. Research on lawyer-client relations shows that one of the biggest predictors of clients trusting their lawyers is that they feel understood and heard.[16] Undeniably, you could have all of the technical knowledge and the best training in the world, but if your clients do not feel understood and heard, you will struggle to retain them. Making your clients feel understood and heard can be accomplished with emotional intelligence.

Additionally, feedback loops that increase a client's understanding of a situation also lead to an increase in their trust in the lawyer.[17] Thus, lawyers can increase trust when they actively use listening and empathy in creating the attorney-client rapport.[18] For example, "five factors a public defense attorney should address that may prove to be very important in obtaining client satisfaction and cooperation [are] engaging the client for input, listening to the client, examining the prosecutor's evidence, focusing on the client's case during meetings, and informing the client of potential consequences."[19] While technical and intellectual skills certainly matter, lawyers need to be able to make clients feel heard and understood. As you will learn in these pages, good listening skills come from strong EI skills, the combination of which results in resonance or strong interpersonal connection.

Lawyers are often surprised to learn that high-performing relationships begin with self-awareness. In order to trust others and show your authentic self at work, a prerequisite to relationship development, you must first trust yourself. Lawyers high in emotional intelligence have spent time thinking about who they are and how they arrived there. They know themselves well and have developed self-acceptance, which allows them to be open in relationships, trusting that others will like them, too, when they reveal their true colors. This self-trust and authenticity, in turn, allow lawyer leaders to be comfortable with their discomfort, showing vulnerability, which is a key way to connect with others, whether clients, colleagues, or employees.

CLIFF TAKING THE LEAD → The first student issue I had to handle as dean of students was on the first day, and it was student on student. The complainant was adamant that I do something about what the other student said to him, which he found offensive and threatening.

I needed to hear the other side of the story; and because I did not know what to expect, and did not know any better or worse, I asked university police to station a plainclothes officer in the office waiting room area. At the time, I was kind of proud of my approach (not a plan, mind you). Grab the bull by the horns. Zero preparation. Zero consultation. I was doomed.

The other student arrived. In a suit. "I would never say such a thing," he pleaded. "The other guy's a bit off, you know." After more conversation, I sent him on his way. I then thanked the officer, walked him to the door, and sent him on his way as well.

Standing at the door, puzzling over what to do next, I turned back to see the entire office staff standing and staring at me, several with their mouths open. I quickly switched the tracks on my train of thought to them. Thinking quickly, I said, "I am guessing that my predecessor never had the police in the office like that." Without a word, they all shook their heads from left to right and back again. No words, just shock. In trying to solve one problem, I had inevitably created another.

I quickly apologized and explained that they were not in any danger and that I would never put them in harm's way. I promised them that if someone potentially threatening was coming to see me, I would let them know ahead of time and give them the choice of whether or not to be there. While I flunked my first quiz on supervision by bringing in the officer without giving notice to my staff or having any awareness of how this might make them feel, I passed the second quiz by quieting my own thinking to shift to how they were feeling, addressing their concerns immediately and with vulnerability, and making a promise that I knew I could (and did) keep.

The situation described above helped me to identify key tools that I would need to sharpen to succeed: consultation, communication, consideration of others (i.e., other awareness or empathy), not rushing to judgments, managing relationships, and managing myself (though not necessarily in that order). Despite the seemingly poor start, I had quickly exercised some fundamental EI skills: self-awareness to quiet myself and focus on this new concern, self-management to quiet any remaining emotions from the immediately preceding situation, empathy when I stepped into my staff's shoes and felt their needs, and relationship management in seeing that I needed to give a constructive and responsive answer that would build trust. In that moment, I (subconsciously) chose to be vulnerable and publicly admit my mistake, and that vulnerability and authenticity built lasting trust with my staff.

So maybe I did have what it takes to do this job. My EI skills enabled me to react in the moment based on thought, not emotion; to directly convey strong leadership; and to be positively responsive to the needs and wants of my staff. What I did not learn in law school, I quickly figured out in practice—and, fortunately, with no serious negative consequences.

This example is typical for people at all levels and in all types of law practice, with the results varying by our ability to bring EI skills to play in the moment.

↔

E. A Tough Way to Start Law School

Perhaps the best way to help you understand what emotional intelligence really looks like is to provide a few examples of what we see when it is lacking. We have seen inadequate levels of emotional intelligence in various corners of the legal profession, including at a top law school, though it often manifests differently.

The gunner and the self-doubter. Hardly a week goes by in a law school course without seeing a high-performing and capable law student who tries to answer every question with a know-it-all air but has no clue as to how disruptive that behavior is for the class, how fellow classmates view this behavior, or how off-base some of the answers might be (until the professor or someone else in a position of authority or with more experience tells him). This type of student is typically referred to as a gunner. This same type of person can be found in the workplace: as you read this, are there any colleagues who come to mind?

In contrast, another type of student commonly encountered expresses a deep level of self-doubt and lack of self-confidence. This person does not volunteer in class, fears being called on, and may preface questions with phrases like "This might be wrong" or "Sorry if this is not related." This is the self-doubter. On one level, these two students are endpoints on a continuum of law-student thinking, yet something they share in common is a lack of emotional intelligence. The gunner lacks self-awareness, and the self-doubter lacks self-management. While law students are each unique in their own beautiful ways and these examples are oversimplifications, we share them with you now to point out the fact that we all have a default mode when responding under stress. Our default mode is based in our experience and is marked by a unique collection of coping, thinking, and interpersonal patterns. If not revealed, addressed, and developed, our default modes may turn into more ingrained patterns and become more problematic throughout a legal career. Emotional intelligence is about getting in touch with your natural way of responding under stress and then making slight adjustments to help yourself succeed.

Thinking about the role of stress in the law-student and lawyer experience necessitates another look at the dark underside of the study and practice of law, which can thankfully be avoided or reversed by enhanced emotional intelligence. The practice of law, regardless of area or type, is stressful. Clients are paying high fees and expecting premium results; and lives, businesses, and often immense sums of money are at stake. Lawyers and law students can struggle with stress at times and form bad habits. Those habits, in turn, can lead to unhealthy relationships. Stress, bad habits, and unhealthy relationships are inherently interrelated and can feed off of one another, growing, or snowballing, often out of control. As noted above, the linkage between the stress of learning the law/practicing the law and personal and professional damage is well-documented and occurs well above acceptable levels.[20] These struggles can manifest in one's physical well-being (e.g., depression, substance abuse, and suicide), in relationships with clients and staff (e.g., client mistreatment, employee mistreatment, and harassment), and/or on a broader professional scale (e.g., job turnover, unethical practices, and malpractice).

↑ ↓ ↑

SELF-DISCOVERY EXERCISE 2: ON STRESSORS

As stated earlier, certain stressors may be unique and also, at times, predictable in the lives of law students and lawyers. Such struggles tend to develop and intensify over the career of the lawyer, and pointing to one causal factor is simplistic. Each of our lives is complicated and unique. Surely history, relationships with significant others, and personal expectations are always at play and can vary widely and quickly from day to day. Consider the unique, complicated, and predictable stressors at play in your life, at law school, in your law practice experience (if applicable), and in your personal circumstances.

1. What are the inherent stressors in a legal career? In law school?
2. What are your top stressors currently?
3. How do they impact you?
4. How do you cope with them?

[STOP and COMPLETE before reading further.]

↑ ↓ ↑

REFLECTION ON SELF-DISCOVERY EXERCISE 2

Awareness of current stressors and how they impact you is a key first step in self-management. We all need to learn our default way of responding to stressors, and it is difficult to do so without awareness of what is currently stressful in your life. It is interesting that stressors are frequently good things in your life: getting married, purchasing a home, taking on more responsibility at work, getting a new job, or acquiring a top client. Emotionally intelligent lawyers know their stressors, what their thinking is about these events (e.g., "I hope this client likes me and my work"), and how their thinking leads to feelings and actions. Developing greater awareness of your top stressors and how you cope with them enhances your emotional intelligence. (We'll come back to this topic in Chapter IV on self-management.) It is critical to develop emotional intelligence given the stress points and stressors referenced above. It is often helpful to think about people who do this really well (reflect back on your answers to Self-Discovery Exercise 1 in the Introduction).

Now compare your answers to Self-Discovery Exercise 2 with the common stressors listed below:

For Law Students

- competition for admission
- in-class engagement
- peer group encounters
- competition for grades
- competition for jobs
- the accumulation of education-related debt
- self-doubt as one encounters vastly new information and analytical methods
- going from being the best of the class to thinking you might not even be in the top half of the class
- the constant worry about getting and keeping a job to validate the decision to go to law school

For Young Lawyers

- paying new bills as well as accumulated debt
- getting experience
- taking on new responsibility
- demands to perform
- professional achievement
- job and career satisfaction
- job market volatility

For Experienced Lawyers (6–12 years)

- continued high performance
- client retention
- continued job and career satisfaction
- additional job responsibility (generally)
- demand to bring in new business
- maintaining relevance
- learning to mentor
- growing personally
- leading

For Lawyer Leaders

- leading
- mentoring
- developing systems
- growing the organization
- sustaining individual and group performance
- inspiring excellence
- client retention and development
- philanthropy

REFLECTIVE WRITING 2

→ What comes to mind when we say "great lawyers"?
→ What does being a great lawyer mean to you?
→ How will you define *success*?
→ What do you see as the biggest impediments to your success?
→ Do you know of personal weaknesses that may be impediments to your success?

□ □ □

Your answers to these questions will give you insight into your values and motivations as a lawyer. You want to make sure to be clear about what it is that drives you. Great lawyer leaders recognize the importance of knowing what is driving them, where those measuring sticks of success come from, and how those measuring sticks guide their decision-making and actions. With self-awareness of these beliefs and narratives about the practice of law, you have the power to choose how you want to proceed—that is, the type of lawyer leader you want to be! In order to develop these social and emotional skills that make up the basis of exceptional leadership, we want you to have a solid understanding of the theory of emotional intelligence. You need to know what it is so that you have a language and framework to reference.

CHAPTER II

Understanding Emotional Intelligence

What It Is

CHANCES ARE HIGH that you picked leaders in the "best boss" self-discovery exercise (Self-Discovery Exercise 1) who have a high level of self-management. For them to influence you the way that they did, they likely possessed the differentiating competencies inherent in emotional intelligence: self-awareness, emotional regulation, empathy, inspiration, and optimism, to name a few. Emotional intelligence is our "*capacity for recognizing our own feelings and those of others, for motivating ourselves, and for managing emotions well in ourselves and our relationships.*"[1] It is a significant force behind professional success.[2] People with high emotional intelligence are better able to understand and express themselves, "understand others and relate with them, and cope with daily demands."[3]

So, how does this relate to the study and practice of law? EI, even more than IQ, has been found to be an important predictor of academic and job performance,[4] strong leadership,[5] ability to accomplish many tasks required of lawyers (e.g., negotiation),[6] and mental health among legal professionals.[7] If that is not enough, higher rates of emotional intelligence have been shown to lead to increased happiness, life satisfaction, and well-being—and, therefore, are thought to decrease lawyer burnout.[8] Furthermore, EI skills can be taught and developed.[9] Thus, emotional intelligence evolves and increases with one's desire to learn and grow, while IQ does not change significantly over a lifetime and only accounts for about 25 percent of overall success.[10] The time is now for EI training in the law. It offers clear benefits for emotional and social intelligence, as supported by the research in neuroscience and psychology as well as key insights that could boost performance in the legal field.

A. A Brief Historical Foundation

The study of intelligence has been a cornerstone of psychology since its inception.[11] The primary research focus has been on cognitive-based practices such as memory and problem-solving, with little work done on the role of social and emotional competence in intelligent behavior. With very few exceptions, most scholars who have worked on understanding the determinants of success have focused on IQ.[12]

One exception is David Wechsler, formulator of the Wechsler Adult Intelligence Scale (WAIS), likely the most commonly administered IQ assessment, who defined intelligence as "[*t*]*he aggregate or global capacity of the individual to act purposefully, to think rationally, and to deal effectively with his environment.*"[13] Wechsler frequently noted the roles of "non-intellective" and "intellective" elements of intelligence, the former referring to affective, personal, and social competencies.[14] He was an early proponent of distinguishing the "non-intellective" abilities and characteristics of success in trying to understand intelligent behavior.[15] His recognition is ironic in many ways because it was his work on intellectual measurement that, in part, drove the field of psychology and society at large toward a bias for IQ over EI (or EQ, as it is sometimes referred).

Some four decades later, Howard Gardner revived an interest in the "non-intellective" aspects of intelligence and developed the theory of "multiple intelligences."[16] In his book *Frames of Mind: The Theory of Multiple Intelligences*, Gardner takes a more holistic view of the definition of *intelligence* that encompasses eight unique aspects.[17] Two fundamental aspects of his theory are "interpersonal intelligence" (the capacity to understand the intentions, motivations, and desires of other people) and "intrapersonal intelligence" (the capacity to understand oneself and to appreciate one's feelings, fears, and motivations), both of which now make up the core of EI models.[18]

B. Current State of Emotional Intelligence Science: The Top Frameworks

The early researchers set the stage for the explosion in psychological research and theory that has taken place in recent decades.[19] Defining *emotional intelligence* is currently the object and subject of investigation and research by some of the greatest minds in psychology and neuroscience, resulting in competing conceptualizations and frameworks.[20] Three major conceptual models hold true today: (1) the Salovey–Mayer model (perceive, understand, manage, and use emotions to facilitate thinking); (2) the Goleman model (competencies and skills across four domains: self-awareness, self-management (sometimes called *self-regulation* or *emotion regulation*), social awareness, and relationship management); and (3) the Bar–On model (interrelated emotional and social competencies, including self-perception, self-expression, stress management, decision-making, and interpersonal).[21]

While all three models share overlapping properties, we consider Goleman's four-domain model[22] to be especially applicable to training lawyers. The model most closely resonates with our experience in helping lawyers and leaders develop into highly effective, happy people: that is, leadership is about knowing oneself well (self-awareness), recognizing how what you are feeling and thinking influences your leadership actions and decision-making, managing those reactions, and using that insight to resonate with others. We had already identified the centrality of self-awareness to our work with law students and in leadership development, so the Goleman model* clearly fit with our values and experiences.

Goleman developed his four-domain approach over several decades of work with Richard Boyatzis.[23] The Goleman model presents self-awareness as the cornerstone of the four domains, with the other three domains (and their respective competencies) flowing from self-awareness. Two of the four domains focus on managing the self (self-awareness and self-management), while the other two focus on managing others (social awareness, or empathy, and relationship management). This four-domain model was also used to develop the Emo-

---

* We use the phrase "Goleman Model" to indicate the framework initially developed by Daniel Goleman, Richard Boyatzis, and the Hay Group.

tional and Social Competency Inventory (ESCI), a widely administered 360-degree EI-assessment tool. We administer the ESCI at the beginning of our Leading in the Law class as a way to help students identify key areas of strength and potential growth.

This is an important time to distinguish between *ability* versus *trait* models of emotional intelligence. The two types of EI models and associated measures—ability and trait—differ with regard to both definition and methods of assessment. While ability models[24] view emotional intelligence as an ability to perceive and express emotions, trait-based models[25] rely on individuals' self-perceptions of their emotional abilities. This distinction highlights the conceptual differences between frameworks that approach emotional intelligence as being another intelligence (ability) and those that approach it as being personality-based (trait).[26] Goleman's model can be considered a *mixed model* in that it combines what has since been separately identified as ability EI and trait EI. The Goleman model focuses on emotional intelligence as a "wide array of competencies and skills that drive leadership performance."[27] Thus, we apply the Goleman model for lawyer emotional intelligence development.

C. The Emotional Intelligence Competencies That Matter for Lawyers

The remainder of this chapter briefly introduces the four domains. The remainder of the book applies this four-domain model of emotional and social intelligence to lawyer leadership development. We provide vignettes of lawyers and law students to illustrate and exemplify the need for and power of these competencies. We have developed our own self-discovery exercises, tailored the content for lawyers, and created reflective writing prompts to help you become the lawyer leader that you want to be.

The domains and their respective competencies are listed around the square in Figure 1. Taking the time to understand this EI framework will not only help you to familiarize yourself with the language of EI but also will help you to better understand what emotional intelligence really is.

FIGURE 1
THE EMOTIONAL AND SOCIAL COMPETENCY FRAMEWORK

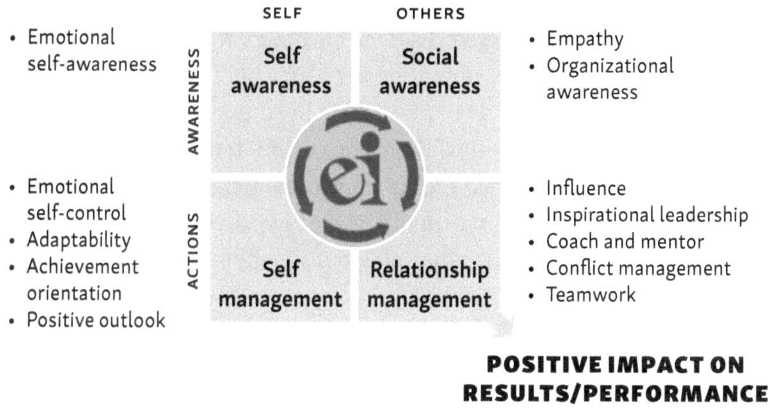

1. Self-Awareness

Self-awareness is the ability to understand your own emotions, what triggers these emotions (a thought or stimulus), and the effect of having the emotion. It is the only domain in the Goleman model that does not have distinct underlying competencies; emotional self-awareness is the only one. For purposes of training lawyers, we expand the notion of self-awareness to incorporate awareness of your thinking, emotions, and behavior patterns, as well as deep insight into who you are and the key defining moments and individuals who helped you become who you are. Self-awareness is about being aware of your reactions to events (such as stressors) throughout the day. It is also about knowing yourself, for example, your strengths and weaknesses, on a deeper level. Self-awareness is about being conscious of cognitive, affective, and interpersonal habits and applying the best reaction to meet the demands of any situation.

Furthermore, Rob's leadership consulting with C-suite executives and Cliff's work with law students have highlighted the importance of a much deeper form of self-awareness, which we refer to as *insight* and expand on in Chapter III. By insight we simply mean being able to tell your story, that is, who you are on a deep level and how you arrived where you are. In addition, Cliff has taught law school courses focusing on and written about personal narrative and professional identity, material that is relevant here.

Indeed, the most effective leaders have a rich self-understanding: they know who they are, how they arrived where they are, and what matters most to them as a result of their lived experiences. Self-aware lawyers have deep insight into their personality tendencies and the defining moments that shaped them. They know where these characteristics originate, whether from genetics or the environment, and they know how these tendencies and values play out for them, positively or negatively, in their work and life.

ROB TAKING THE LEAD → When I was a freshman in college at the University of Mississippi, I felt frustrated with higher education and career development and, at times, disenfranchised. In high school, I was an accomplished athlete in basketball and soccer, and the loss of that identity, mixed with a desire to understand the meaning of life and find real purpose in my career, led me to question public higher education and several societal norms. I grew skeptical of the ability of traditional modes of pedagogy in higher education, such as large lecture halls and static syllabi, to really lead to the type of learning and meaningful impact that I wanted to make in my life. I was bored in my undergraduate classes. The college admissions process had made me feel like a number. I felt that many of my peers were not thinking deeply enough about what they wanted out of their lives and careers, while I was looking for something more meaningful during that formative time. But I also remember feeling like I could not leave school, as it had been ingrained in me that earning a college degree was the path to financial success and happiness. As a result of all of these feelings, my grades suffered and I found myself floundering.

I remember showing up uninvited to the Athens, Georgia, apartment of my older sister, who was then a business major at the University of Georgia, to "experience" life with her. We would engage in late-night discussions about the meaning of life and the purpose of all the hoops we were jumping through. I would skip class and drive around the Southeast visiting friends, engaging with new people and cultures, and going to music festivals, all while staying enrolled in Ole Miss and paying tuition. Not the greatest plan, I know. But in my self-righteous, immature, 18-year-old mind, "real" purpose and meaning could not be found in the packed lecture halls on campus, where all of the other freshmen seemed to me, at the time, like cattle making their way through chutes established to keep them in line as they headed to their destiny (or fate).

With my parents' questioning my motives and priorities, I decided to leave Ole Miss in the spring semester of sophomore year for a semester-long course with the National Outdoor Leadership School (NOLS) in the great American Southwest. While earning college credit through the University of Utah, I backpacked, canoed, rock climbed, and learned about ecology and plant biology, environmental studies, and geology. I had no idea at the time that it was exactly what I needed. I spent my days accomplishing significant physical challenges, such as free climbing in the Dragoon Mountains in southern Arizona, and my evenings reading, journaling, and engaging in discussions about the purpose of life, the state of the planet, and what really matters in the "good life" as we all sat around a campfire. It was my chance to take a step back and revel in nature with a supportive group of leaders. It was a privileged way to get in touch with what matters most—an opportunity few receive—and I will never lose my appreciation for that.

Outside the reach of societal pressures, and with the stillness around me, I was able to see how my uncertainty about my future career and the meaning of life was impacting my academic motivation and affecting my college performance. Through meditation and reflection, I developed an awareness of the overwhelming feelings I was experiencing in response to questions by family, friends, and elders I respected about what I was going to do with my life and what I wanted to study. This newfound self-awareness allowed me to see that that these overwhelming feelings had led to my negative thinking about school, contributed to a negative narrative about higher education and several societal structures at large, and pushed me away from what I really was good at and wanted to do with my life: make a difference.

Lacking self-awareness at the time, I had gotten off track. I had always been an A/B student in high school and never got into trouble. During those three months of sleeping under the stars, walking through desert landscapes, and reading the works of poets and authors like Walt Whitman, Jack Kerouac, and Victor Frankl, I gained self-awareness and found my authentic self. I clarified my values and reworked my core beliefs toward a love of education and an appreciation of many of the societal norms that I had previously judged with disdain.

The experience taught me the essence of emotional intelligence—that is, keeping in tune with your emotional journey and how it impacts your thinking and actions. I also recognized the importance of reflection in clarifying values and guiding principles. My time connecting with the natural world while in deep mindfulness revealed to me the significance of being authentically in touch with who you are and staying true to that through life. From that experience, I learned several key values that guide me to this day: always try to see others and their beauty; there is no right way or one way to live this life; we are doing our best; treat everyone with dignity and respect; spread kindness and love; strive for self-acceptance as well as acceptance of others; and pursue your passions with vigor.

My journey of working through my own career decision-making also illuminated the importance of work as a means to finding a calling. I learned the critical lesson that our work should align with what matters to us. I came to recognize the significance of career decision-making in general, how heavy it can weigh on the young adult psyche, the importance of finding meaning and purpose, and the reality that we will be happy and most effective at work if we pursue what we care about. Through this process of developing deeper self-awareness, I realized that my life's purpose was to help others find their calling.

With this level of self-awareness, you, too, can find your purpose, discovering what matters most to you and realigning your life to match it, no matter what career stage you are in. I am certainly not saying that your values need to align with mine or that mine are the best—or that I would wish on anyone else the circuitous route I had to take to find my calling. But if you have not engaged in deep self-exploration—reflecting upon your past and then connecting the dots between your past experiences and how they have shaped who you are today—it will be nearly impossible to self-actualize and lead with emotional intelligence at the level you are capable of. But have no fear—that's why we wrote this book and developed a course to help you get there. (And by the way, all these years later, we have the empirical research to support the notion that finding your purpose and pursuing it with passion are central to exceptional leadership. So that's pretty cool!)

↔

All that is to say, we view self-awareness as having two distinct branches that form the foundation for emotional intelligence: (1) deep insight and (2) present-moment awareness. As you reflect on my story and your own, think about who you are and how you got here. Do you know your prime default personality tendencies and from where they originate? Do you know what values drive you and their origin? If not, no worries—we will get to that recognition. If so, good for you (seriously, nice work!)—now start to think about your narrative (and life story) because that is what has led to your having the tendencies you possess today and is also what forms the basis for the leader you are. (In the next chapter, we guide you through an array of exercises developed to strengthen your insight into how your life journey contributes to your leadership tendencies and how you can use that insight to manage yourself and those around you most effectively.)

2. Self-Management

The next domain is self-management (also referred to as *self-regulation* or *emotion regulation*), which involves regulating your emotional reactions to reach a desired outcome. This is probably the skill set that most people think of when they think about emotional intelligence. While self-awareness is truly the core of emotional intelligence, self-management is what we can see in others and what has the most overt impact in our lives. We engage emotion regulation all the time. We choose a route to commute to work because it is the least frustrating or most inspiring. We associate with colleagues who are exciting and like-minded because it is inspiring or soothing. We take a deep breath or sigh when overwhelmed with work or frustrated by a colleague to curb the tide of emotion. Self-management involves regulating both positive and negative emotions. We tend to think of emotion regulation as being able to manage strong negative reactions, like anger or anxiety, but it also involves keeping yourself optimistic, motivated, and engaged, day in and day out.

The self-management domain includes four competencies: emotional self-control, adaptability, achievement orientation, and positive outlook. In our review of ESCI assessments for hundreds of law students, achievement orientation, not surprisingly, tends to be a top-scoring competency. If you have enough motivation to earn a JD, practice law, and read a book like this, then achievement orientation is a given—but that does not imply strength in other competencies in this domain. Also, in some cases a lawyer's achievement orientation can be so pronounced that it can become an *over-strength*, at which point it is no longer solely a positive attribute but one that may cause difficulties.

We have all seen a movie in which a character can stop time—freeze the action and actors so that the character can think and assess without having to do so in real time. When we think about the decision-making that ties together self-awareness and self-management, exercising both is a bit like making time stop. Accurate self-awareness of emotions is obviously key because it queues up the question of whether you should allow the emotions to continue (as motivation or "fire") or halt them (apply the brakes). It is nearly impossible to regulate your emotions without accurate awareness of what you are feeling.

Lawyers are constantly in positions requiring this kind of real-time decision-making, whether in litigation (during trial or arguments), transactional work (in negotiations), or regulatory work (during drafting, hearings, or floor debates). For example, imagine a client counseling scenario in the most basic setting and without regard to any particular practice area. Unless you are devoid of feelings, when a client starts to present reason(s) for coming to you for help, you will have emotional and cognitive reactions. You may also react to the client personally, whether you have met him/her/them previously or not. Does the person appear truthful or not, attractive or not, well-dressed or not, hygienic or not, worthy of your time or not, dull or not, and so on? While this is basic human nature, the emotionally intelligent lawyer will practice self-awareness in this situation by recognizing those reactions and judgmental impulses, notice the influence of those reactions and impulses, and adjust accordingly with self-awareness, to be able to continue to connect with the client. These reactions are healthy and provide the beginning of empathy.

The key point here is that self-management involves paying attention to where you are placing your attention nonjudgmentally so that you can acknowledge those thoughts and feelings, adjust them accordingly or regulate yourself, and continue to listen closely to your client's story. Being aware of your emotions allows you to regulate them, listen effectively, and probe professionally—all of which is the essence of self-management. (In Chapter III, we introduce mindfulness, which is a key tool for effectively managing your emotions.)

HERM'S STORY → Herm is a partner in a boutique law firm. Today he is meeting a new potential client, Laura. She approached the firm because it had handled the IPOs (initial public offerings) for many similar, small tech companies. Laura walks into the office and smiles warmly. She immediately reminds Herm of a former adversary in a case that did not end well. Herm has harbored ill-will toward that attorney ever since and feels a rise of negative emotion within him. Initially, Herm and Laura make some small talk about lawyers and the business of law.

At this point, the conversation could go one of two ways: Herm could check his feelings or not. If Herm does not check his emotions, then he might unknowingly use an inappropriate tone, be too dismissive when he should be listening, or give her the impression that he is antagonistic toward her or not genuinely interested in her business. If Herm checks his emotions, then he might assess that he is reacting to Laura in a way that could negatively affect her decision on which firm to hire, as well as his ability to gauge her legal needs and provide legal services objectively and professionally.

"Checking in" allows Herm to tell himself that this is about Laura and not about Herm's reaction to Laura. Recognizing his emotional reaction, realizing its inapplicability here, and not letting it enter the conversation allows Herm to focus on her and listen closely to make sure that he focuses on her needs. After checking in, Herm asks Laura to talk about her business model and what her business means to her. He is able to refocus his mindset toward one of curiosity, empathy, and getting the job done for her with care. He then uses the time in which she is answering his questions to redouble his focus on her business. He listens closely and writes some notes about follow-up questions and potential legal issues to research. He maintains steady eye contact with Laura and interjects several times to acknowledge things she says that are pertinent or of interest.

Herm is using his knowledge and experience with emotional intelligence to make sure that his focus is both in the moment and on what is important in the moment and not on emotions stemming from a prior experience.

↔

Your reactions have a role, after you acknowledge them. Acknowledging and pausing them allows you to prioritize what to follow up on now versus later, what you think you need to know versus what is unnecessary (and perhaps inappropriate), and what you think the client wants to hear from you. Often the best response you can get from a client conversation (or a conversation with anyone, for that matter) is something like "I really appreciate that you listened and understood me." Not only is that person more likely to hire you, but that person is more likely to recommend that others hire you. We know from research on this topic that making your client feel heard comes from your ability to manage your attention and emotional reactions to stay engaged and present.

Thus, we have an initial one–two punch of overarching EI competencies that matter for lawyers: recognizing one's emotions in real time and managing them in a way that is beneficial under the circumstances. When we bring the unconscious to the conscious, we have the power to choose our response, as opposed to being driven by automatic responses that do not always serve us well.

To be blunt, how many times have you been talking with someone and had your thoughts drift away? It happens, and it happens for a million reasons. You smell some good food. Poof—you are no longer listening but instead are thinking about lunch or dinner. The person mentions a place that you have visited. Poof—you are remembering your last visit there, and how much fun you had, and wondering when you will be able to go back. The person mentions how much they need to do. Poof—you are worrying about how much work you need to do later that day. And so on. The commonality among all of these is that you have lost your focus, driven by a core emotion (hunger, pleasure, fear) and not what you should be engaging with in the moment.

3. Social Awareness and Relationship Management

Another important aspect of emotional intelligence for lawyers is managing relationships. The domains of social awareness (Domain 3 of the EI Model, which includes empathy and organizational awareness) and relationship management (Domain 4 of the EI Model, which includes the competencies of influence, inspirational leadership, mentoring, conflict management, and teamwork) are all about how you engage with others. We dedicate a subsequent chapter to social awareness, mostly focused on empathy (Chapter V), and another chapter is all about relationship development (Chapter VI). If you go back and look at Figure 1, you can see that the final two domains of emotional intelligence are on the right side of the model, which has to do with how we work with others. The key here is that emotional intelligence flows into social intelligence, highlighting the reality that the best path to being able to read the situation, find empathy for others, and have healthy, successful relationships starts from within—that is, with self-awareness and self-management.

Social awareness is a highly desirable and sought-after leadership skill. It is well-known in business and law, in particular, that being able to read others and social situations is key to success. Leaders need to be able to accurately pick up on social cues and the emotions and motives of their clients and law partners, and then use that knowledge to inform the best way to work with them to achieve their desired outcomes. In much the same way that self-awareness lays the groundwork for self-management, social awareness (or, more accurately, understanding others) creates a path to building healthy and thriving relationships with others.

Before we dive much deeper into the development of each domain, we want to take some time up front to help you understand at a high level what each domain is. Leaders in the law who are self-aware are highly skilled at being able to connect with their clients, and not just the ones they like or with whom they find immediate similarities. They work to stay curious about the people in their lives with a value toward hearing and trying to understand others. This is an important time to say that empathy—being able to put yourself in another person's shoes—does not mean that you agree with the other person. (We have heard lawyers and law students say this repeatedly over the past decade.) Agreeing is not what social awareness is about. To have empathy or a capacity for empathy does not mean that you have to agree or accept another person's beliefs, values, or way of life. Rather, it means that you value and recognize the importance of hearing about another person's way of life beyond some financial or vocational gain. Emotionally intelligent lawyer leaders bring a curiosity about the people in their lives and seek to understand where they are coming from. They actively maintain their focus on what drives others and who others are on a deep level, and they see others' strengths as well as ways to work together. Relationships are all about how you make others feel and what you bring out in them.

Without being able to understand who the people you lead are and what makes them tick, you will find it quite difficult to accomplish your leadership goals. When we approach leadership from a focus on the virtues and strengths of those around us and we are able to monitor our tendencies to get sucked into conflict or adversarial narratives about them, we are able to bring out the best in others and help them flourish. This requires deep social awareness. It requires understanding what others are thinking, why they are thinking that way, what cultural or personal experiences led to those beliefs, how those thoughts and beliefs influence their feelings, and how those feelings relate to their actions. Social awareness requires perspective—being able to understand others' way of seeing things.

If there is one universality about the law, it is that one can (usually) ethically make an argument for either side of an issue, for one approach over others, or for one outcome being better than others. Coming to terms with this choice necessarily means that a judgment—whether legal, moral, ethical, or otherwise value-laden—is being made. In making judgments, we try to fully understand three things: (1) the law, both the legal foundations for the choices and the legal ramifications of them; (2) the facts, both the facts at hand from our client and potential factual changes that could alter the outcome or make someone question the validity of the choice; and (3) our clients' needs so that this judgment does not have an unforeseen and unexpected impact on their business or interests. In law school, lawyers are trained to gather this vast array of information and knowledge, often by questioning their own beliefs, by confronting twists and turns in the facts, and by firmly stepping into alternative positions to examine the issue. In this process, the EI question is whether we recognize our initial reaction in real time such that we can most effectively shift from any emotional attachment to that position and engage another, regardless of our emotional feelings about it.

In the ancient story of the seven blind travelers and the elephant, the travelers encounter the great animal and are asked to describe what they have found. The one who is by the trunk says that an elephant is like a large snake. The one who is by the tail says that an elephant is like a rope. The one who is by a leg says that an elephant is like a tree. The one who is by the tusk says that an elephant is hard as a rock. The one who is by the ear says that an elephant is as soft as a baby's skin. The one who is by the hindquarter skin says that an elephant is rough like sandpaper. The story, then, has many different possible paths to the ending as the seventh traveler imparts a moral lesson. In some versions, the final traveler says that you cannot all be right; in others, the last one says that everyone is right. The moral, though, is that you have to be willing to shift into a position from which you can examine and appreciate the whole from varied perspectives without judgment—otherwise you are just a blind traveler touching but one part of a much larger and diverse entity.

ROB TAKING THE LEAD → I was brought in to work with a young female attorney who had tremendous potential but was increasingly seen by others as inflexible and difficult to work with.* She was also starting to isolate and appear disengaged after only a few years at the firm. By all measures, she was a rising star in the corporate law scene, who had a law degree from a top university where she graduated at the top of her class, outstanding work experience, and promising early career experience in the trial practice group. But there was one glaring problem: she was perceived in the workplace as having a negative attitude and being difficult to work with. Some even saw her as grandiose. While this did not matter much in her first five years due to her wins and successes in the courtroom, she was progressively ruffling more feathers in the office and had recently had a run-in with the managing partner. So the firm hired me to be her coach.

After just a few coaching sessions, she opened up to me about a performance review she had received at the end of her first year in the firm that made her feel ganged up on and blindsided. She repeatedly wanted to tell me about how she had been wronged. With no specific recommendations in the review, she did not know what the problem really was. She had also decided that the partner who conducted her review did not like her and was out to get her. She repeatedly said, "The system is flawed," "He doesn't like me," and "It's not fair."

While there may have been merit to these claims, her repeating them indicated that they had become her story, or narrative, and were deeply ingrained in her thinking. She had started to tell herself that the entire workplace was unjust and that she was unsupported. Again, there may have been validity to these claims, especially given the reality of persistent gender bias against women in the legal world. But what this attor-

* This story is but one example of how young female attorneys are viewed and treated in Big Law—a definite problem; however, the point of the example is that a person should focus on controlling what she can control in a given situation.

ney did not realize was how strongly she was holding onto these reactive statements, how they were contributing to her defensiveness, and how her defensiveness was creating an image of her as being a difficult and inflexible coworker.

We quickly realized, however, that the issue she was really dealing with was not the flawed performance system that was beyond her control but rather how she reacted to it. Once she let down her defenses with me, we were able to identify that she was actually *worried* about the review and *hurt* by the feedback—not angry, as others, including herself, had started to believe. She lacked emotional intelligence. She lacked self-awareness of what her core emotions were and could not see that her way of coping with pain and fear was to appear more action-oriented, direct, and strong, which only came across as angry, difficult, and inflexible to others. We were only able to reach this realization by first validating her experience and then acknowledging that workplace bias is real.

These negative storylines were starting to impact her mood and work satisfaction because she repeatedly told herself that she was unsupported and that things were unfair. After realizing the amount of time that she was spending on thinking this way (i.e., dwelling on the negative), and after feeling validated and heard (especially when I agreed that she was right about many of her thoughts about the flawed system and how unfairly female leaders can be treated in professional settings), she was able to see that she was not benefiting from it. Not only was this negative thinking not solving the problem, it was impacting her mood.

With a new self-awareness and the accurate identification of her emotions, she was able to start to work on her true feelings and offer more empathic responses to her coworkers. Her increased self-awareness enabled her to self-manage her responses to others, and as a result, her relationships in the office improved. After gaining more clout in the organization, she was eventually able to share her feelings with her colleagues about the performance system and its inherent gender biases in a calm, confident manner. This resulted in lasting changes in the way these performance reviews are conducted with young lawyers, particularly with young women.

↔

D. Strong Emotional Intelligence: Achievement, Performance, and Leadership

By looking at what lawyers do that involves managing themselves and managing relationships, it is obvious that emotional intelligence can enhance a person's ability to work, their work ethic, and ultimately their success in any endeavor. The following are some of the things lawyers do that involve self-awareness, self-management, social awareness, and relationship management (some or most of which you may already know):

- Balance the demands and deadlines of many clients and many bosses within stringent time constraints
- Be very detail oriented—that is, not letting small points escape them—in reading (researching the law in its many sources and forms), in listening (to a client, in getting an assignment, or in team strategizing with regard to how to solve a problem), in investigating the facts underlying a client's matter (turning over every possible stone in searching for relevant, damaging, and helpful facts); and in drafting documents
- Deliver negative, unexpected, or complex results to a client, associate, superior, or arbiter
- Negotiate complex matters among competing parties
- Prepare large, complicated documents, deals, and regulatory filings
- Prepare lengthy, complicated court filings
- Prepare for trial
- Know and follow complex rules of practice (court rules, practice rules, regulatory rules, statutory rules)
- Adhere to the highest ethical standards (those of the profession or the organization that they work for, or their own), particularly when there are pressures or gaps that yield advantages for their client, their employer, or themselves
- Maintain social relationships with other people: ranging from those with whom they have strong personal relationships to those with whom they have strong professional adversarial relationships, and everything in between

- Maintain a strong sense of self, self-worth, self-esteem, success, pride, humility, integrity, honesty, etc.
- Achieve personal and professional growth and development such that they are presented with additional opportunities

Feel free to add anything that you do as a lawyer that is missing from this list and could be related to emotional intelligence. And keep in mind that, in each instance, maximizing your EI ability is essential to the legal work.

Now let's look at ways that lawyers can improve their work, work ethic, and success:

1. Humanize self and work
2. Maintain ethical legal practice
3. Prioritize self-care and personal wellness*
4. Improve compassion and empathy
5. Improve their ability to work with others, ethically and in a diverse workplace
6. Maintain and enhance integrity
7. Be a leader**
8. Improve professional performance (beyond having a high IQ): achieve results, gain competitive advantage, strengthen client retention through relationship development, improve networking, and do more with less
9. Find work-life balance: follow values and passion, stay motivated, and still achieve professional goals (not one at the expense of the other)
10. Control attention and maintain focus (emotional intelligence and mindfulness versus perfectionistic tendencies and ADHD medication)

---

* It may strike you as odd that this item is number 3. But after some thought, it could be number 1. If you are not feeling as close to 100 percent as possible, then how can you expect to perform at that level? Yes, we all know anecdotes about people performing while ill, but that is not how a professional operates on a regular basis!

** Early in your legal career, you are not going to be in traditional leadership positions like policy and decision-making. Rather, you will be a lateral leader (among peers on a team) and seek leadership-type responsibilities (responsible for a section of the work) and leadership opportunities (serve on a committee), particularly among highly diverse groups of individuals.

11. Maintain connections and avoid feelings of isolation and loneliness***
12. Prevent burnout, depression, and substance dependence
13. Maintain strong self-confidence
14. Market their skills, pay for their talents, and advance professionally

↑↓↑

SELF-DISCOVERY EXERCISE 3: GOALS FOR IMPROVEMENT

You can think of the preceding list as goals for improvement. Now look at the chart below. Think about the different areas of legal work in relation to the years of experience, regardless of the location of the work (big law, midsize firm, small firm, NGO (non-governmental organization), government, etc.), and place each of the previously numbered goals for improvement where you think they fit (or fit best) for you, or generally.

	Litigation	Regulatory	Transactional
As a Law Student			
As a Young Lawyer (1–5 years)			
As an Experienced Lawyer (6–12 years)			
As a Lawyer Leader (13+ years)			

[STOP and COMPLETE before reading further.]

↑↓↑

*** When you think that you are the only one, the bottom can drop out—fast. Personal isolation can lead to social isolation—a warning sign of worse to come. Building individual courage and social connections is the cure.[28]

REFLECTIVE WRITING 3

As a debrief of Self-Discovery Exercise 3, refer to your completed chart while thinking about your area of work and your trajectory through time. Consider how these goals for improvement, emotional intelligence, and your path can coincide.

- → How is leadership important in your area of work?
- → Where do you anticipate leadership will come up?
- → What types of teams will be involved in these leadership situations?
- → How will your EI skills be critical in leading in your specific area of law?

□ □ □

Nice work! You've successfully navigated the background and foundation sections of this book. Everything that has been included up to this point helps to set the stage for your leadership journey. You now know the importance of emotional intelligence in legal education and the practice of law. We hope you see the true power of emotional intelligence in your own well-being, in your effectiveness as a lawyer, and in your leadership, both in your career and in your personal life.

Over the course of the next few chapters, we take a deep dive into each domain of emotional intelligence, incorporating our experience, knowledge, and guidance throughout. This exploration culminates in the final chapter, where we bring it all together in our leadership model that we refer to as *twenty-first-century leadership*. We hope that you enjoy the process!

CHAPTER III

Know Thyself

Self-Awareness in Legal Practice

EVERY JOURNEY STARTS WITH THE FIRST STEP—and on the journey to becoming an emotionally intelligent lawyer and exceptional leader, that first step is building self-awareness. Carl Jung said, "Who looks outside, dreams; who looks inside, awakes."[1] Indeed, self-awareness is the cornerstone of emotional intelligence as it allows you to see your immediate *reactions* and have the conscious awareness in real time to choose the best *response*.

Leaders who are high in self-awareness know their personal shortcomings and then learn how to make adjustments in those areas, not only to perform optimally but also to experience the most career satisfaction. Developing self-awareness is also a prerequisite to improving the other areas of emotional intelligence. Without self-awareness, it is virtually impossible to manage your emotions and relationships at the level that you want or that is most beneficial to you. A professional, like a lawyer, who lacks self-awareness is like a ship at sea without a compass, at constant risk of going off course. For instance, self-awareness of personal values, such as family, keeps you driven by what truly matters, as opposed to being driven by other factors, such as wealth, prestige, or glory. As previously noted, staying focused on what really matters can be particularly challenging when law students or lawyers are presented with extrinsic goals that can subtly supplant personal values.

So how do you develop self-awareness? Like all social and emotional growth, you first have to understand what it is before you can actually practice it. Self-awareness has been defined in several ways over the years and with various interchangeable terms, such as *insight*. It is generally agreed that self-awareness is recognizing and understanding your own emotions, thoughts, and behaviors and the interplay between them. In each domain of emotional intelligence, two types of learning need to take place: (1) cognitive learning and (2) experiential learning (in which you try out the new skills and competencies).

In this chapter, we present our model of self-awareness so that you have a cognitive framework to understand it. We then introduce various exercises to help you become more self-aware. Your life is a story full of chapters that have influenced and shaped who you are; better and continual understanding of that story, or narrative, heightens your self-awareness. We spend the bulk of this chapter helping you to connect the dots from your background to the type of leader you are today. We also spend substantial time on mindfulness, which is the primary vehicle for greater current, or in-the-moment, self-awareness. Self-awareness as attained through the practice of mindfulness allows you to understand what you are thinking and feeling in real time. This is self-awareness in the EI sense. Mindfulness practice has been found to be one of the best ways to develop the muscles of self-reflection.

In the final section of this chapter, we highlight the power of psychological assessment in gaining greater self-awareness. You have default settings, or subconscious strengths and weaknesses, that take over your thoughts and actions in times of stress. The Myers-Briggs Type Indicator (MBTI®) is one personality tool that reveals these default, or subconscious, settings, which in turn raises your self-awareness. We give you just enough background on these default settings so that you can identify some of your top personality characteristics and how they influence your leadership.

A. The Two-Branch Model of Self-Awareness

We approach self-awareness as having two distinct branches: (1) *deep insight* and (2) *present-moment awareness*. While some EI models focus solely on the latter, we believe strongly that self-aware lawyers and leaders have and need both. We also want to be clear that we developed this model from years of practice, so it is not based in empirical research. We have seen, time and again, that great leaders know what is coming up for them in the moment. We refer to this branch simply as *present-moment awareness* because it involves being aware of the thoughts, feelings, and behaviors happening in the moment and their interplay. At time same time, great leaders are keenly aware of their deeper story, or personal narrative, which allows them to know where their emotional, behavioral, cognitive, and coping reactions originate. By *deep insight*, we mean knowing who you are with regard to what drives you—your values, motivators, and purpose. This form of self-awareness is about knowing who you are on a deep level and how you got there. It is also about knowing your deeper default patterns and habits, your strengths and weaknesses, and where they originate. These deeper aspects of yourself, such as core beliefs and values, directly influence how you respond as a leader or lawyer in the moment. With deeper insight into your default mode of responding, present-moment awareness comes more naturally.

To highlight the difference between the two, let's consider a common lawyer tendency that is advantageous for lawyers to monitor: negative thinking.

GEORGE'S STORY → Rob has been coaching a lawyer (let's call him George) for the past few years who had a tendency to be critical—of himself, of others, and of much of what is around him. He is a perfect example of someone who has been successful by all metrics but felt agitated and alone, and he had difficulty understanding how it was possible for him to be unhappy when he looked at his life on paper. He spent his time dwelling on the negative with minimal awareness of how negative his thinking had become and the ramifications of that thinking. His default attitude and coping style were to complain and expect that things will not work out. In order to think more positively, he had to first gain awareness of his narrative about work and life. As George shared his experiences, Rob repeated his thoughts back to him. Through that sharing, George started to distance himself from his thoughts, noticed the inherent negativity, and gained clarity about how his own outlook was affecting his life. He also did the work to recognize where these default thinking-patterns originated.

The real change will happen when he can practice present-moment awareness and catch his negative thinking in real time; however, this is more difficult to do than one might expect. His chances of success are much higher if he first understands where this cognitive habit originated. He has to gain (1) deep insight in order to practice (2) present moment awareness.

↔

1. Deep Insight: Understanding Your Personal Narrative

The first branch of self-awareness is deep insight. In other words, the first step in self-awareness is to understand how your life experiences shape who you are. Emotionally intelligent people know who they are and what they value, and they have identified their purpose. They found their calling by self-analysis and live their life aligned with their values. Self-aware lawyers know how they arrived where they are and where they are headed—that is, they understand their "story," or personal narrative.

Defining moments and influencers. Understanding your story begins with knowing from where your habits and values originate. If you think about it, your patterns of coping with and reacting to the world around you have a long history. You are the result of your experiences. The way that you deal with others and manage yourself is the result of the circuitous route that led you to the present moment. Having deep insight means understanding how that route led to who you are today. In our combined work with lawyers and other professionals, it became clear that insight has to do with knowing two key things: defining moments and influencers. Indeed, it is about understanding the defining moments in your life in combination with the most influential people in your life. After all, experiences and people molded you into the law student or lawyer that you are today.

By *defining moments*, we do not mean single isolating events or major changes, although they certainly could be either. Rather, defining moments may be entire phases or chapters of your life, such as a year of work or marriage, or they could be shorter experiences, such as a particular global adventure. Later in the chapter we help you to identify your defining moments and truly understand how they contributed to who you are today.

Influencers are just that—the people in your life who have or had the greatest impact on you. They are the individuals you watched and observed and decided to emulate—the people who consciously or subconsciously taught you how to live and what to value. These individuals can be people you know personally or not.

In order to have *deep insight*, you have to understand how these defining moments and influencers led you to where and who you are today. With this level of self-awareness, you will find your authentic self and others will believe in you, which is the essence of great leadership. Thus, the critical first part of this branch of self-awareness is being able to understand who you are on a deep level—that is, how the defining moments and the most influential people in your life got you here.

Personal narrative. These defining moments and influencers are the foundation of your *personal narrative*—that is, *who you are, why you are here*, and *what is important to you*.

Chances are good that you are well past your first year of law school, either literally or figuratively, and can probably think of more times than you have fingers when you barreled forward doing something without thinking. As should be clear by now, that drive to act before thinking is a product of a lack of emotional self-awareness. Sometimes you still get where you want to go because your actions are the product of good training and instinct, such as when a lawyer asserts an objection immediately upon the completion of opposing counsel's question (and then has to think of and articulate the rule on which the objection is based), when adding standard clauses to a contract or other agreement, or when drafting legislation and regulations that follow a standard format. Equally often, emotions arise before you cognitively register what is going on, such as when you hastily respond to an incendiary comment from an adversary without thinking about the best way to address the point, or when you hastily write and send an email responding to an irritating one that you just received without thinking through how that new written record may show up later and hurt you or your client. Some of this difference is accounted for by your personal narrative, which consists of your lifelong experiences, formative events, understanding of your values, and impact of your influencers.[2]

These days you hear myriad terms and phrases related to personal narrative: *story, narrative, tell your story, control the narrative, listen to their story, wait for the narrative to develop*, etc. Stories and narratives have been with us forever. Before we had writing, we had stories. Stories were passed down orally. Stories were drawn in caves. If you examined the droppings of a dinosaur, you would find a story that might be a formative moment for you!

How do you best understand your story? You can turn to science and explore your heritage by having a DNA sample analyzed, then tell others where your ancestors came from. You can emulate others by watching different people in varied media as they try to create narrative around events as they unfold. You can listen to politicians who try to present a compelling anecdote to convince you to be for or against some policy. You can wait for the next large-scale sporting event (e.g., the Super Bowl or Olympics) and read compelling stories about how particular athletes came from nowhere, came back from a horrible place, or have always dreamed of being here and are all here now. You can go to your house of worship and hear your spiritual leader retell the stories from the book of your faith and relate them to your life and the larger world with a moral message. You can watch stories presented on television and in movies that tap into these same stories of redemption, whether religious, sports-related, political, medical, and so on. Perhaps sometimes you even tell the stories of others when they are related to the moment. You may tell these certain stories to others in the hope that they will take a moral lesson, to your clients so that they will better understand the ramifications of particular choices, or even to others about your clients so that they are better able to understand your clients and their needs.

But what are you doing about your story? Do you know your story? Do you tell your story? Have you connected the dots between your youth, your life's defining moments, and your current behavioral and leadership patterns? Sure, you wrote your story in an essay for your college admissions application and another one for your law school admissions application. Who did you write those stories *for*? Someone else. You have a story, and it is chock full of your life's lessons and experiences, successes and failures, friends and family, and values and morals. There are parts you tell readily and parts you may not want to share. You tell your story if it is compelling. But never forget that your entire story, your whole personal narrative, is a core part of defining who you are. As Brené Brown has so eloquently stated, "Owning our story can be hard but not nearly as difficult as spending our lives running from it."[3] These stories, whether told to others or to yourself, make up your narrative identity[4] and form the foundation of your leadership style.

Using stories of a law student and a lawyer, let's look more closely at personal narratives to unpack the concepts therein.

SINEAD'S STORY → It was May. The first week of spring 1L exams. A female student with a decidedly non-Jewish name (let's call her Sinead) went into Cliff's office in tears. The Constitutional Law exam was scheduled to start in thirty minutes, and Sinead said that she could not do it. She said that law school had been a struggle and that she hit a wall studying for Con Law. She did not think that she could go on.

She was clearly not being melodramatic. She definitely could not take the exam. But there was a more important question below the surface of her exam distress. So Cliff asked Sinead what she wanted to be. She paused and stared at Cliff. Cliff asked again, "What do you want to be?"

Still stymied, she said, "Of anything?"

"Yes," said Cliff.

She said that she always wanted to be a rabbi. After a pause to absorb her answer, Cliff said, "Well, then you should be a rabbi."

"I can?"

"Has no one ever asked you what you wanted to be?"

"No."

"If you want to be a rabbi, then you should be a rabbi."

The tears left, replaced by a smile. Cliff and Sinead decided that she need not take the exam, then or ever. Sinead left law school that day and entered rabbinical studies the following year.

↔

Sinead was suffering from both a lack of emotional intelligence and a lack of connection with her personal narrative. She was feeling strong emotions and acting on them without understanding the impetus. There was a gap in her personal narrative because she had lost sight of why she went to law school—that this was someone else's idea and that she was "following the crowd" and doing what she thought she was supposed to do. With respect to emotional self-awareness, Sinead was in a bad way, feeling sad, unmotivated, and perhaps depressed. She was that way because she was on a path that did not align with her own purpose and interests, she could not recognize that, and she was, for quite some time (almost a year), willing to accept that this was to be her lot in life.*

Sinead had lost touch with her personal narrative and the values, goals, and important elements of her life. She was so overwhelmed by the

* Biblical pun intended.

conflict that her brain shut down and just would not let her study another subject. She was (and still is) extremely intelligent, though she could not read the barometer of her feelings or navigate back to her narrative.

Although Sinead's eventual self-awareness took her away from the law, this example precisely exposes how many law students quickly lose sight of their personal narrative. The story also illustrates how easily law students are swept into and carried away by the fast current of legal education.[5] It happens so quickly and completely that some do not even realize that they are drowning until some part of their system shuts down. This is equally true for lawyers who find themselves working in areas that are at odds with their narrative and values. Because law was not what Sinead wanted, and because she was so unaware of what was driving her emotions, her train ride through law school was bound to be extremely bumpy, eventually going off the rails. But on the bright side, Sinead's story shows the impact that even a small but salient degree of emotional intelligence can have in getting oneself back on course. Rather than sit for the Con Law exam, she sought help from someone because she recognized a deep emotional feeling that things were not right.

How is your personal narrative fitting in with your current chapter in life? Do you know what you have learned from your story? Do you use those lessons to improve your life and the lives of those around you? When events occur in your life, you need to try to learn from them. We all have a (natural) tendency to take lessons from the successes and try to distance ourselves from the failures, but that is completely backwards. In the success stories, we know what we did, we know the result, and chances are that we learned nothing new. We are pretty sure that should the same thing happen again, it will happen under the same circumstances.[6] Ironically, the same thing can be said of the failures (definition of insanity: doing the same thing over and over and expecting a different result); but in the case of failures, we need to figure out what went wrong so that we can make changes for the better should the same or similar circumstances arise.[7] Our mistakes always catch up with us if we try to ignore them. Do we consider them in our personal narrative? We should. In his novel *Even Cowgirls Get the Blues*, Tom Robbins eloquently wrote,

> So you think that you're a failure, do you? Well, you probably are. What's wrong with that? In the first place, if you've any sense at all you must have learned by now that we pay just as

> dearly for our triumphs as we do for our defeats. Go ahead and fail. But fail with wit, fail with grace, fail with style. A mediocre failure is as insufferable as a mediocre success. Embrace failure! Seek it out. Learn to love it. That may be the only way any of us will ever be free.[8]

All events in our lives, whether positive or negative, are formative. Things happen in life that shape us. The question is how much we should embrace the experiences and incorporate them into our personal narrative so that we gain further insight into who we are, where we have been, where we want to go, and how we get there.[9] What we think of these events as they fit into our personal narrative (either as stories in our overall narrative or as chapters in the story of our life) helps shape what we believe in, or our values.[10] While this is important for everyone, it is even more so for those who lead (politically, spiritually, economically), those who are responsible for lawmaking and its enforcement (lawyers, legislators, criminal justice), and those whom we look up to (you can fill in this parenthetical).

In learning from your stories, it is very important to take personal responsibility, to not place blame on others to make yourself feel better, to not judge others unfairly, and to not extend any experiences unfairly to others by association. Think about this in the context of losing a key client: if you are to truly learn from the experience, then you must try to ascertain fairly what contributed to the loss. What were your actions? What feedback was given to you about your work or firm that can be used as a lesson for growth? In this type of evaluation, try not to judge based on the type of client or person with whom you had the experience.

With so many people on the planet, we are constantly crashing into each other. By *crash*, we mean to say that life circumstances bring us together—and not always in comfortable ways. We have to deal with those situations and learn from those encounters. That is how our own narrative develops and how we learn the lessons that guide our lives.

Through Cliff's role as dean of students in a law school, he learned much about life, relationships, himself, his values, and what it takes to be a good carbon being among the more than seven billion other carbon beings trying to survive on this planet. Personal narrative, though, is not as clear or linear as one might think. We are constantly rethinking our stories in search of better understanding, a greater sense of coherence, and consistency or a through line—all of which relate to defining who we are, why we are here, and what is important to us.[11] Let's look at Cliff's story from several different angles.

CLIFF TAKING THE LEAD → "And you may ask yourself, 'Well, how did I get here?'"* To the outsider, my career looks like a neat, planned, upward climb: a nice liberal arts education, then straight to law school (K–JD), working summers in litigation, and landing a job with a boutique litigation firm. Success after success. All my work had been in civil rights- and civil liberties-related fields, and every plateau on that route was squarely within those realms. Then, like the associate who had preceded me, I started teaching law. After teaching at one institution for ten-plus years, I catapulted to teach at a top law school. Then I took on the academic counselor duties, working closely with the dean of students. Based on our experience working together, when she announced her departure, she recommended to the dean that I be her replacement. After a lengthy tenure in that role, I stepped aside to return to teaching full time.

Upon closer inspection, this "neat upward climb" narrative may actually resemble less a cleared path and more a pinball bouncing off bumpers. I chose my undergraduate institution because it was the college or university that accepted me and was farthest from home. I went to law school because I did not want to have to find a job and start working. While my politics have always been left of center, I had long hair when it was in fashion, so people assumed I held progressive views, and I felt comfortable with those people. Thus, I was welcomed into the civil rights community as a trial lawyer. Five years post-graduation, the firm divided. Unable to decide which of the partners to follow and learning of an open teaching position, I opted to teach instead, even though I had no teaching experience. I went from one law school to another because of the fortuity of calling a colleague to congratulate her on a promotion only for her to ask me to interview for her old job. Never having supervised anyone, and after a little over a year of working with the outgoing dean of students, I segued into a managerial, supervisory, decanal position. Not having taught full-time for over a dozen years, I dove into

* This is from the song "Once in a Lifetime" by Talking Heads.

teaching those courses the law school needed that related to or overlapped with areas in which I had practiced.

Which personal narrative is mine: the stock story of climbing from one successful position to another or the alternative story of luck and happenstance? Is it a combination of the two, or is there another story missing, one requiring a high degree of self-awareness of underlying emotions and values and which brings those emotions and values to bear in the narrative? As but one example, what is in the personal narrative that explains my being able to take on an extraordinarily challenging leadership role despite having no prior experience in supervision or management?

Let's be clear: when I was approached to be dean of students, the totality of my knowledge of what a dean of students does could fit in a shoebox. The dean of students when I was in law school only seemed to aggravate students, hide in her office, and attempt friendly but microaggressive appeals to students. She was offensive yet harmless, intrusive yet ultimately ineffective. At my first law teaching job, I had only indirectly encountered the dean of students. One day shortly before spring break, one of my first-year students rushed into my office in tears. She explained that she needed to have surgery over break and that the recovery would be tough, but that she thought she could come back and finish her first year of law school. That seemed reasonable to me, so I said so and asked why she was crying. She said that she had just seen the dean of students and told her of the very same issue, but the response she got was that she should drop out of law school. This dean of students did not seem to understand just how much it meant to law students to get to and through law school, something that was readily apparent in the student in front of me. I told her that the dean's response sounded like an overreaction, that the choice should be hers and hers alone, and that she should find trusted sources of information to help her make the decision. She was very grateful and no longer crying. By the way, she came back from surgery and finished both her first year and her legal education as she had planned, in one and three years, respectively.

Despite that one-off conversation, the job was seemingly about as far from my skill set as possible. I knew that office hours and student conferences drained me. Individual conferences were such a struggle for me that, at least once in every set of conferences, my mind would wander until I was no longer mentally present in the conversation. Suddenly I would snap out of it only to find the student staring at me, waiting for an answer and not knowing that I had little recollection of where the conversation had just been. The job of dean of students would require this precise level of interaction with all students, at the most challenging times, with no space or tolerance for losing focus.

So back to the question, what is my personal narrative? It is only through thinking about self-awareness and the values that I hold deeply and have lived by that the narratives sort into the one that is my own. Not surprisingly, then, pieces of each of the narratives make sense for me. Allow me to clarify.

All throughout, though not known to me as such, I had strong EI skills—from knowing the importance of self-awareness to strengthening empathy to understanding the organization and the need to respond positively and inspire those I worked with and who worked around me. I say "not known to me as such" because I think others recognized and responded to this characteristic long before I knew or understood this about myself. No one ever connected the dots for me, and not being a self-promoting type (in fact, like many law students and lawyers, I do a healthy job of suppressing self-esteem), I repeatedly failed to see the signs.

In retrospect, I see not only how EI skills carried me forward but also the role that my values played in building my personal narrative. One of my most important values is independence, which explains my effort to break free from my upbringing and go to college as far from home as possible. This independence gave me the confidence to take on tasks even when I was unsure whether they were a good fit or whether I had the right skills and experiences. My family is of the utmost importance to me, and this love for my family served as the driving force behind my decision to leave the practice of law to teach. My wife and I were having our first child, and I wanted a work-life balance where I could prioritize my family over the demands of my work, so I left my known job for an unknown job in the hope of finding this balance. Notwithstanding the story about student conferences above, I am a good listener, and people have always sought me out for that purpose. In addition, every job I have taken has focused on helping others, and my caring and empathic attitude permeates my work and life. I value being able to pay close attention to details without losing sight of the big picture, and this ability helps me solve problems of any scale. Clearly, strong EI and a strong value orientation frame my personal narrative. As a bonus, in recognition of that combined strength, I am able to deal with low self-esteem by acknowledging it and continually trying to address it without being perfectionistic, losing balance, or inflicting self-loathing.

Going to law school gave me the chance to recognize how my values and narrative would fit together. Lawyers, particularly litigators, plan ahead. They investigate claims to be sure that they have and can prove sufficient facts to support their allegations. They interview their clients, visit the scene(s), interview witnesses, collect documents, request information, and verify and verify again. They do this because they want to be strategic and see all the possibilities. Lawyers who make mistakes get reprimanded and punished, their clients get hurt, they can be fined, and they can lose their law license. As one judge told a group of our students, "You have one thing when you walk into my courtroom: your integrity. Only you can lose it, and the decision is yours." So lawyers plan ahead, and my studying and practice in the law brought this out in me.

Heading into the dean of students role, I was about to learn an incredible amount about people and what they are made of—their hopes, dreams, and challenges—and how to help them get to where they want to be. I was about to become open to the need to more consciously understand myself as well. When I walked into the dean of students' office in May 2004, it was facing multiple crises, and strong emotional intelligence is what helped me get through them. The office carpet was wet and smelled of mold. The employees (ten) smelled fresh blood in their new leadership and wanted some changes. The first student complaint I received was a student-on-student threat.

The key, though, is that as dean of students I learned how to help students find missing, damaged, or hidden pieces of their narrative. Once located, they could relearn how to value them and grow them into a foundation so that they could then learn what they had hoped to learn in law school. I knew the research on how law students lose sight of their intrinsic or core values in law school, particularly as law school substitutes them with shiny baubles of extrinsic values that eventually ring hollow for many (think about replacing integrity with money, or honesty with prestige). While this does cause problems for some students (particularly depression and substance abuse), many other students encounter different, more personal challenges, such as loss, peer pressure, family expectations, an inability to deal with failure (lowercase "f", not the grade "F"), loss of identity, and the like. These same challenges can extend into practice or appear anew to lawyers in practice.[12]

Our values are at the core of the answer to the question "Which narrative is accurate?" We have and hold these values, but they are only beneficial if we are aware of what they are and how we feel about them. However, trying to get law students to reacquaint with their values is tough; a direct message would surely come off as preachy and not be taken seriously. Slowly, through taking a training course on administering the MBTI®, by sharing the assessment's impact on me, and by learning more about leadership, personal narrative, formative events (particularly the ones that bring law students to see the dean of students), redemption (learning from those events), generativity (giving back to others), and ultimately professional identity formation, I found ways to address values and narrative with the law students.[13] I also found my calling, or purpose, in the process, which was essential in helping me with present-moment awareness.

While I cannot remember why I decided to get MBTI® training (it seemingly fits into my pinball pattern of education and job movement), I do have the fondest memories of the course, which was tailored to law school faculty and administrators. I found the MBTI® fascinating not because it answered the be-all and end-all questions but rather because it raised my level of self-awareness. I finally understood why I did certain things, like blurt out reactions to ideas even though I like to think on things, perhaps even overnight, before voicing my views. I was often frustrated by this tendency, and the MBTI® gave me the self-awareness to recognize it and then address it in ways that I had never considered. It is clear how such knowledge would help me in my leadership role at the law school (I was associate dean at the time), particularly with regard to working with the dean and other associate deans. It also led me to recognize the need to hire a law school psychologist and the need for immersion in emotional intelligence.

↔

ROB TAKING THE LEAD → When I started working as the law school psychologist, it quickly became clear that while law students may present with various surface-level or context-specific problems in therapy, some key underlying themes were present. One of the themes was a lack of awareness of personal narrative. Indeed, lawyers need help reconnecting with what matters most to them in life, as well as tools to stay grounded to these values in the face of pressure. This is key for law students charting their course, but it is equally essential for lawyers in leadership roles as their success depends heavily on their ability to follow their purpose with passion. The data we cited earlier on lawyer mental health pointed to the tendency for lawyers to measure their lives by extrinsic factors, such as salary, when in fact they have not been found to be strong predictors of success and can actually be quite detrimental. I needed a way to help them gain clarity about what really mattered to them (their values) so that they could align their lives with these work/life motivators, be driven by passion, live out their life's purpose, and be happy. How hard could that be, right?

↔

As we explored and researched how to make this process as tangible as possible—how to really help leaders in various industries tell their story and identify what truly matters to them—the idea of passion mapping emerged. In this next exercise, we will walk you through a process of reflecting on your defining moments and influencers, how they impacted you, and how they ultimately led you to who you are today. By connecting the dots between the key moments in your life and who you are today, you tell your story and find purpose-driven leadership.

↑↓↑

SELF-DISCOVERY EXERCISE 4: PASSION MAPPING

The "passion-mapping" self-discovery exercise will help you create a map between *influencers* and *defining moments*, where you are in your career now, and where you hope to go. Having deep-insight self-awareness is central to becoming an authentic leader. When you follow what is most important to you (values) and what you are most passionate about, you will lead authentically, and people will naturally want to follow you. Your passion can be derived from your life story (also known as your personal narrative), and only you can determine what it should be. Complete the following exercise to discover what you are passionate about and the purpose behind your leadership.

STEP I: Identify your influencers.

Who have been the most influential people in your life? These may be the people who first recognized your potential, people who inspire you, people to whom you look for guidance, or others. Who had the greatest impact on you? Write their names in your leadership journal or notebook, or create a Word doc.

[**STOP and COMPLETE before reading further.**]

From your list of influencers, pick the top three. For each of the three, answer the following questions:

1. Why was this person so influential?
2. What did you learn from this person?
3. How did this person impact you? For example, what beliefs and/or values do you have as a result of this person's influence? What behaviors and habits—good and bad—did you pick up?

Before leaving Step I, be sure to fully reflect on these people in your life. Maybe at different points in the past, the first list and/or the top three looked different—and five years from now, it is probable that they will look different from the way they look now. How did these people fit into your life: Are they relations? Did other people bring you together? Did you seek them out, or was it more like happenstance? How are these people alike or different from each other and from you? How deep and long-lasting was or is their impact on your life? Were they trying to shape or mold you, or did they provide space for you to grow and develop while providing outer boundaries to keep you safe in the process? All of these thoughts and reflections might make you add to your answers above and will help you to answer the prompt below.

TAKEAWAY: How did these influencers collectively influence your career development and what you want to do with your life? How did they lead you to where you are today?

[**STOP and COMPLETE before reading further.**]

STEP II: Identify your defining moments.

What are the top defining moments in your life? Starting with your earliest memories, consider which experiences marked key turning points in your life. Maybe these were times of key decisions at a fork in your life's path; maybe they were happy or sad life events, or events that just arose, for better or worse. These defining moments may be one single moment or a period of time. Write these moments in your leadership journal or notebook, or in a Word doc.

[**STOP and COMPLETE before reading further.**]

From your list of defining moments, pick the top three. For each of the three, answer the following questions:

1. Why was this experience so influential?
2. What did you learn from this experience, then and since? What was the takeaway or lesson? (You can have more than one.)
3. In what ways does this experience define who you are today? Is there a connection to the way you are (e.g., socially, habitually/behaviorally, career wise)?

Before leaving Step II, be sure to fully reflect on these moments in your life. Maybe at different points in the past, the first list and/or the top three looked different—and five years from now, it is probable that they will look different from the way they look now. Think about how these moments fit into your life more broadly. Are there multiple ways to interpret how these events came to be, what you take from them, or how they fit together? Can you identify any threads of commonality? How deep and long-lasting was or is their impact on your life? If you think of your life so far as a linear path, did these moments simply appear on that path, or did they alter your direction? All of these thoughts and reflections might make you add to your answers above and will help you to answer the prompt below.

TAKEAWAY: How did these defining moments influence your career development and what you want to do with your life? How did they lead you to where you are today?

Look back at the takeaways that you came up with for each influencer and each defining moment. Choose one defining moment *and* one influencer that especially resonates with you and is significant at this point in your life. What was the takeaway from each? Create a chart like the one below in your leadership journal and write them in the space that says "Takeaway." (You can start with one influencer and one defining moment, or you can do this for each influencer and each defining moment.)

How have these takeaways made you who you are? How did the combination lead to your values and life's mission or purpose? Try to write out your mission statement using the combination of these takeaways.

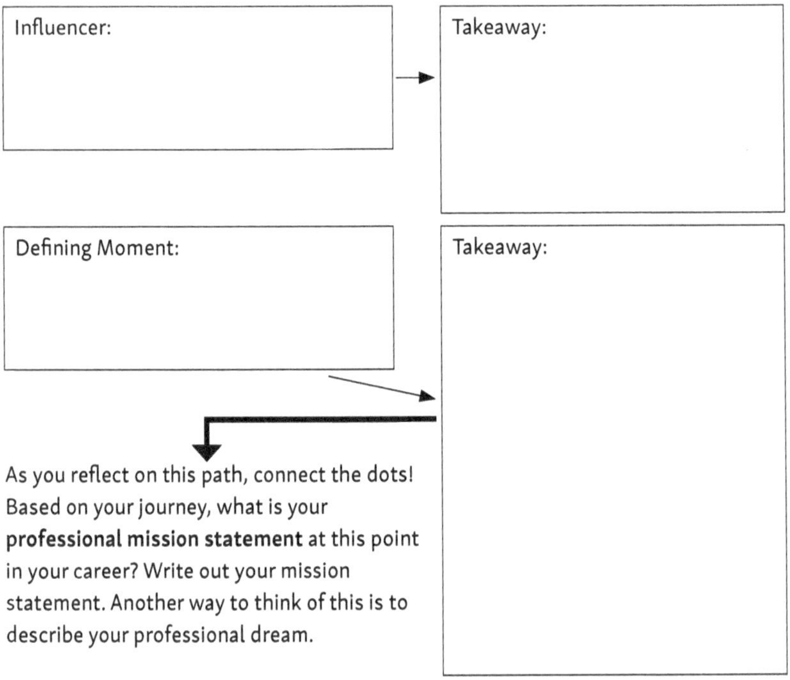

[STOP and COMPLETE before reading further.]

↑ ↓ ↑

REFLECTIVE WRITING 4

Now that you have completed the passion-mapping self-discovery exercise (Exercise 4) and are thinking about the influential people and defining moments in your life, it is a great time to do some reflective writing on what you have learned, using this newfound insight to engage with your personal narrative and your self-awareness. And remember, reflective writing trains the muscles in the brain necessary for self-reflection, which brings about self-awareness.

The sum of your answers to the following prompts will help define your personal narrative and then extend it toward defining your professional identity. Professional identity is defined in many ways by many people.[14] We think of it as the totality of your personal narrative and personal values as expressed by you through your work, your actions, and your decisions.

- → Who are you? (personal narrative)
- → How have your life experiences led you to where you are today?
- → Are there different ways to interpret how these pieces fit together?
- → What is important to you? (values)
- → What core values do you bring to your leadership as a result of early influencers and defining moments?
- → Why are you here? (your path, journey, and goals)
- → What are you most passionate about at this point in your life?

Now consider these additional questions that relate to your answers to the previous questions:

- → How do you define *success*?
- → What do you see as the biggest impediment(s) to your success?
- → Do you know of personal weaknesses that may be impediments to your success?
- → What does it mean to be self-aware?
- → What are the qualities of people who are self-aware?
- → Who in your life and career has moved you?
- → In your experience, think of the best boss, mentor, or teacher. What qualities made that person the best?
- → In your experience, think of the worst boss, mentor, or teacher. What qualities made that person the worst?
- → What skills will make you a better lawyer?
- → Think about and describe a time when after doing something, you realized that you could have done it much better if you had thought about X (fill in something that you did or did not do) ahead of time.
- → What would you include in your personal and professional mission statement?

2. Mindfulness: Developing Greater Current-Moment Self-Awareness

Now we are going to move into the second branch of self-awareness, which is the cornerstone of self-awareness and emotional intelligence: present-moment awareness of your emotional life in real time. As you begin to understand your personal narrative and passion map, your reactions to current-moment experiences should become more obvious and clearer. You now know where your default tendencies originate and can see them more clearly. You know how the defining moments in your life impacted you, what they brought out in you, and how your response to those experiences led to your present-moment reactions.

Basic brain function. In order to master the skill of present-moment awareness, you first must understand a bit more about your brain. Emotional intelligence is a collection of emotional skills that can be trained based on the science of neuroplasticity. *Neuroplasticity* is an umbrella term referring to the ability of your brain to reorganize itself, both physically and functionally, throughout your life due to your environment, behavior, thinking, and emotions. The concept of a flexible and adaptable brain has replaced the formerly held belief that critical developmental periods occur only in childhood and so the adult brain is pretty much a hardwired, physiologically static organ. But it turns out you can teach an old dog new tricks! While it is true that the brain is much more malleable during the early years of life and that capacity declines with age, the potential for change remains present throughout your life.

Start by thinking of your brain as being of two minds: the emotional and the rational. The emotional brain responds to an event much more quickly than your rational or thinking brain; when your brain responds more emotionally than you would like, it is essentially operating on autopilot. Given a little extra time to process a stressful situation, you may take a different approach, usually a better or more thoughtful one, from the initial one driven by your automatic response or reaction under pressure. You get smarter when your rational, or logical, brain has the time and opportunity to kick in.

Expanding on this point, think for a minute about the lawyer or leader (we will use leader to avoid confusion and repetition) who has all the potential in the world (high IQ) but struggles to control their temper (low EQ). When that IQ leader is in a meeting and an employee says that he is not feeling supported, the leader might react on impulse. Under those circumstances, the emotional brain quickly responds, telling the leader to be defensive regardless of the impact on the employee's feelings, and the leader says something dismissive or directs the employee to leave. We all have probably seen this scenario play out first-hand, whether between others or personally. You could be the most intelligent leader in the organization, but if you do not have self-awareness in order to manage your emotional reactions, you will not get very far.

While the focus of this book is on EI skill development to enhance your leadership in the law, providing some basic understanding of the neuroscience of emotion can be useful. The neuroscientific research behind emotional intelligence, which is still in its infancy in many ways, is based on human lesion studies. Despite advanced neuroimaging technology, there are a few consistent findings,[15] including growing evidence suggesting that brain regions and neural circuits play a central role in how we process and manage emotions.

The neuroscience behind our emotional life is dense and complex and we are not going to provide a neuroanatomy lesson here (and we are sure you are not looking for that). That said, leaders need to understand several key points about the biology at work in emotional life. The way the brain is wired has not only kept us alive from an evolutionary perspective but also makes emotion regulation quite challenging in our modern society. We are hard wired for survival so certain brain regions throw us into an emotional response so we can move without thinking (and avoid being eaten by a sabertooth tiger). Surely you have noticed this in many instances. You actually feel before you think about it. You are surprised, so you react. You feel anger, so you pounce. You feel joy, so you smile.

Indeed, evolutionary psychologists teach us that over time, the brain evolved from the bottom up and has continually been shaped by what works for survival, all the while retaining that basic survival instinct. Our brains evolved to code and detect emotions because emotions are key to our survival. Researchers are growing in their agreement that neural pathways for feelings bypass the thinking regions of the brain. This is especially true for our strongest emotions, which explains how these emotional responses can overpower rationality. In other words, these neural pathways ignite an emotional response before the thinking regions of the brain are active. While this was quite advantageous in our natural environment, nature, such as responding with force or fleeing a dangerous situation (the sabertooth tiger), it can lead to significant negative consequences in a corporate office or courtroom, when someone says something that offends us.

Several key brain regions have been found to play a central role in emotional life and they are collectively referred to as the Limbic System. The limbic system, or *emotional brain*, involves the amygdala, hippocampus, and hypothalamus. The amygdala, a specialized structure in the midbrain (core), has received the most attention in EI training for its role as an emotional scout and in receiving direct input from the senses to start a response before everything has fully registered with the neocortex (thinking brain). The amygdala is thought to be responsible for detecting threats and triggering potent, core emotional responses like anger and fear. The brain works to protect us by sending signals to the regions that bring about emotional responses, to move us to safety (the latin root of the word emotion is to move).

The amygdala allows us to respond while the slightly slower but more thoughtful neocortex maps out its more refined plan for reaction. Neuroscientific research explains how the amygdala can take control over what we do even as the thinking brain, the neocortex, is still gathering information to come to a decision. With self-awareness, we are able to catch our natural, emotional (and cognitive and behavioral), default reactions and then choose to proceed mindfully or more rationally once the thinking regions of the brain catch up. That's why taking a "time-out" works for kids. In this sense we have two brains, two minds, and two different kinds of intelligence: rational and emotional, IQ and EQ. Both matter for how well we do in life. Indeed, intellect cannot work optimally without emotional intelligence. Typically, the complementarity of the amygdala and neocortex means that each is a full partner in mental life. When they interact well, EI rises—as does what you can do with your IQ.

Thus, Daniel Goleman wrote about two minds, one emotional (that feels) and one rational (that thinks): "There is a steady gradient in the ratio of rational-to-emotional control over the mind; the more intense the feeling, the more dominant the emotional mind becomes—and the more ineffectual the rational."[16] Most of the time, these minds are "exquisitely coordinated; feelings essential to thought and thought to feeling. But when passion surges[,] the balance tips."[17] This overlap, or balance, between the logical mind and the emotional mind is where the wise mind lies. Wisdom is borne of balance, and learning self-awareness creates the fulcrum needed to achieve that balance.

FIGURE 2
SELF-AWARENESS BALANCE

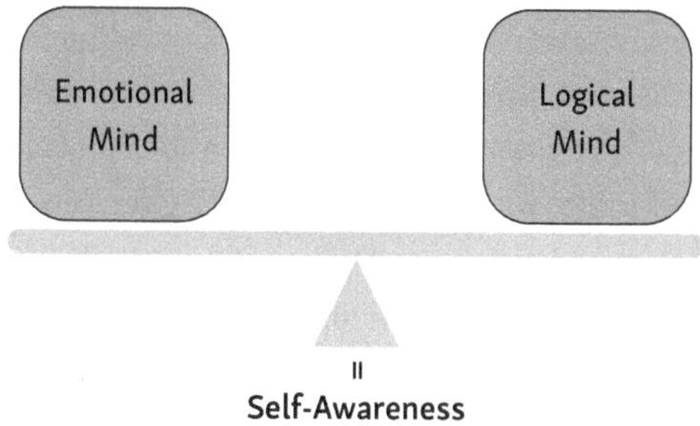

Self-awareness, mindfulness, and training our brain. To increase awareness and in turn alter your response, you first have to train your brain to be able to pay attention to unique aspects of the human experience. It always feels funny and in some ways seems counterintuitive to tell leaders that the first step in becoming more *emotionally* intelligent involves a *cognitive* skill, but it is true. We have to begin with attention training. Self-aware, emotionally intelligent leaders have trained their brain to pay attention to where they are placing their attention. They have learned the value in choosing to focus their attention on their emotional and default reactions in situations instead of on just the content of the situation. Mindfulness, or mindful meditation, is an essential vehicle for developing greater self-awareness because when we practice it, we are actually training our brains to focus on emotional responses nonjudgmentally. Mindfulness helps to build self-awareness because it develops the regions of the brain responsible for attention regulation. It trains you to notice what you are feeling, describe it as objectively as possible, and then proceed with mindful awareness.

While there are several competing models of emotional intelligence and debate persists about what exactly emotional intelligence is and how it compares to personality, most psychologists and academics agree that the cornerstone of emotional intelligence is present-moment *self-awareness.* Without self-awareness, it is virtually impossible to manage emotions in order to achieve the desired outcome. There is no greater skill for a lawyer, law student, or leader to have than an acute and accurate awareness of the intra- and interpersonal dynamics in their work. Often we are consumed by the content of a particular situation when, in fact, it is underlying interpersonal dynamics and emotions that are influencing the outcome. When most people think of emotional intelligence, they think of someone who is "always calm and collected," poised under pressure, or seemingly unrattled by high-stakes situations. Although this representation of high emotional intelligence is absolutely true, reaching this outcome is the result of several key skills at work below the surface, the first being an acute and accurate awareness of your internal reaction to any environmental trigger. How can we expect ourselves to be poised under pressure, cope with stress in a balanced way, or manage anger in a productive manner without first being aware that we are feeling pressure, stress, or anger?

Put simply, self-awareness is the ability to understand your own emotions and their effects. Self-aware people know what drives them, accurately identify emotional triggers throughout their day, and understand how their values play out in their professional lives. In the first phase, known as *attentional deployment*, an emotion begins to arise: a random trigger captures our attention, and we start to interpret, judge, and respond to it. This *cognitive appraisal* leads to the emotional response that follows.

With present-moment awareness, or paying attention to your default emotional responses, you have the power to choose how to respond. And when you know yourself on a deeper level, your choice will be more aligned with your true values and purpose, you will lead authentically, and people will naturally want to follow you. Thus, your current-moment awareness is linked to your deeper story.

The following story of a physician leader (let's call him Evan) illuminates this point. Evan struggled to address conflict as it arose, and Rob coached him to develop greater self-awareness to address this issue.

EVAN'S STORY → As a result of being raised in a family that rarely shared emotions and instead preferred to avoid difficult conversations, Evan had become conflict avoidant. If conflict arose in teams or between him and his subordinates, he would let it fester or just move forward without addressing the issues. This approach had been working out fine given his strong clinical skills and efficient work ethic, but as his responsibilities increased in a new and more advanced leadership role, his teams started to experience dysfunction, and he lost the respect of key constituents because he had let certain issues go unresolved. He had grown to be all head and no heart.

He had not connected the dots between how his family patterns (both influencers and defining moments) had led to an avoidant style of handling difficult situations, which was significantly impacting his leadership and team. With time in coaching, he eventually learned that he was socialized to believe that talking about feelings was weak and pointless and that the best way to handle conflict was with intellect. Having attained deeper insight about his default mode of handling conflict and leading, he eventually recognized that he needed to address conflicts as they arise and bring issues out into the open so that they could be dealt with timely and efficiently.

This was a great coaching goal; however, what Evan and I missed initially was that his conflict-avoidant responses were so engrained, so "conditioned," that he could not even recognize when he was in a conflict. His "default mode" had become so automatic that he was only able to realize after the fact that conflict had occurred. We had to work to raise Evan's awareness of key aspects of conflict so that he could respond in a timely manner. Essentially, we needed to bring Evan's conditioned responses into conscious awareness so that he could choose a better strategy (i.e., address the conflict head-on). In EI training, this is referred to as "bringing the subconscious to the conscious" in order to make the "compulsive more conscious."

The physician leader needed greater self-awareness. He needed greater self-awareness of how he processed and coped with emotions and where those tendencies originated. As he developed greater insight about his coping patterns and their origin, he was able to notice emotions arise in himself and others in real time and create space to process those emotions in a collaborative spirit as part of his approach to difficult conversations.

↔

Self-awareness means being able to see ourselves objectively. To do so, we have to acquire the ability to examine our thoughts and emotions from a third-person perspective—that is, we have to avoid getting swept up in our own emotions to the point that we cannot identify what we are feeling. This requires having the ability to place stable, clear, nonjudgmental attention on our emotions and thoughts.

Mindfulness as the essential vehicle. Practicing mindful meditation (again, we will use the terms *mindfulness* and *mindful meditation* interchangeably) is essential in developing self-awareness. *Mindfulness* is typically defined as nonjudgmental attention to experiences in the present moment.[18] It is a process of focusing our attention on our immediate experience from an orientation of curiosity, experiential openness, and acceptance. Mindfulness is attention training in that it changes the relationship between our thinking and our emotions, allowing us to become more aware of our emotions such that they are not a fixed reality to which we feel fused.[19]

For lawyers, the core of professional practice is thinking about things without judgment. However, because we have been trained to know the answers, at times we think about—and judge—things even before we have collected all of the facts and done all of the research. We need greater *response flexibility*, which is a fancy way of saying "Pause before you act." The practice of mindful meditation encompasses focusing attention on the experience of thoughts, emotions, and body sensations, simply by observing them as they arise, not judging them in that moment, and letting them pass away. As we practice this on a regular basis, we live more mindfully and become more emotionally intelligent.[20]

Practicing mindfulness helps you avoid a common thinking trap that many lawyers fall into: *cognitive fusion*. Cognitive fusion is treating your thoughts as reality. Perfectionistic thinking, in general and among law students and lawyers, is a common example of cognitive fusion. For example, you might think to yourself, "I have to write this contract perfectly." When you fuse with a perfectionistic thought like this, you truly believe you cannot make mistakes. You have then become fused with your thinking and perfectionism becomes the reality. Mindfulness allows for *cognitive diffusion* by being able to distance oneself from the thought and then being able to treat it as it is, just a thought. Cognitive fusion, as seen through the lens of perfectionism, is quite simply unhealthy.[21]

Metacognition refers to thinking about thoughts, attention to self-talk, and awareness of emotions.[22] Goleman describes this as "the sense of an ongoing attention to one's internal states."[23] Self-awareness serves as the foundation upon which the other EI competencies are built because it allows us to know what we are feeling and thinking in real time and to live more mindfully. Lawyers who are self-aware can step back from their experience to create space between recognizing feelings and managing their reaction to their feelings, and this enables them to fulfill their job, to meet their clients' needs, and to reach success commensurate with their values.[24] Austrian psychiatrist Viktor Frankl, author of *Man's Search for Meaning*, noted that "[b]etween stimulus and response, there is a space. In that space lies our freedom and our power to choose our response. In our response lies our growth and our happiness."[25] Not surprisingly, then, without self-awareness, it is nearly impossible for lawyers and leaders to regulate their emotional reactions "because they are being guided by the emotion itself instead of a balance between emotion reaction and rational thought."[26]

While this ability to regulate emotional reactions is the second quadrant of emotional intelligence, sometimes called *self-management* or *emotional regulation*, we mention it here to highlight its connection to self-awareness. A study assessing business managers found that with self-awareness, they had a fifty-fifty chance of demonstrating self-management; without self-awareness, they had virtually no chance.[27]

The critical work of lawyers makes developing self-awareness even more imperative. Their work involves demanding clients, competitive compensation structures, large sums of money, intricately constructed deals, high-stakes negotiations, and the fate of clients' individual rights and personal freedoms (in the criminal cases). This type of work environment requires lawyers to have strong self-awareness and self-management skills; without these skills, lawyer-client relationships will be damaged, office dynamics will devolve, and attorney effectiveness will be diminished.[28]

↑↓↑

REFLECTIVE WRITING 5

Practice mindfulness. If you are not doing so already, then find a mindfulness app or recording to follow. The Northwestern Pritzker School of Law has a web page on student wellness, where you can find eleven guided mindfulness meditations that we recorded.[29] To become comfortable with mindfulness, you may have to experiment with different mindfulness recordings (perhaps at different times of the day) and become attuned to the mood you are in. Push through these circumstances and build experience as you would if you were learning any other skill (rare is the person who sits at a piano for the first time and can play a concerto!).

Once you have found this comfort and tried enough sessions to feel a difference (the number will vary by person), we suggest that you track your experiences either in a dedicated mindfulness journal or in the journal that you started at the beginning of this book. As you experience some change as a result of practicing mindfulness, reflect on the following:

- → What opportunities exist to apply mindfulness in your life now?
- → How can mindfulness apply to success in law school? In a legal career?
- → What obstacles do you see to developing your own formal practice of mindfulness and informal integration of mindfulness into your current life?

B. The Power of Psychological Assessment in Gaining Greater Self-Awareness

Self-awareness speaks to knowing how your emotions drive subconscious behavior and raising those subconscious matters to your consciousness. Likewise, you have subconscious strengths and weaknesses. How can you learn what those are? We all have natural, or default, ways of responding in various situations to accomplish our goals. These built-in reactions are stronger when emotions rise. What are your default settings? And how do they relate to being a lawyer and a leader?

One tool that reveals some of these default settings (strengths and weaknesses) is the Myers-Briggs Type Indicator® (MBTI®). The indicator has been rigorously tested across people, professions, and cultures and found to be a good predictor of what it tries to predict (like how a thermometer tells you the temperature). This tool helps to explain why we do certain things reflexively (our default settings) and where we should work on building strength. In our experience, this tool greatly complements the development of your EI self-awareness.* The MBTI® gives you a sense of your default settings in the following areas: how you get your energy, gather information, make decisions, and organize. These dimensions lie at the core of all Myers-Briggs personality types.

Examples of personality type in action. Let's look at a simple, and somewhat embarrassing, example.

CLIFF TAKING THE LEAD → In MBTI® terms, my personality type is an ISTJ. No need to know what that means at this point other than that the greatest strength of an ISTJ is thinking about matters before sharing an opinion on them. In fact, this is a comfort for the ISTJ. Take in information, process it relatively slowly, and reach an assessment that you are then comfortable sharing with others. Conversely, an ISTJ's greatest weakness is to uncontrollably share unprocessed opinions; it just happens. I sometimes share views in personal settings that are well-intentioned but wholly unprocessed. For example (and yes, the following dialogue really happened),

> "What do you think of that picture on the wall?"
>
> "It's nice, but what if, instead, we hung something small and tasteful?"

In a professional setting, this weakness has the potential to manifest itself in responses that are intended to be neutral but sound like insensitive criticism. In a personal setting (where the example occurred), the insensitivity is magnified.

I did not recognize that weakness (and particularly not relative to that strength) until learning my personality type. Here is where emotional intelligence and the MBTI® come together—I am now much more aware of each. I know that quick, initial responses are not my strength, and I understand that sometimes sharing sooner than I want to will be necessary; thus, I work hard to maintain the balance when I am in that space. I try to process a bit faster so that my emotional response reflects better

* Some people think the MBTI® is the be-all and end-all of who they are and what they will be, while others think it is pop science. Thus, people either accept the results as gospel or reject the tool. We take the middle ground. Knowing your personality type raises consciousness but does not answer all questions.

judgment in the moment. At the same time, I also know that there will be times when I need to say that I need more time to respond. (We will talk later about the willingness to be vulnerable, which is needed here as well.) This knowledge resulted directly from learning my personality type.

You should not think that this example is any kind of outlier. Every one of us and every personality type has a weakness like this—and 20 percent of all lawyers are ISTJs, just like me!

↔

Let's look at another example. You just finished an important two-and-a-half-hour presentation with your work partner. He is exhausted and just wants to go back to the hotel to decompress. You are tired as well but want to celebrate that the talk went so well. You want to check out happy hour at the hotel, then find a great place to eat and talk about how you did and what comes next. Each of you might wonder why the other does not feel the same way. Or you might not wonder and just accept that it is attributable to some "personal" differences. Regardless, these differences could lead to friction or unfounded assumptions about the other person, your work together, and the presentation—and they certainly would impact your work together if this were a multiday presentation. The point is that these differences may emanate from your personality type and where you find energy. Some of us (so-called introverts) recharge by going solo for a while; others (so-called extroverts) reenergize through social interactions.* At a party, for example, introverts and extroverts look the same, but introverts are using up their energy while extroverts are actually recharging. Knowing this might make either work partner, after their joint presentation and with true understanding, say, "Go do your thing for a bit, and then let's meet up later."

An overview of the MBTI®. Everyone has a personality type, one of sixteen, none of which are better or worse than others, and truly all of which have a place in the law. The better lawyers know that you need to

* Considering the social isolation and mandatory work-from-home period many people experienced during the pandemic, this distinction should ring true with everyone. Some of us, the introverts, were less likely to feel cramped by a stay-at-home order or other limits on social gatherings. We were plugged in and recharging at home. Meanwhile, the extroverts were totally depleted and knew or felt this need for social contact to recharge their depleted internal energy.

develop your nonpreferred skills (such as sharing opinions quickly, referred to in the example above) so that you can channel any one of the sixteen personality types and their associated strengths as the situation demands. Similarly, you can think of personality types as rooms in a house: while you might feel most comfortable in the kitchen, you know that you have to use (and get used to using) every other room in the house (including the attic, bathroom, and basement) in order to maximize use of that house.

Let's start with a short quiz:

- → How do you see and think about the world?
- → How do you perceive or absorb information?
- → How do you organize and process that information?
- → How do you come to conclusions or decisions?
- → Where do you find energy or strength?[30]

If you know the answers to these questions, then you have a good sense of your default positions. If not, then you need to learn more so that you better understand how and why you start from certain default positions.

Here's a bit on the intricacies of the MBTI® and personality type, from *Working Together in Law: Teamwork and Small Group Skills for Legal Professionals*:

> There are systematic methods of answering the questions raised above, ways to engage in self-analysis as well as to increase your understanding of the communication and problem-solving styles of other members of your group.... The MBTI is not a diagnostic psychological test, that is, it is not intended to indicate abnormalities in reasoning, personality, or perception. Instead, the MBTI authors assume the person answering the MBTI questions is relatively mentally healthy, and has certain preferences that are clustered by personality type. An MBTI "personality type" describes a person's preferred ways of approaching the world, thinking, and communicating, but does not measure or predict aptitude or ability.
>
> ... [U]nderstanding your own preferences can help you understand why you gravitate toward certain information, or why you find some people easier to work with than others. Under-

standing your own MBTI preferences can also alert you to aspects of your communication and problem-solving approaches that others may misinterpret or misunderstand. This kind of self-analysis is an important activity for any professional.

Thus, a growing number of lawyers and judges are using the MBTI personality instrument to increase their professional effectiveness. Some law schools are using it in their career counseling.... One corporate attorney gave [us] an example of how the MBTI could be used:

> We have an annual retreat for all lawyers in the company. We tried to build our EQ. We all took the MBTI and talked about group dynamics. Especially for less senior lawyers, it enabled us to talk about how lawyers should talk to corporate clients.

...

The MBTI is based on psychotherapist Carl Jung's theories about personality difference among healthy persons along four dimensions: their preferences for

1. obtaining mental energy,
2. gathering information,
3. making decisions, and
4. dealing with their environments.

... The results of the MBTI are reported as scores that indicate a person's preferences along four different dimensions, represented by their initials:

- Extraversion or Introversion (E or I)
- Sensing or iNtuition (S or N)
- Thinking or Feeling (T or F)
- Judging or Perceiving (J or P)

The usual process for taking the MBTI involves learning about the different personality type preferences, completing the full type indicator questionnaire, engaging in further self-assessment, and participating in a feedback session with exercises to illustrate the differences between your self-identified type and the types of others.[31]

The literature about the MBTI® far exceeds the scope of this book. How much or how little you delve into your personality type and its meaning is up to you. To take the MBTI®, you can find a certified administrator through the Association for Psychological Type International or through the Myers & Briggs Foundation. Some websites purport to administer the MBTI®, but none will help you interpret the results.

Figure 3 contains readily available descriptions of the kinds of self-inquiry that help in self-assessment of personality type.

FIGURE 3
PERSONALITY TYPE SELF-ASSESSMENT

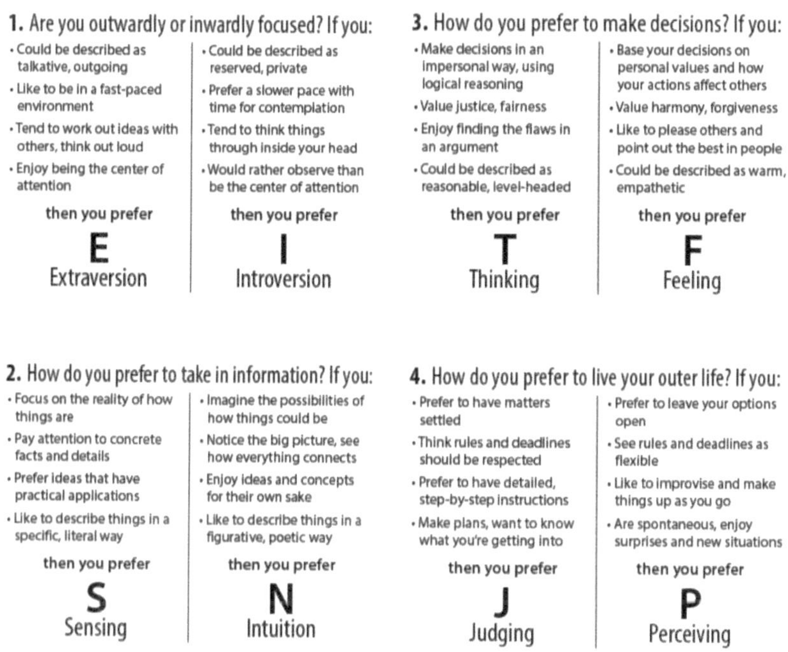

↑↓↑

SELF-DISCOVERY EXERCISE 5: YOUR MBTI® PERSONALITY TYPE

After taking the MBTI®, answer the following questions:

1. What is your personality type?
2. If you are on the border on any letters, read more about the personality types to determine which you think is more descriptive of you (not who you would want to be, but who you are). Which one is more accurate, and why?
3. What are identified as the strengths and weaknesses of your personality type?
4. With respect to the weaknesses, can you think of an example where a weakness arose? What would greater self-awareness have meant for you in that situation?
5. What might your personality type (strengths and weaknesses) mean for you as a leader? A lawyer? A problem solver? In relationships?
6. In terms of having greater consciousness of your default settings, what are the top two or three aspects of your personality type on which you need to focus going forward? Explain why you chose those aspects. Why are they most important to you?

[STOP and COMPLETE before reading further.]

↑↓↑

REFLECTIVE WRITING 6

In this chapter, we discussed several critical aspects of the self-awareness domain of emotional intelligence, particularly in-the-moment awareness and a larger realm of deeper, narrative awareness, including your passions and values. Practicing mindfulness, learning your story, realizing your values, and knowing your subconscious strengths and weaknesses all go to unpacking what has gotten you to where you are today and give you a consciousness to deliberately move ahead with focus.

In this regard, answer the following questions:

→ What does your personality type tell you about how you have managed to get where you are today?

→ Was that journey conscious (in the sense that you had a deep understanding of your narrative and values, you made thoughtful and in-the-moment decisions that aligned with both, and others around you were engaged with you)?

→ Or was the journey fueled more by unconscious providence than planning?

→ Or was it somewhere in between?

□ □ □

As you think about your answers to these questions and reflect on these new insights about who you are and what drives you, our discussion turns to how to harness the power inherent in that self-understanding to effectively manage your life and accomplish your leadership goals. Strong leaders know their strengths and areas of growth, where their interpersonal and emotional patterns originate, pay attention to their reactions throughout the day, and know how to build relationships from the connections that arise in that awareness. Now let's take these insights and put them to use in the next chapter, which focuses on self-management.

CHAPTER IV

Self-Management for Lawyers

ROB TAKING THE LEAD → Growing up in a small, Midwestern college town, I had dedicated most of my childhood to playing basketball with friends and family in the driveway. High school sports are center stage, and I loved the game and worked hard to be the best I could be.

My aspiration was to play on the high school varsity basketball team, which came to fruition in my senior year. Part of the draw for me was the longtime, legendary coach, so I was particularly disappointed when he took a different job just before I started high school. The school hired a new coach who came with a lot of buzz, having coached most recently at a junior college and at a Division I school prior to that. He was knowledgeable about the game and had a good strategy, both offensively and defensively. Our team was also loaded with talent, so expectations were high.

We started the season strong, but as the year progressed, we fell short of our hopes of a state championship run. Our new coach had been a basketball star himself. He loved the game and cared deeply. But when mistakes were made on or off the court, he lost his cool, got frazzled quickly, and would often explode with anger. Practices and half-time speeches became marked by open displays of anger. When our top players made mistakes in the game, he was quick to yell in their faces and resort to slamming clipboards. His lack of insight into his own emotions and his increasing frustration became visible to everyone around the program. Players started to get down on themselves and question their abilities. Time and again, I watched as his disciplining tactics impacted the team's spirit, confidence, and motivation. It became apparent that he lacked emotional intelligence—and was not only negatively impacting everyone currently around him but was also likely the issue at his previous programs. He became an influencer for me, but not in a good way.

↔

The same thing happens to lawyers, as evidenced by many published opinions and anecdotal stories. For example, in an intellectual property case alleging that Mattel infringed on his client's Barbie look-alike, a lawyer "lambasted his client in plain view" of opposing counsel for a damaging deposition admission and "tossed Barbie dolls off a table" during a meeting with opposing counsel.[1] This is a clear example of a lawyer with limited emotional intelligence, particularly a lack of self-awareness of his emotions in the moment and an inability to manage those emotions.

When asked why emotional intelligence matters for leaders, most people think about emotion regulation, or *self-management.* Indeed, while self-awareness is the cornerstone of emotionally intelligent leadership and the first step toward managing emotions, self-management is really the ultimate goal. Leadership, at the end of the day, is about managing cognitive, emotional, and behavioral reactions in real time through various complex situations to achieve optimal relationships and decisions. Star leaders effectively manage their emotional and behavioral reactions in a manner most conducive to positive workplace culture and individual and organizational success.

While this sounds easy, as a lawyer leader you are surely challenged emotionally in various ways on a daily basis. Self-management, the second core domain of emotional intelligence, is about keeping both yourself and others motivated and being able to manage the intensity of an emotion—what Daniel Goleman coined *fire* (positive use of emotion intensity) and *brakes* (self-management of emotion intensity).[2] Although the processes underlying self-management are quite complex, most lawyers manage their emotions every day in a variety of ways. Many different activities can count as self-management, including small actions like pushing a chair away from a desk when too frustrated to work or simply taking a deep breath to calm nerves before commenting at a firm meeting, and more complex acts such as trying to change one's own interpretation of a setback in an effort to stay positive or asking for a break during a tense meeting.

In the previous chapters, we laid the groundwork for self-management. You now know how managing your emotional and social reactions to be able to effectively lead begins with self-awareness. You also have the tools and exercises to keep building your self-awareness. But a high degree of self-awareness alone is not the goal. Rather, you must be able to use your self-awareness to effectively manage your emotional reactions as a leader so that you can act and think in ways that lead to successful outcomes in your life. If Rob's coach in high school could have noticed his escalating anger and recognized the underlying anxiety about performance and job security driving that anger, he would have had the opportunity to manage his reactions in a manner that was more conducive to player and team development. Likewise, the lawyer's actions and the judge's opinion in the *Mattel* case are memorialized forever due to the absence of that level of awareness. The research shows that we can learn the tools necessary to manage our emotions. Through impulse control and adaptability or flexibility in responding to change, we can manage ourselves and our emotions.

On the other hand, we can motivate ourselves through achievement orientation and positive outlook. These are the brakes and fire, respectively. You may respond by saying, "Sounds great! But how do I know when to do which?" The answer is that self-awareness (particularly through mindfulness) gives you the chance to decide which is appropriate and when it is appropriate. The ability to manage your emotions will not happen instantly but will grow (remember neuroplasticity) with experience. For example, if you think back to your first year of law school, you will recall that you had to brief cases and chart or compare their similarities or differences in order to synthesize the rules across several cases. Do you still do that? No. Why? Because you took that slow and arduous process, learned it, and became efficient at it—and now it happens, instantly at times, in your head. The same will be true for self-management if you continue to work on your self-awareness. To be sure, at times you will have to stop yourself, but many other times you will automatically respond in a strong, positive way, as leaders do. Thus, self-awareness leads into self-management as illustrated in the Goleman model.

FIGURE 4
THE EMOTIONAL AND SOCIAL COMPETENCY FRAMEWORK

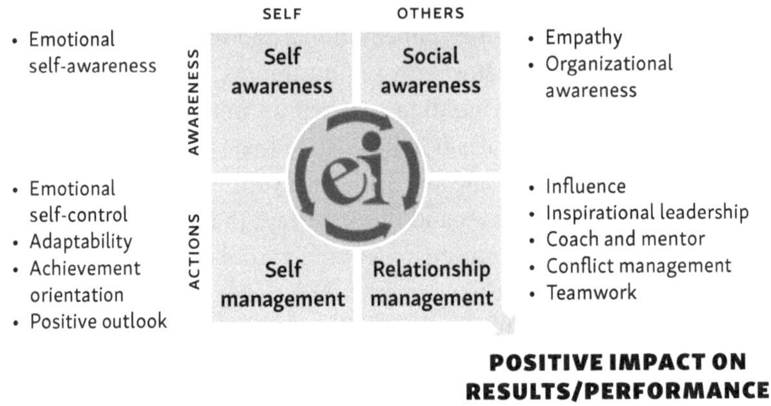

In this chapter, we walk you through what an emotion is so that you have a baseline intellectual understanding of it, and then we share evidence-based strategies to effectively manage your emotions. We also cover seven concepts and practices from psychological science essential for emotion self-management. Finally, we discuss ways to increase happiness and boost your mood—key elements of self-management.

A. Learning When to Brake

One of the greatest challenges for a lawyer arises when everyone looks to her for how to move forward. In traditional legal work, this could be plaintiff's counsel, the lawyer who knows the most about the transaction, or the lawyer who drafted the regulation or legislation, any of whom might not necessarily be the senior-most attorney on the matter. The way this lawyer leader exhibits self-management of her emotions, to either motivate herself or to cool off and take a different path, will be read by those whom she leads and result in either good consequences or bad ones, as in the preceding examples.

Another example, from a published opinion, fits here. The judge recounted a lawyer's emotional spiral that was so taut that he could not break out of it even with some time to reflect. Defendant's lawyer (we will call him Smith) requested documents in discovery, and plaintiff's lawyer (we will call her Jones) responded with files loadable into any standard e-discovery software, which would organize the files for easy review. Because Smith was unfamiliar with the format (but should have been), the "production appeared to be a randomized, unorganized, and duplicative mess."[3] Unable to see an innocent explanation for the situation, Smith "concluded that [Jones] had willfully committed the unprofessional and odious discovery foul of providing a 'document dump.'"[4] Because of this, Smith failed to meet and confer to resolve the issue and decided to address the issue during his deposition of Jones's client. Not surprisingly, this resulted in Smith's asking a multitude of argumentative questions and making a multitude of argumentative statements; asking questions lacking a good-faith basis; walking through the produced documents in the order they appeared in the file (which was random); and assuming that when a document mentioned attachments, the attachments were not provided in response to his discovery request. As but one specific example of Smith's downward emotional spiral, he asked Jones's client fourteen times in the deposition for a reason *why* the client did not pay a bill after the client said that he did not know if the bill was unpaid.[5] As a lawyer and a leader in his case, Smith failed to manage his emotions and could not slow down, or brake, his emotional response to the original document production.

When you have self-awareness of your emotions, you can decide whether to brake or let them fuel you in the moment.

CLIFF TAKING THE LEAD → In an educational institution, the dean of students is, at times, the leader. Everyone looks to this person to know how to react, how to proceed, and what degree of fervor or hesitation should be applied in doing so. I did not experience this situation until we had a student death. Very few students die, but the impact of that event hits everyone: students, staff, and faculty. Naively, I thought that this responsibility would lie with the dean; but when the first student passed away while I was the dean of students, I had to gather the student body to share the news.

I wept openly as I told them what I knew about what had happened. I am not one to cry or show a lot of emotion, but I wept openly and did nothing to stop the tears that fell from my eyes. Even though this was not my usual behavior (which would be to restrain my emotions), it was a reflection of what I felt in my heart—and it fueled my words and actions and allowed others to do the same. We all cried together for our loss, for the student's loss, without any restraint.

I knew that showing my emotions and sharing them, including, if need be, in public, could be very positive both for me and those around me, and I used this knowledge not only as the dean of students but also as a practicing lawyer. On occasion, in practice, I would get angry with a client. Once I got angry over a client's nonchalance about something very important. The client left my office quickly, and I immediately questioned the wisdom of not reining in my anger. A short time later in the day, though, the client returned to my office, contrite, and said, "You know, you should get angry more often."

↔

Self-awareness allows you to determine when to let your emotions motivate your actions, which counterbalances being able to pump the brakes on emotions when you recognize that you are mired in the thick of something and struggling. A large part of a lawyer's job is about making this determination and modeling behavior for the profession, on both levels. Self-awareness allows you to self-manage. In exercising both the fire and the brakes, that is, by exhibiting behavior that is very intentional for others to see and value, you form your professional identity.

To be sure, this behavior is learned and differs by background, culture, and even gender and gender identity. However, the answer to the best way to act in a given situation does not lie in doing what stereotypes dictate (e.g., men don't cry, women shouldn't be assertive, successful lawyers don't show weakness); rather, the answer lies in having the self-awareness to make the time to properly manage your emotions to what fits you, as a leader, in that particular situation.

B. Learning How to Brake

CLIFF TAKING THE LEAD → As a young associate responsible for a status conference, I was prepared for the discovery issues that we needed to resolve, the schedule that we thought would suit our case, and a couple of legal issues that necessitated both. I was not prepared for the judge to not know anything about the case. At the conference, I could not stem my emotions and froze when the judge asked me what the case was about (I am still not sure if it was frustration, fear, or surprise). I was in the trees and could not present the forest because my emotions had shut down my ability to think and understand.

Later in my career, while presenting a novel gender discrimination theory before the state supreme court, I was similarly asked a very basic question that had nothing to with what I was arguing or my part of the argument. Having had lots of practice in noticing and paying attention to my emotions, I was able to pump the brakes on my frustration, fear, and surprise and answer the question. And then when I was done, I shifted back to my argument on the novel cause of action.

↔

You may say that Cliff learned from experience. And while that is true, what is essential is learning *how* to do the same so that you can adjust regardless of the similarity of the situation.

CLIFF TAKING THE LEAD → One year when I was the dean of students, a male student was sending unsolicited emails to female classmates about the most innocuous of things. For example, one said "It was raining. I saw you had no umbrella. I have an extra one if you need it." On its face, this is a kind offer. But just below the surface, it is creepy. Very creepy. It implies, *I am watching you.* He sent a couple of these emails to different women ("I like the sound of your voice when you talk in class."). Each recipient independently went to the 1L class representative who, upon receiving several concerns, discussed the issue with me.

I asked the student to come in for a talk. I tried many ways, over the course of forty-five minutes, to explain to him how uncomfortable his unwanted messages were. No dice. Was it possible that he had so little self-awareness? So little social awareness? Or was he feigning innocence and toying with everyone? Did he know exactly where the line was between acceptable and proscribed behavior—and how to get very, very close to that line while not crossing it (and leaving himself enough space to have arguably not crossed it)? Technically, he had done nothing wrong (or at least nothing that I could comfortably say was actionable).

I could let it go, wait for him to dance near the line again, and see if he crossed it. That approach made me distinctly uncomfortable. There were students whom he had already impacted, and I did not want to be in the position of explaining to the next email recipient why he had the right to continue this intrusive behavior.

I decided to act but did so with the best emotional intelligence I could muster. Before speaking, I spent some time thinking about what I was really feeling. Was I feeling like I was in a struggle with him? Was I angry at him? Was I scared for the community? I finally identified that I was feeling frustrated with him, and that frustration was pushing me to react more strongly than necessary. I also thought about what was motivating him and his perspective. I thought about his motivations and realized that whether his conduct was intentional or not did not matter in its effect on other students. My self-awareness could then move to think about how to include those other students in my response. With self- and other-awareness, I could then proceed mindfully. I told him that he was not to email any female members of the community about anything that was not related to school. No personal emails. I thought he might push back, and I was not sure how well I could support the prohibition. But he blinked and agreed.

↔

So what can we take from these scenarios in relation to learning self-management?

Crying in front of the state supreme court would not have been beneficial. On the other hand, if I had tried not to cry that day that I addressed the students, then I probably would not have been able to talk or surely would not have shared the same kind of deep and meaningful message. Feeling those emotions allowed me to talk from the heart. Anything else would have been contrived and inauthentic. Certainly, hiding those emotions (totally dampening reactions) would lead to lost opportunities to connect, to emote, and to manage.

Likewise, I was frustrated by the student's lack of awareness that he was harassing women. I could have gotten angry as I had before in practice, but that was probably what he wanted me to do—lose my cool. Furthermore, the student had stomped on the brakes of his emotions too much, which shows how overcontrolled emotions can lead to others questioning your presentation, digging deeper to figure out what is going on, and ultimately questioning whether you are authentic or reliable.

These scenarios highlight that the key to leadership is being attuned to our emotional reactions so that we can respond effectively. Successful lawyers do not avoid or suppress their emotions. That is not self-management. Rather, they invoke a constant process of awareness of their emotional, cognitive, and behavioral reactions so that they can align their actions with their values and the demands of the situation.

C. Regulating Attention, Psychologically Speaking

Now let's talk a bit more about how to manage emotions from the psychology side of things. As we mentioned previously, becoming an emotionally intelligent lawyer is all about mental habits. It may sound funny that to become better at managing our emotions, we must first start with a cognitive skill, such as attention regulation. But we know through cognitive science that emotions are preceded by cognitions (thoughts): *where the mind goes, the energy (emotion) goes.* Thus, in order to manage emotions, we must first tune into our thinking. As we pay attention to our thoughts and the emotional and behavioral reactions that they evoke, we increase our power to choose how to respond.

Self-awareness paves the way for self-management. This is very important given our understanding of how one central brain region, known as the amygdala, works and the nature of emotions: emotional reactions are often set into motion before we know it consciously. The amygdala triggers emotional impulses to act, far quicker than our cognitive brain does or can keep up with, under normal circumstances.[6] Thus, we are often thrown into emotional responses before we are intellectually aware of it or can think about how advantageous that emotional reaction will be. Modern theories of emotion largely agree that this is because emotions played a key role in survival during human evolution[7] and emotions are biologically determined.[8]

Contemporary research also supports Darwin's original hypothesis that emotions played a key role in adaptation and that core emotions have universal meaning for people in different parts of the world.[9] Paul Ekman, one of the modern era's most influential scholars on the study of emotion, found consistent with Darwin's biological approach that some basic, primary emotions are universally recognized cross culturally, such as anger, fear, joy, sadness, disgust, and surprise.[10]

While there is general agreement on the idea of universal primary emotions, there is considerable cross-cultural differences in expression of each emotion. That is where *emotional self-control* comes in, which involves managing disruptive emotions and impulses effectively.[11] Emotional self-control involves being able to curtail negative behaviors when provoked, when met with opposition or adversarial circumstances, or when working under pressure—circumstances that law students and lawyers know quite well. Lawyer leaders who exhibit emotional self-control are often those who come to mind when we think of emotionally intelligent leadership. They are able to not only stay focused under pressure and manage the tide of distressing emotions as they arise, but also stay positive and elicit specific emotions when appropriate. It is not about only limiting negative emotions or at all about suppressing emotions. In fact, it's quite the opposite. Emotional self-control entails being able to allow the full range of emotions to surface in a culturally appropriate, adaptable manner.[12] People who demonstrate this competency are able to maintain their effectiveness under stressful or hostile conditions.

The challenge is that when emotions are riding high, we tend to act before we think.

↑ ↓ ↑

REFLECTIVE WRITING 7

How about you? Has there been a time recently when you did something out of impulse and regretted it later? Maybe a time when you lost control, but then, as more time passed and you gained some emotional awareness, thought that you would have responded differently?

- → What was the situation?
- → What were your initial thoughts about the triggering event?
- → What emotions were evoked?
- → What actions were evoked from your initial thinking about the situation?
- → As time passed, did your thoughts subsequently change?

[STOP and COMPLETE before reading further.]

↑↓↑

Tuning in to your modus operandi. It can be helpful to step back a bit and learn your modus operandi (MO), or patterns of behavior, when emotions run high. When emotions get going, you can fall into hard-wired patterns of thinking and responding as a means to cope with the demands of the situation. So your MO becomes a conditioned response, which is a learned response to a previously neutral stimulus. Individual MOs affect individual as well as team performance. By understanding your patterns of behavior under certain high-stress situations, you can be better prepared to adjust negative behaviors and channel your stress in a more productive way. If you become aware of the patterns that high-stress situations bring out in you, you can choose to react in a healthier manner. Without awareness, you are doomed to repeat negative reaction patterns.[13]

↑↓↑

SELF-DISCOVERY EXERCISE 6: I TEND TO ...

To develop this aspect of self-awareness, you should take some time each day to observe how you react to other people and stressful situations. What is your typical emotional and behavioral response? Do any of your classmates, loved ones, or professors trigger a particular emotional response? How do you manage this? Reflect back over the past few weeks and try to think of a time when you experienced a strong emotional response. You can also think about situations you encounter regularly—like an additional school or work assignment, a difficult person in your life, or the discovery that you're running late for something. What is your typical way of responding? You may start to notice some patterns, or maybe close people in your life have noticed how you tend to respond and have commented on it. Think about those triggering situations in your life and then complete the following prompt:

1. "I tend to ..."

[STOP and COMPLETE before reading further.]

↑↓↑

REFLECTION ON SELF-DISCOVERY EXERCISE 6

In the "I Tend to ..." self-discovery exercise, what situation did you choose? How did the starting point come to your attention? What was your first, or initial, reaction or thought? How did you cope with the emotional reaction you had? That is your MO. For some, you may allow the emotion to come on strong and express what you are feeling directly to others either through venting or retaliating. For others, you may internalize it, suppress it, and avoid it all together. What is your MO in these emotionally charged situations? As time passed, how did your thinking change? As a result of that change in thinking, how did your emotional reaction change? Were you able to move out of your MO and offer more conscious strategies?

□ □ □

Tuning in to the Modal Model of Emotion. At this point you may be asking, what exactly is an emotion? The questions in the reflection exercise that you just completed are explained through the Modal Model of Emotion, which is a theory on the core features of emotion, that will help you to grow your self-awareness and thus manage your emotions.[14]

According to the Modal Model of Emotion (see Figure 5), emotions arise through a cycle of four elements: in the context of a *situation* that compels *attention*, has a particular meaning to an individual (*appraisal*), and gives rise to a coordinated yet malleable *response* to the ongoing situation (looping back to the original situation).[15] In other words, the model explains the emotion generative process by outlining four key features of an emotion beginning with a situation that grabs your attention, evaluation or appraisal of the situation, and a response to the situation.

FIGURE 5: MODAL MODEL OF EMOTION

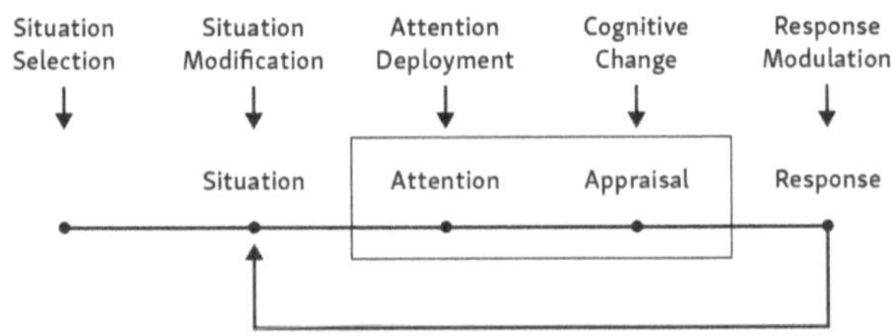

Appraisal is a core feature of emotion. Emotions arise when a situation is interpreted, or "appraised," as relevant and important to a particular goal. "Emotions are elicited and differentiated on the basis of a person's subjective evaluation or appraisal of the personal significance of a situation, object, or event on a number of dimensions or criteria."[16] For example, you notice that a lawyer is directing concerning facial expressions at you during a meeting, and it gets your attention—and then emotion arises.

Scholars suggest a two-stage process of appraisal:

- Primary appraisal involves determining if the situation is of positive or negative significance for one's well-being.
- Secondary appraisal is the ability to cope with the consequences of an event.[17]

Appraisal theory teaches us that the meaning given to a situation related to a particular goal will lead to the resulting emotion.

A clarifying example of the primary and secondary appraisal concepts occurred while Rob was coaching a midcareer real estate lawyer (let's call him Kendrick) from an East Coast law firm.

KENDRICK'S STORY → Kendrick had been putting in his time for several years, steadily working toward partner with the firm. He reached out independently for coaching because he was struggling with burnout, motivation, and attention issues that caused him to miss a few deadlines. Shortly after Kendrick and Rob started working together, Kendrick was notified that the firm had hired a real estate lawyer at the partner level from outside the firm. He was devastated. Based on his years of hard work, and his share of grunt work, he thought he was next in line for partner.

By the time of the next coaching session, only about forty-eight hours later, Kendrick had already decided that the firm did not value his work and "only looks out for themselves" (primary appraisal). He also decided that he was not a good fit and needed to immediately look for a new position in a firm where he would be a better fit (secondary appraisal: exploring coping options or ways to respond).

His primary appraisal was clearly negative. At best, it was contributing to his anger and potentially clouding his judgment. At worst, it could result in his leaving a job he actually liked. The fact that he liked his job was clear because he had talked at length about how the firm was a good fit for him in regard to both its size and its culture. After talking about his appraisals, he gained the perspective (self-awareness) that he was latching on to a negative interpretation of the external hire and really personalizing it. He realized that he needed and wanted to stay poised on the partner track, show optimism, and take the high road (positive secondary appraisal, which led to personal happiness and a sense of integrity rather than anger).

↔

The role of *accurate* self-awareness was key for Kendrick. His initial appraisal of the situation was leading to anger when in fact he was not angry but hurt. Anger is a secondary emotion that feels less vulnerable and is frequently chosen unconsciously over more vulnerable emotions like sadness or fear. Accurate emotional self-awareness is key to finding the right path forward. Kendrick's right path forward could only come once he was able to slow down and really understand how his initial appraisal was contributing to anger.

↑ ↓ ↑

REVIEW OF SELF-DISCOVERY EXERCISE 6 AND SUBSEQUENT REFLECTION

Briefly look back at the "I Tend to ..." self-discovery exercise and the subsequent reflection. What were your primary and secondary appraisals?

□ □ □

Tuning in to Gross's process model of emotion regulation (see Figure 6). The self-management branch of most EI frameworks is conceptually linked to Gross's process model of emotion regulation. The process model outlines five different techniques, or strategies, that can be used to regulate emotions according to the point at which they have their primary impact in the emotion-generative process. During the milliseconds and seconds following the occurrence of a potentially emotion-eliciting situation (microlevel), there are five points in time at which individuals might intervene in order to modify their emotion trajectory. Think of them as falling on a timeline of an emotion, from when something first grabs your attention to the way the emotion impacts you. These points represent five families of emotion-regulation strategies:

1. *Situation Selection:* approaching or avoiding particular people, places, or objects
2. *Situation Modification:* active efforts made to address the situation at hand, similar to problem-solving or task-focused coping
3. *Attentional Deployment:* a shift in focus through distraction, concentration, or rumination
4. *Cognitive Change:* modifying one's evaluation of the situation, including cognitive reframing and reappraisal
5. *Response Modulation:* directly influencing the physiological impact of emotions through the use of, for example, drugs, exercise, and relaxation techniques

The following chart gives a visual presentation of their relationship and interaction:

FIGURE 6

FIVE FAMILIES OF EMOTION-REGULATION STRATEGIES

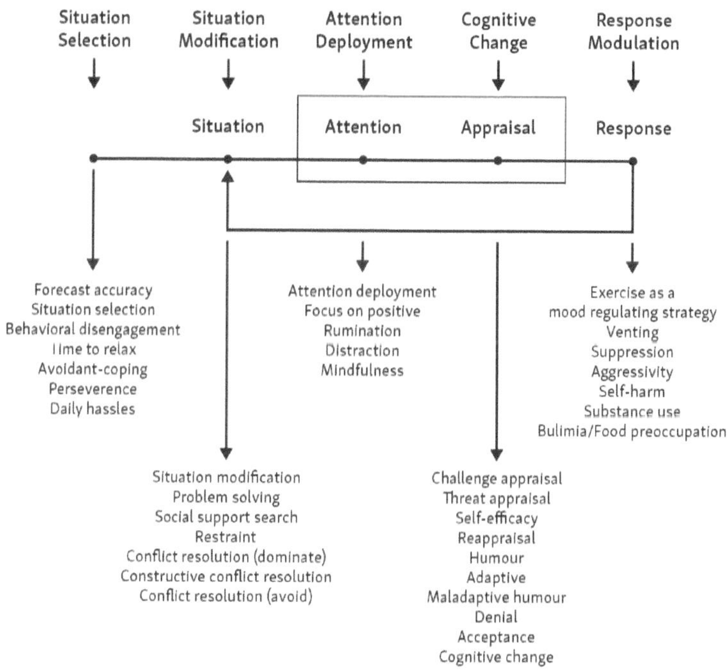

Although sequential at the microlevel, these strategies can be used in parallel or in any order at the macrolevel (i.e., at the level of minutes, hours, or days following the emotional situation). Put differently, if the emotion trajectory was not altered or if the emotion was ill-regulated at the microlevel, one can still regulate it later by using any of the five families of strategies.

Think about this in relation to what causes ethical breaches. Sometimes ethical breaches result from not knowing the law or process—that is, technical matters. However, most ethical violations are a failure to manage personal activities, such as mishandling funds, failure to communicate, and/or failure to share and seek help for one's mental health.[18] Think about how this emotion-regulation model could help avoid the two latter ethical lapses.

Tuning into other self-management research. Researchers are investigating the affective, cognitive, and social consequences of different types of self-management. A lot of work focuses specifically on *re-appraisal* versus *suppression. Re-appraisal* simply means re-framing the initial appraisal of a situation so that it has a more adaptive or positive outlook. Suppression leads to decreased positive, but not decreased negative, emotion experience and increased sympathetic nervous system responses. Allowing negative emotions to surface can be hard. It does not feel good to process and experience negative emotions, such as sadness. Nevertheless, it is important and healthy to do so. In other words, suppression may temporarily alleviate negative emotions but in the long run leads to greater stress. Another point to make here is that there are really no "bad" emotions. We have positive (e.g., joy, excitement) and negative (e.g., fear, sadness) emotions, and it is vital to our psychological health that we experience the full range and not suppress the difficult ones, because they are equally important. The same goes for effective leadership. When leaders find meaningful and professionally appropriate ways to express more difficult feelings with colleagues, it leads to a culture of openness and trust.

Related to this is the development of our emotional responses. An emotional response is mediated by our experiences, specifically, our beliefs about the world and ourselves, which begin in childhood and—because they are so early born and deeply held—are viewed as truths, for better or worse! Thus, distorted or maladaptive thinking, which is guided by beliefs, influences our mood and behavior.[19] Remember, where the mind goes, the energy (emotion) goes. In other words, what you dwell on will lead to how you feel.

This is why perfectionism can be so pernicious—it supplants the positivity of the work product and becomes a negative mood.[20] "[S]elf-critical perfectionists are more likely to withdraw from pursuing their goals and engage in avoidant behavior, which helps them prevent experiencing any distress in the moment but also enhances their propensity for avoidance over time."[21]

To sum this up in layman's terms, the research on self-management has produced some clear conclusions. We experience a range of emotions throughout our life, and that is normal. Our emotional responses are often brought about not by the situation itself but by how we think about and react cognitively to the events in our life. It is what we tell ourselves about the situation, how we appraise it, that leads to the emotional reaction. Given the distress that comes with experiencing negative emotions, people often cope with them by engaging in suppression, which has been found to be a counterproductive coping strategy. For lawyers, one of the dominant beliefs has been that there is no place for emotion in legal practice. This belief leads to suppression of key emotional experiences, which then often go unresolved and lead to burnout, interpersonal conflict, and a host of other challenges.

↑ ↓ ↑

REFLECTIVE WRITING 8

Thinking a bit more about beliefs and norms in the practice of law as it relates to emotion and self-management, let's do some reflective writing:

- → What is there about lawyers' work that could be detrimental to one's well-being?
- → Think about aspects of a lawyer's work that include having to think negatively.
- → Think about an ethical lapse that could be avoided with better self-management.

□ □ □

This naturally leads to a discussion of how you can develop a variety of skills designed to help you achieve better self-management. For example, you will need to alter habits that lead to thinking patterns that correlate highly with mental health issues and burnout. You have heard the adage that insanity is doing the same thing again and again and expecting a different result. And you know what happens when you view a problem as a wall and just put your head down and ram forward—the wall wins. Positive psychology provides a range of tools that will enable you to start strong, persist in light of failure, and learn from experience.

D. Strengthening Self-Management

Over the years in teaching the Leading in the Law class, we have come to realize that certain essential concepts and practices truly build self-management in leadership. These are tried and true, evidence-based emotion-regulation and mood-boosting strategies from psychological science. In this section, we cover our top seven.

1. Explanatory Style

One of the most influential psychologists of the past century is Martin Seligman, considered by most to be the father of positive psychology. His work on optimism and the role of thinking styles in self-management has been well received in the business world for decades. One of his greatest discoveries was "explanatory style." Explanatory style is how we explain events in our lives to ourselves. Research shows that it is not as simple as thinking the glass is half full or half empty. Rather, it is about how you explain setbacks and victories in life and at work.

Three dimensions of explanatory style. Whether you think about something with optimism or not depends on your explanatory style, which consists of three dimensions: stable/unstable, global/specific, and internal/external.

- *Stable* versus *unstable* is about unchanging across time or changing across time, respectively. This represents whether a person believes a repeated event will be the same or subject to change (see "ramming your head into a wall," above).

- *Global* versus *specific* is about whether something is universal throughout one's life or specific to a part of one's life. This relates to whether or not a person's explanation generalizes the event beyond the specific event at hand.
- *Internal* versus *external* is about whether the cause of an event is within oneself or outside oneself.[22]

A person with an *optimistic explanatory style* is said to explain the causes of negative events as *external*, *unstable*, and *specific*. Optimistic people place an appropriate amount of blame on themselves but do not blame themselves for everything, believe that there is room for change, and believe that the bad experience was specific to that particular event and is not to be generalized to all others. When optimists have setbacks, they believe "It's temporary, I can change it, and it's just this one situation." When pessimists have setbacks, they believe the opposite: "It will last forever, it's going to undermine everything I do, and it's my fault." Conversely, when optimists experience victories, they believe "I did it, it will last forever, and it will help me in every circumstance."

Three elements of pessimism. How are you explaining life events? Seligman has identified three elements of pessimism that hold us back from being successful when things do not go right. The three Ps of pessimism align with the three dimensions of explanatory style described above, and they are personalization, permanence, and pervasiveness.

Personalization can reveal itself in two ways: (1) when you believe that you will never amount to anything and that all obstacles are there because of you ("Everything bad that happens to me is my fault.") and (2) when you take negative interactions personally. Personalizing things is taking an internal explanatory style ("It's because of my faults").

Permanence is believing that the setback you are explaining will always happen. The words *never* and *always* are very dangerous when it comes to maintaining a resourceful attitude during difficult times. If you catch yourself saying, "I'll never be able to change," make sure that you challenge yourself on this false assumption, as you are explaining the setback with permanence.

Finally, for some people, if one thing goes wrong, then that one thing impacts every other aspect of their lives. This is called *pervasiveness*. Pervasiveness comes along with a global explanatory style. For instance, let's say you lose a client due to a personality difference. If you find yourself saying, "No clients like working with me," then you are globalizing the setback to all clients and falling into the trap of pervasiveness.

↑↓↑

SELF-DISCOVERY EXERCISE 7: EXPLANATORY STYLE SELF-TEST

1. Think of a time when you failed to meet a deadline.
2. How do you explain it to yourself?
3. Do you notice any of the Three Ps involved in your explanation of the missed deadline?

Again, we are not advocating that you dismiss your errors, not take ownership, and pretend that you never make mistakes. The key takeaway is that if your explanatory style is consistently marked with these three Ps, then you will struggle to manage yourself or lead others effectively. Start watching for the three Ps and see if you can practice reframing them into more specific, unstable, and external ways. You can manage your own mood with an optimistic explanatory style as well as the culture of your team.

[STOP and COMPLETE before reading further.]

□ □ □

Did you use the terminology and framework above in writing your answers? If not, no worries, but go back and try to layer the framework over your answer. Did you address all of the parts? If not, can you fill in the gaps? Try to be as complete as possible so that the next time an issue arises, you are prepared to fully address your reaction. For example, did you notice any personalizing in your explanation? Watch for those three Ps.

2. Resilience

Resilience is often identified as our ability to recover from a difficult situation. Recovery has two components: (1) the ability to move past the situation (and not let it define your life and circumstances) and (2) the ability to learn from the situation (think of learning from failure in this sense). Resilience in leaders enables them to try things and not fear failure or fear the process of moving past a less-than-successful endeavor. Resilience in lawyers is the ability to learn from and move beyond not getting your clients what they want, whether in whole or in part. Because complete success is rare (unlike in the movies), lawyers often temper their clients' expectations. But who tempers the lawyer's expectations? Lawyers must do that themselves.

Let's discuss failure a bit more. Many of us were taught that failure was unacceptable. You took on a task and completed it successfully; and if you did not, then you kept at it until you got it right (if you were lucky) or you were criticized for your lack of success and told how your life would be negatively affected by this failure (if you were unlucky). Research has shown, though, that from failure comes great wisdom, which can eventually lead to future success.[23] Legendary coach John Wooden put it simply: "If you are afraid to fail, you will never do the things you are capable of doing."[24] So failure is something to be embraced and accepted—not feared or shunned.

Another point that arises in this context is the law student's (and lawyer's) perfectionism. Seeking perfection will make you anxious and drive you crazy. Most perfectionists also move the goalposts: if they achieve their goal, then they question whether that was truly a lofty enough goal and move the goalposts to a more distant yard line. Perfectionism plunked down in a workplace will make you spend too much time on a project, make you appear to others to be unreliable and not capable of managing your priorities, and generally undermine your ability to perform and succeed. Perfectionism is driven, in part, by fear of failure. If something is perfect, then it has no flaws and must be right. Embracing failure is one way to countermand the pressure for perfection.[25] Another way is by accepting that if your performance is not perfect, you will learn from those flaws and overcome whatever negative results occur—the essence of resilience.

3. Cognitive Interaction

In case you have not noticed, there is a conceptual pattern here. Your thoughts, feelings, and behaviors are interconnected. The way you feel (emotions) and how you respond (actions/behaviors) are the direct result of the interpretations you make. Your automatic thoughts and beliefs guide your emotional and behavioral reactions. Oftentimes, though, we treat our automatic thoughts as reality instead of having awareness of them and deciding if we like the interpretation. In other words, the space between stimulus (e.g., the law client you find annoying) and response ("I can't stand him") is where we can intervene (consciously choose the most adaptive cognitive response) to achieve the best outcome.

ROB TAKING THE LEAD → In executive coaching with lawyers and physicians, I am always struck by the power that negative thinking has on well-being and performance. It is remarkable how much overlap professionals present in their dysfunctional cognitive habits at the core of their job dissatisfaction and performance issues. One of the most common patterns I see affecting attorneys is a lack of recognition of their storyline, or narrative, about their professional work, which ultimately impairs their performance and contributes to burnout.

↔

Emerging neuroscience findings indicate that the brain's resting place is marked by concern over what is not going well, and the negative thinking exhibited by these individuals likely stems from this resting state. In other words, when idle, the brain tends to think about what is not going well, what we could have done better, and how we have fallen short. You can think of this as the negativity bias. By developing self-awareness habits of our thinking, we can catch these patterns—and with consciousness of them, choose to think in a more adaptive manner.

ASHLEY'S STORY → An exceptional transactional lawyer (let's call her Ashley), like many of the lawyers discussed in this book, made partner at a young age and checked all the little boxes marking success but found herself depressed and floundering. Ashley was struggling to maintain the performance level that she attained during her first decade out of school. She decided that her job was pointless and that it should not exist because she was just a middleman, collecting a lot of money and profiting off of others' work. Her narrative, or storyline, about her specialty area had become so negative that it was affecting her mood on a constant basis.

↔

Ashley completely lacked awareness of how this negative storyline about her work might be contributing to her depressive symptoms and general malaise in life. More importantly, she lacked awareness that it was just her narrative and not reality.

The point is that each of us is a complex system. To become more emotionally intelligent, you need to break down what is really happening internally. You have (1) thoughts, (2) feelings, and (3) behaviors—and they interact with one another in ways that affect your affective states and performance. You could start at any of these three and cycle through the others, the speed and reinforcement continuing with each cycle. However, by becoming aware of your thoughts, feelings, and behaviors, you can increase insight and make effective changes where and when needed.

↑ ↓ ↑

SELF-DISCOVERY EXERCISE 8: SELF-MANAGEMENT

1. Describe a situation in which you did something out of impulse and later regretted it.
2. What was the specific *trigger*, or activating event, that caused your emotional reaction?
3. What were your *thoughts* about the situation?
4. Describe the *emotions* that caused you to act as you did.
5. What were the resulting *actions*?

[STOP and COMPLETE before reading further.]

□ □ □

Let's take a quick mood and pulse check here. The preceding information can feel (cognitively) dense and (emotionally) personal. How are you doing at this point in the chapter? What are your reactions so far? Pay attention to what you are telling yourself (appraisal), how that is making you feel, and the consequential behaviors. If you find yourself at all dazed, maybe stand up and stretch, refocus, and tune in, because what we are about to share with you now is likely the essential ingredient of all self-management, and emotional intelligence in general for that matter.

The parts you identified in your responses to Exercise 8 will match up with parts in the discussion below, so be sure that you have identified something in each category. If you have not, be prepared to go back and fill in the missing pieces once you have read further. It can be especially helpful to realistically track what you tell yourself—your thoughts—about the situation (which will match up with step B of the ABC model below). How did you explain, interpret, or appraise the situation? Be specific. Pause briefly now to consider how these appraisals influenced your emotional reactions and subsequent actions.

ABC model of human functioning. One of the most useful models of the interaction between events in our life and our reactions (i.e., thoughts, feelings, and behaviors) is the ABC model of human functioning. The ABC model is a time-tested framework for behavioral and cognitive psychologists. Daniel Goleman wrote about metacognition (awareness of thought processes) and meta mood (awareness of one's own emotions).[26] Long before Goleman, Albert Ellis developed an ABC model in the 1950s.[27]

Figure 7 is a graphic representation of the ABCs of human functioning.

FIGURE 7
ABCS OF HUMAN FUNCTIONING

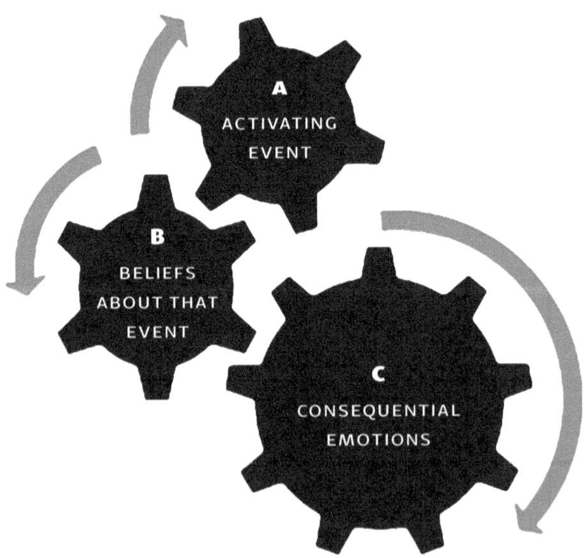

The ABCs are powerful because they highlight the role of thinking in our emotional and behavioral responses to events in our life.

Imagine you are the managing partner of a midsize law firm. During your quarterly board meeting, a colleague makes a direct attack on your decision-making over the past year. Like most, you feel a rush of anger. Depending on your MO, you will likely withdraw, lash out in retaliation, or respond somewhere in between. When you break this down later to your partner over dinner, you are likely to explain that "she was out of line" and "I felt pissed." You attribute your emotional response, feeling pissed, to her actions. However, there is a key step in that process that is often overlooked: how you explained her actions. Your explanation, automatic thought, perspective, interpretation—or whatever you want to call it—is what made you feel pissed and ultimately led to your leadership action, not her actions.

The best way to understand this is to practice mapping out the ABCs. We will highlight some of the most common thinking errors at step B that tend to lead to the most dysfunction in teams and organizations.

↑↓↑

SELF-DISCOVERY EXERCISE 9: DOING THE ABCS

1. You studied harder than ever, knew the material better than anyone else in your study group, and felt great after the exam.
2. Then you got a B+ on the exam.
3. Map out your ABCs.

Be sure that you have an A, a B, and a C here. We have given you the A, but you need to fill in the B and C. If it helps you to complete all parts of this exercise, feel free to think of a more dramatic surprise (A) than receiving a B+ on the exam. Having some detail on B and C are crucial because the next reading helps you to better understand what they are and how to manage them. Furthermore, in combination with responses to prior self-discovery exercises, details from this self-discovery exercise are critical for the next self-discovery exercise, which provides you with a way to track multiple situations.

[STOP and COMPLETE before reading further.]

□ □ □

Common distortions. Below are some common distortions (dysfunctional ways) of thinking that we all experience at one time or another, first identified and published by David Burns and appearing in a variety of sources since.[28] Understanding them—cognition—is key to not letting them take hold to begin with or addressing them if they do. These would be thinking patterns—at "B" in the ABC model described above—to keep an eye out for as they can easily lead to unhelpful emotional reactions. We try to frame each in terms of law school or law practice.

All-or-nothing thinking (polarized thinking). This distortion is essentially an inability or unwillingness to see the space in between polar points. It is the propensity to think in terms of binary opposition: "friend or enemy" or "good or bad." You can liken this kind of thinking to an on-off light switch, which has only two settings, rather than a dimmer switch, which allows for many shades of light. In our class, we call this *living on the edge*, that is, thinking in absolutes, and it is a dangerous way to go. Much of legal education and the practice of law reinforces this view when matters are presented as zero-sum. Fortunately, the world and the law is full of ambiguity and the issues are complex and multi-factored, which can result in thinking that reveals other or more outcomes. To lead, we have to be able to practice cognitive flexibility which allows us to see all of the varied aspects and perspectives—the nuances—that are essential in good decision-making. An inability to see the nuances makes leading oneself and others quite difficult.

Overgeneralization. This distortion occurs when we see one instance or example and take it as exemplifying an overall pattern. Many law students fall into this trap by thinking that grades define them—that a low grade reflects continued low ability, that a particular employer will not talk to them because of that grade, and that they are unworthy of being hired. When we overgeneralize, we may extend and apply a specific negative thought, be it personal or professional, to other situations, thereby creating even greater negative thoughts about ourselves.

Mental filter. Somewhat like overgeneralization, mental filter is a distortion where the focus on a single negative is used to exclude all of the positives. One example of mental filter would be where a student receives one lower grade and several higher grades but dwells or focuses on the lower one as the accurate reflection of reality, without considering the positive grades. Another example would be where a young associate receives a mixed performance review, one that includes numerous positive points and several negative ones requiring improvement, but focuses only on the negative points and what they portend for the future.

Disqualifying the future. Disqualifying the future is similar to mental filter, but it also involves actively rejecting the positive matters. Using the prior example of the performance review, an associate with this distortion would recognize the positive praise and dismiss or discount it for reasons that have little or no basis in reality ("Well, she had to say something nice."). This distortion enables negative thought patterns even when strong reasons and evidence that are positive exist, and in this way distortion plants the seeds of negativity deeper.

Jumping to conclusions. One version of this distortion is also referred to as *mind reading.* Jumping to conclusions refers to going beyond what someone says to attribute negativity to what is underlying and unknown. While you certainly might have a sense of what someone else is thinking, this distortion is about the inferences and interpretations one makes. Our preconceived notions of others and implicit biases also creep in here. When a professor or partner walks past you with a serious or angry look on her face, that does not mean they are thinking about you in that moment.

Another version of the *jumping-to-conclusions* distortion is called *fortune telling.* Here, the lack of an event is used to foretell the future, such as when a student who has not applied to any jobs assumes that he will never get a job, or when a young associate who has never had to try to land a client assumes that she is incapable of doing so. These predictions are based on little to no evidence, and there is no way to know what outcome will come to pass, yet they are held up as truth.

Magnification, *catastrophizing*, or *minimization* is also known as the "binocular trick" because it skews your perspective. This distortion involves exaggerating, in either direction, the meaning, importance, or likelihood of a matter. A good example would be the student or lawyer who makes one mistake and believes that the mistake, however small, has monumental implications. To be sure, missing a filing deadline or letting a statute of limitations run is monumental, but that is not what we are talking about here. The types of mistakes we are talking about here are typos, missing a meeting, or not returning a call as promptly as someone expected. This distortion causes you to believe that making one of these relatively minor mistakes makes you a weak or mediocre student or lawyer.

The distortion of *emotional reasoning* is, perhaps surprisingly, even more prevalent in the law. With this distortion, one accepts emotional feeling as fact. Even though legal education and the law both downplay the importance and role of emotions in the law, we all still feel emotions. For example, when a fellow law student or associate says something that is praised by the professor or law partner, we might feel less smart or jealous. Likewise, in our personal lives, we may feel a twinge of jealousy when a friend or partner gives more attention to someone else. Yet this jealous reaction does not reflect the truth of the matter in either scenario. We all know that with more time or additional opportunity, we would have had the same thought or comment, or that others sharing time with a wide range of people is normal and not a negative reflection of us. The frustrating part of this distortion is that we all know it is an unreasonable feeling.

"Should" statements. This particularly damaging distortion involves telling yourself what you *should*, *ought*, or *must* do. It imposes expectations and sets limits that likely will result in guilt if not achieved: "I should read more for class," "I should have written a longer memo," "I must get to work earlier (than expected)." The resulting guilt can also lead to feelings of anger and resentment toward either ourselves or to others who seemingly are doing what we think we *ought* to do. We even have a joke we like to make with our students and clients: *Stop "should"ing all over yourself.*

Labeling and mislabeling. This distortion is an extreme form of overgeneralization. Here, one takes an event and assigns it a judgment or value. The judgment is negative toward oneself or others, and it usually involves a severe label. For example: the partner (or professor) who used red ink to excessively mark up your memo or who called you out in a meeting (or class) rather than taking you aside to point out an issue is a pompous jerk. Our emotions drive the mislabeling such that the descriptor is loaded, inaccurate or unreasonable, and goes beyond what is appropriate to the setting.

This leads us to the distortion of *personalization*, where one takes everything personally or assigns self-blame without there being any underlying reason for doing so. For example, just because a client you work with fires the firm and the partners get upset, or just because everyone is confused in a class session in which you were speaking, does not mean that you are to blame for how others are feeling. This distortion gives too much weight to what you did or did not do in the grand scheme of things and places on you a false feeling of responsibility for how others are feeling.

Our hope is that by naming some of these common and unhelpful thinking patterns, you will be able to catch yourself falling into them, take a pause, and reframe your thinking in a more adaptive and healthy way.

↑↓↑

SELF-DISCOVERY EXERCISE 10: CREATING A THOUGHT RECORD

As mentioned in Exercise 9, "Doing the ABCs," your goal is to track these distortion-of-thinking situations, your responses, and your assessments of these responses. This self-discovery exercise gives you a framework in which to do so. The first step is to replicate the chart on the following page in your journal (or Word doc) and record your answers to the prior self-discovery exercises in it. Be prepared to continue to do so going forward.

Date & Time	Situation	Automatic Thoughts	Emotion	Cognitive Distortion	Rational Response	Outcome
	What led to the unpleasant emotion? *What distressing physical sensations did you have?*	*What thoughts or images went through your mind?* *How much did you believe the thoughts at the time (0–100%)?*	*What emotion did you feel?* *How intense were these emotions (0–100%)?*	*What was your logical error?*	*What was your response? Rate your belief (0–100%).*	*Re-rate your belief in thought and specify subsequent emotions.*

Be sure to think about the common cognitive distortions described above. Which ones have you experienced?

[STOP and COMPLETE before reading further.]

↑ ↓ ↑

REFLECTIVE WRITING 9

Creating a thought record in which you write about these times, detailing the situation, your thoughts, and how you might rethink those circumstances if and when they come up again is a challenging exercise. Reflect on that process. How will you make sure that you apply a positive explanatory style here (as opposed to simply rehashing how you see situations)? Your growth in self-management depends on developing that explanatory style!

4. Do You Have a Mantra?

The term *mantra* makes most of us think of Buddhist monks sitting all day long, repeating a word to themselves. While this is a very real circumstance and a beautiful image, in everyday parlance, a mantra is simply a personal phrase that provides some individualized motivation. Everyone has or should have one.

Rob and Cliff are both runners.* Cliff likes to tell himself, particularly after a long run when only a short portion is left, "You've run X miles hundreds of times—this is very doable." When Cliff looks to large projects that seem overwhelming as a whole, he says to himself, "Just chunk it," meaning break it into manageable pieces so that the overwhelming nature dissipates. And to maintain optimism and excitement at work, Rob thinks "The best is yet to come!" Try practicing repeating that one to yourself on a regular basis—it can be quite uplifting!

↑ ↓ ↑

---

* Runners include those who take short jogs, who run/walk, who race often, or who run longer distances. We fall into this spectrum of runners.

SELF-DISCOVERY EXERCISE 11: WHAT'S YOUR MANTRA?

What do you tell yourself when you hit a tough spot and need to reframe your thinking?

1. What's your mantra?
2. Do you have more than one mantra?
3. If so, what is the difference in your use of each?

[**STOP and COMPLETE before reading further.**]

5. Adaptability

If there is one thing that we have all learned from the COVID-19 pandemic, it's that things can change at the drop of a hat. Most of us will never forget the barrage of information and varying instructions coming out nearly daily about safety protocols and best business practices, shortages on meat and toilet paper, and complex decision-making about when it was safe to visit family and friends. Leaders' adaptability was tested in ways that had rarely been seen throughout modern history. Adaptability is the ability to be flexible, handle multiple demands within a variety of changing situations to fit fluid circumstances. Leaders with this competency challenge their own ideas or views on the basis of new information. They are able to modify systems and practices when necessary and juggle multiple demands smoothly.[29]

Developing your adaptability will help you deal more positively with change. Unexpected change happens to all of us and tends to be out of our control, but we can control our reactions to it. Being able to accept the change, be flexible and adapt to it, and then move forward is a real skill.

People who demonstrate adaptability willingly change their own ideas or approaches based on new information or changing needs. Does this mean giving in to every suggestion that is made? No. But it does mean listening to what others have to say and not immediately rejecting the idea (as your amygdala might want you to do, just because the idea is different). If you are one of the seven blind men, adaptability through listening lets you see and appreciate everyone's perspectives rather than be stuck in the one perspective that you had. The firms that persevered through the COVID-19 pandemic are a great example of this adaptability. They did so with emotionally intelligent leaders at the helm who exhibited superior adaptability, often referred to now as *adaptive leadership*.

ROB TAKING THE LEAD → The primary theme in my coaching since the pandemic began has been on this exact topic! I have frequently been asked, "How do I keep up with the constant barrage of change?" Many leaders were put to the test throughout the pandemic, forced to make swift changes to their protocols and systems in the face of new information about the virus itself and about any number of things impacted by the virus (e.g., supplies). One strategy that has proven helpful is talking with leaders about the idea of *triaging*, a term used in the medical field. Triaging involves assessing a situation to determine the urgency of the need for treatment. In leadership, *triaging* involves constantly assessing your beliefs and actions with self-awareness and empathy in order to rise to the moment. Executives who demonstrate this form of adaptability champion flexibility, but it does not come naturally to many; business as usual is often easier, initially, because familiarity is comfortable. But change is always happening around us (e.g., the need to offer virtual/remote workplace, meeting, and event formats to employees and clients), and transitions brought about by these changes affect us. Great leaders spend more time thinking about how changes are affecting them and their teams.

↔

You increase your adaptability by being curious about new ideas and diverse perspectives, keeping tabs on how attached cognitively and emotionally you become to one idea, and, probably most importantly and in the spirit of emotional intelligence, monitoring your own emotional reactions to change (i.e., how it makes you feel). Indeed, a great body of literature in leadership is about the difference between change and transitions. What changes are you going through currently, and what is the transition you are required to make? Often, transition involves more vulnerability and threats, such as the loss of control or power. You will thrive as a leader when you are keenly aware of this emotional transition and can adapt in a successful way.

People who are adaptable are able to juggle multiple demands, or multitask, as it was once known. Neurological research has shown that we do not truly multitask—that is, we do not actually do two or more things at once. Rather, the brain, very quickly and adeptly, switches from one task to another. This entails juggling multiple demands. When your plate is full and you get another serving of work, your amygdala tells you to stress out, sending you messages like "Not another assignment!" "I can't handle the load." "Something's not going to get done!" or "I just want to run away and hide from it all! Binge *Game of Thrones*, now!"* But being adaptable means that you think about how to manage the pile.

People who are adaptable change their approach: Let's make the plate bigger. Let's add a second plate. Let's move from a plate to a cooktop and divide the work among the burners, where some things will simmer while others are on high heat. Lawyers and law students can be just like the cooks who do that all the time. It is just a matter of being more flexible in how you approach changes, particularly changes that add more stress to an already stressful environment.

6. Achievement Orientation

Self-management also involves relentlessly striving for excellence, constantly working to do things better, and taking calculated risks to surpass expectations, all of which has collectively been referred to as Achievement Orientation. Similar to adaptability, achievement orientation plays a key role in innovation as leaders high in this EI competency urge and support entrepreneurial ideas. They challenge themself and teams to be results-oriented, seek ways to improve performance, and meet challenging goals. Achievement Orientation has been identified time and again as a distinguishing characteristic between typical and the highest performing leaders, and for rather obvious reasons. Leading in the law is not easy, as you likely know. Busy leaders face various challenges on a daily basis. Leaders high in EI pay attention to their cognitive and emotional reactions to business challenges, remain committed to new and innovative ideas, and reorient themselves on a daily basis to be their best self.[30]

For law students and lawyers, this may require some adaptability. Perfectionism is an evil infused in many of us. It makes us wary of letting

* We are acutely aware that binge-watching a series (new or old) is not necessarily an outlet for everyone, but you get the idea!

go of things (because they are not yet perfect). It makes us move the goalposts once we achieve a goal (because we think that goal was not good enough, or because we got there too fast and so must have set too low a goal). It makes us unable to feel satisfaction in completing our work and in the success that stems from completing it. To be sure, sometimes we need to perfect something. A document improperly or incorrectly completed is a problem (such as a Securities and Exchange Commission or Internal Revenue Service filing). But that is about diligence and attention to detail, not perfectionism. Perfectionism keeps us from accepting more on our plate, setting realistic goals, and feeling real job and life satisfaction.

Achievement orientation is about healthy striving. As you know from the groundwork laid earlier in this book, it is about setting intrinsic motivators, like doing your best or trying your hardest, not judging yourself on unattainable perfectionistic standards. Leaders who are high in achievement orientation have a drive to succeed, competitive spirit, and want to do the best they can in their work. Our work with law students and lawyers has shown us that success comes to those who recommit to excellence on a regular basis. They are constantly looking for ways to improve how things work and challenge themselves to bring forth big ideas. This requires a deep self-awareness to know when they get off track, and strong self-management to realign with accomplishing even the most rigorous goals. A quick study of leadership stars throughout history would reveal this level of commitment to excellence. Luckily for you, lawyers tend to score high in this competency.

CLIFF TAKING THE LEAD → When I was in practice, I knew of our (collectively, in the firm) perfectionistic tendencies. This included hanging on to briefs for a couple of extra days before filing, hoping for those words of wisdom that would win the motion. The partners always asked the judge for a Monday due date for just this reason. But that brought with it extra pressure on that work, on other work that needed to be done, and on us personally. Thus, I always pushed for a Friday deadline. (This dance was never adequately resolved in practice as I had limited final say.)

This lesson carried over into teaching, where I always try to give Friday deadlines. However, I recall one illustrative instance where a student had strong reason to need the Monday due date. The student was asking for an extension over the Thanksgiving holiday weekend, and I knew that even with the extra days, it was not likely that she would markedly improve the assignment. So, I made a deal. I told the student that I would give her the extra time on one condition: that she submit the paper on Wednesday at 5:00 p.m. (before the long weekend) and again first thing Monday morning. I would grade the Monday paper, but I would also compare the two and meet with her to let her know what, if any, difference the weekend made in my assessment. The moral of this story lies in the fact that the papers were virtually identical, with no difference rising to the level of a grade advancement. Most valuably, it taught the student that the extra time to perfect the paper was not really in her best interest.

↔

Remember, achievement orientation is about realistic expectations and measuring our success based on intrinsic values, such as doing our best, while perfectionism often involves measuring success by extrinsic motivators, such as money or accolades, and unrealistic or unattainable outcomes.

↑↓↑

REFLECTIVE WRITING 10

Think of a time when you had a similar experience—that is, when your achievement orientation was more about perfectionism or chasing an unrealistic goal and could have otherwise been moderated. Write out the circumstance, your assessment at the time, and your reflection on it now.

[**STOP and COMPLETE before reading further.**]

7. Positive Outlook

Unlike Achievement Orientation, lawyers tend to score lower on Positive Outlook. Any thoughts on why this might be? The answer often lies in the way 'thinking like a lawyer' training in law school can impact lawyers' underlying thinking patterns. Indeed, legal education serves law students well in terms of being able to pinpoint weaknesses in arguments, but this ability to look for what is going wrong can become an over-strength when it is applied, by extension, to situations in many areas of life. Positive outlook is the ability to see what is possible, what is good, and where there are opportunities. It is about training the mind to stay focused on opportunities instead of threats, hopeful thoughts versus fears, and seeing lessons in setbacks and difficult situations.[31]

Affirmations. Have you ever found yourself truly thinking something positive about yourself? Like, a really genuine and authentic positive self-statement? If so, hold onto that moment and try to repeat that message to yourself. That is known as self-affirmation and the practice has been found to increase neural activity associated with well-being and performance.[32] An affirmation is simply a self-statement or thought that affirms your adequacy and value. While it might sound simple or like pseudoscience, it can be difficult to muster up during times of setback, and takes intentional practice. We have to train our brains to focus on what we are doing well, especially in a profession that can be rather critical and inherently focused on outcome. You can think of affirmations like a magical wand that you wave internally to refocus your attention on your strengths. You might think, "You got this. This is your sweet spot," or "Nice work, you really do care so much and give it your all," or maybe, "You really are good at leading team meetings." You will feel a rush of positive neurochemicals associated with well-being, calm, and high performance when you engage in a practice of repeating self-affirmations.

"[E]vidence suggests that affirmations can help you to perform better at work." For example, "spending just a few minutes thinking about your best qualities before a high-pressure meeting [such as] a performance review, can calm your nerves, increase your confidence, and improve your chances of a successful outcome."[33]

Writing an affirmation statement. If you take some time to practice writing affirmations, they will become more natural over time. The following tips can assist you in writing an effective affirmation statement:

> **Think about the areas of your life that you would like to change.** For instance, do you wish that you had more patience? Or deeper relationships with your friends and colleagues? Or would you like a more productive workday? Write down several areas or behaviors that you'd like to work on. Be sure that they are compatible with your core values and the things that

most matter to you so that you'll feel genuinely motivated to achieve them.

Be sure that your affirmation is credible and achievable. Base it on a realistic assessment of the facts. For instance, imagine that you're unhappy with the level of pay that you currently receive. You could use affirmations to raise your confidence to ask for a raise. However, it probably wouldn't be wise to affirm to yourself that you're going to double your salary: for most people, and most organizations, doubling what you're earning in one go isn't feasible. Keep it realistic! After all, affirmations are not magic spells—if you can't believe in them, it's unlikely they'll impact your life.

Turn negatives into positives. If you are struggling with negative self-talk, note down the persistent thoughts or beliefs that are bothering you. Then choose an affirmation that is the opposite of that thought and belief. For example, if you habitually think, "I'm not talented enough to progress in my career," turn this around and write a positive affirmation such as, "I am a skilled and experienced professional."

Write your affirmation in the present tense. Write and speak your affirmation as if it's already happening. This helps you to believe that the statement is true right now. For instance, "I am well-prepared and well-rehearsed, and I can give a great presentation" would be a great affirmation to use if you feel nervous speaking in front of a group.[34]

A great affirmation about a law school exam would be "I know this material and am comfortable discussing it." (Contrast this to a mantra, which would be something like "I've taken many law school exams and I've got this one.")

Say it with feeling. Affirmations can be more effective when they carry emotional weight. You need to want this change to happen, so every affirmation that you choose to repeat should be a phrase that's meaningful to you. For example, if you're worried about a new project that you've been tasked with, you could tell yourself, "I am really excited to take on new challenges.

Examples of Affirmations

By definition, your affirmation will be personal to you and specific to what you want to achieve or change, but the following examples may provide some inspiration:

- I have plenty of creativity for this project.
- My work will be recognized in a positive way by my boss and colleagues.
- I can do this!
- My team respects and values my opinion.
- I am successful.
- I am honest in my life and my work.
- I like completing tasks and projects on time.
- I'm grateful for the job I have.
- I enjoy working with my team.
- I'm bringing a positive attitude to work every day.
- I am excellent at what I do.[35]

Here are a couple more affirmations (from us):

- I am generous.
- I am happy.
- I possess the qualities needed to be extremely successful.

E. Finding Happiness

Are you happy? Really happy? Lawyers *are* typically happy that they chose the profession of law, despite their being unhappy or unsatisfied at times with aspects of their work life. And many lawyers you encounter will tell you positive things about their work and life. This is important because happiness is a key part of self-management.

1. Lawyer (Un)happiness

We talked earlier about how law students' mental health, while equivalent to the general population at the start of law school, declines during law school. The data show that the rates of anxiety and depression among law students are significantly higher than those of the general population, and this is important because it suggests that something happens during the law school experience that tends to increase anxiety and depression. This carries over from law school into the practice of law.

A 1990 study found that out of 104 occupational groups, *lawyers ranked the highest in depression*, with 17.4 percent of respondents screening positive for depression and 20 percent indicating that they had been diagnosed with depression at some time in their life. In fact, that same 1990 study found that lawyers, as an occupation, ranked *fifth in incidence of suicide*, with 6.3 percent having thought seriously about suicide in the previous twelve months. By 2016, these numbers had increased, with 28 percent of lawyers struggling with some level of depression and 11.4 percent having thought seriously about suicide. A particularly telling statistic in the 1990 study was that roughly one-sixth of those with a depression diagnosis had received the diagnosis since starting law school.[36]

While this does not mean all lawyers are unhappy, it does mean that happiness—and the achievement of it—is an issue in the profession of law. This is why we want to introduce some simple habits that you can integrate now to stay healthy and thrive.

↑↓↑

REFLECTIVE WRITING 11

→ Are law students/lawyers happy? Why or why not?
→ Does law practice lead to issues with well-being?
→ Were you happy in your last legal job?
→ Were the people you worked with happy?
→ What affirmations (will) help you through the challenges?

[STOP and COMPLETE before reading further.]

2. Happiness Advantage

We don't know about you, but it seems to us that we are never quite satisfied with what we've got. The moment we reach a goal, we set a new one.

Just think about it for a moment. Can you remember a time in your life when you told yourself that you would be happy if you could just obtain some goal—but then as you were achieving it, you were setting your sights on the next goal?

For instance, when applying to law school, it is common to say something to yourself like, "If I could just get into law school, then everything will be fine." Then you get into law school and pretty quickly find yourself saying, "If I could just . . . [get on a journal board, obtain a top associate position, etc.]."

This raises the question of what comes first, happiness or success? Shawn Achor, an expert in leadership and human potential, addressed that exact question in *The Happiness Advantage*. Achor suggested that you probably answer that question several times each day.[37] You answer it every time your brain says,

- "I'll be happy when I . . ."
- "I'll be happy when I get a good job."
- "I'll be happy when my outline is finished."

In his book, Achor eloquently explains that we have been socialized mostly with this formula: work harder, then you'll be successful, then you'll be happier. Ask most law students or lawyers what will make them happy, and their answer is easy: "I'm working my butt off now so I can be happy when I get . . . [a top job, a 4.0, a partner position, etc.]." But the problem is that it is hard to find happiness after success if, as discussed earlier, the goalposts of success keep changing. Achor points out that our society's formula for success and happiness is broken, and that if you reverse the order of the formula by starting with finding ways to be happy and enjoying the pursuit, success will follow.[38] As is evident from the book's title, Achor called this idea the *happiness advantage*.[39]

And there is mounting empirical evidence showing that if we can find happiness in our current life, we will perform better.[40] Happiness is an advantage—and the precursor to greater success. This makes sense, and it has been shown time and again in research.[41] Just think about a time when you were not happy in a job. Did that impact your performance? Do your mood and attitude impact how you do the work?

Alternatively, think about companies that are supposed to be the best places to work. They have happy employees and therefore outperform most other organizations.[42] Can you think of any companies like that?

Did you pick a law school or firm (or other employer) that will help you be happy and healthy so that you can thrive in a balanced career?

Obviously you are not going to like all aspects of law school. However, you can be happy in your life even as you pursue a legal career, and being happy will help you to perform better. So, what about you? What makes you happy?

↑ ↓ ↑

SELF-DISCOVERY EXERCISE 12: WHAT MAKES YOU HAPPY?

1. Write down three things that make you happy.
2. Are you doing those things?
3. How can you make time for those things?

[STOP and COMPLETE before reading further.]

3. Boosting Your Mood

You have learned that so much of being emotionally intelligent is being able to self-monitor. Here are some evidence-based ways to boost your mood when you find that you are struggling throughout the day:

"Three good things" habit. This is about maintaining focus on what is going well. Law students tend to catastrophize even the most minor of things. Write down three things every day that went well and why. These do not need to be major events; they should be anything that you felt went well throughout the day. *Actually write them down* instead of just thinking about them.

"Three good things" habit—shared. After you have completed this assignment on your own, do it again with a partner (preferably a person you frequently share your anxieties with). Write down three things that went well this week and why, and then share it with your partner. How does that feel?

Letter of gratitude. Gratitude is the general habit of noticing and being appreciative of whatever is good in one's life. Practicing gratitude predicts emotional and physical health. Write a letter, text, or email to someone who has changed your life for the better *and deliver it to that person.*

ROB TAKING THE LEAD → I have an uncle who is a retired CEO. He ran one of the largest health systems in the Southeast successfully for years. I have noticed over the years that he takes time to write texts and emails expressing his gratitude for me, my wife, our daughters, and most people in our family. Having worked with some of the best leadership minds and through years of his own coaching, he recognizes that expressing gratitude is great for him and also builds up those around him.

↔

Gratitude journal. Make it a weekly practice to write in a gratitude journal. Think back over your week and list five things that happened for which you are grateful. Make sure to include both personal and professional items/occurrences and to write *why* you are grateful for each.

Meaning. Take two minutes to journal about the most meaningful experience of the past twenty-four hours.

Mindfulness. Practice mindfulness two to five minutes daily.

Exercise. Research shows that even ten to fifteen minutes of aerobic exercise can boost your mood by increasing your brain's ability to take up serotonin from your blood and increase dopamine production. Serotonin and dopamine are neurotransmitters, brain chemicals that allow signals to pass from one nerve cell to the next. Serotonin affects mood, sexual desire, appetite, sleep, memory, and temperature regulation. Low serotonin levels are connected with depression. Dopamine affects movement, emotional response, and your ability to feel pleasure.

Altruism. Helping others is a therapeutic activity. Do one nice thing for someone in your life today. It may be easiest to first think of someone you know through school, church, family, or elsewhere who could use some help. Start with identifying something that you could actually do for this person, and then reach out to help.

Help others focus on the positive. Ask a friend or family member, "What was the best part of your day?" You also could start meetings by practicing gratitude. When Rob was at the University of Denver Health Center, the weekly staff meeting would begin with an open time during which everyone could share something positive that they had noticed over the past week. The practice contributed to a positive workplace culture and spirit of collaboration going into each meeting.

Listen to upbeat music and move to it. Have you ever listened to a song on repeat because you love the thoughts and feelings it evokes? We have to seek those out. If you find one that really makes you feel good and brings out strong visualizations of your best self, put that thing on repeat. You can also use a song that you associate with a great time in your life. Either way, listen to it and take time to dive in. It may not be a bad idea to "dance like no one's watching," too.

Practice empathy. Take the perspective of someone else in your life. Imagine that person's emotional experiences and how that person thinks about them. Bring a deep curiosity to others throughout your day. You may want to ask yourself, "Where are they coming from?" or "What's going on with them today?"

Can you think of other things to do that help you maintain positive emotions and psychological health and well-being? If so, share them with someone else.

↑↓↑

REFLECTIVE WRITING 12

→ List several "mood boosts" you plan to try this week and when.

→ List four things that you are grateful for in your life—two that are personal and two that are professional.

[**STOP and COMPLETE before reading further.**]

↑↓↑

SELF-DISCOVERY EXERCISE 13: HAPPINESS AT WORK

Beyond the obvious mental health benefits, why does being happy at work and carrying a positive energy matter?

[**STOP and COMPLETE before reading further.**]

□ □ □

With your growing self-awareness and newfound means of self-management, you are now in a strong position to excel further in all of your personal and professional endeavors. You should have a broader understanding of what you do and why, what you do not want to do and how not to, and how to manage your thinking to dampen your emotions or add fire to them, depending on the situation. You should now have the necessary foundation within you to turn to your relations with others.

CHAPTER V

The Empathic Lawyer

IN THIS CHAPTER, we move from focusing on intrapersonal processes to focusing on interpersonal processes. Leadership from the inside → out! The remainder of this book is about how to bring the EI skills you have learned so far (self-awareness and self-management) into your life and leadership. This involves social awareness and organizational awareness.

A. Moving to Empathy

There is a great deal to unpack with empathy, the key component of social awareness. This section starts by connecting self-awareness and self-management to empathy, then branches into clarifying what we mean by empathy, and finally shifts to how to build your capacity for empathy.

1. Visualizing How Emotional Intelligence Leads to Empathy

Let's begin with some visualization.

Car and driver scenario. Imagine you are driving to work one morning and someone cuts in front of you and quickly whips her car into the turn lane. You slam on your brakes, and coffee spills as you come to a sudden halt.

Self-Awareness: What do you think to yourself? What specific thoughts do you have? What is the appraisal? What emotions do you feel?

Self-Management: How do you manage the flood of emotions that take over?

As you pull ahead and look back, you notice that the driver of the car is a middle-aged woman. She slows her car to a complete stop and puts her hands over her face; she is clearly in distress and crying.

Back to Self-Awareness: What do you think to yourself now? What is your appraisal? Is it still the same? Have your emotions changed as result of a new appraisal?

In this moment, you have a variety of choices about how you will interpret the situation. Your interpretation is at a cognitive level, based on your lived experiences and values. The appraisal you make will undoubtedly lead to how you feel (e.g., enraged, frustrated) and react (e.g., whether you drive more quickly or slowly, flip her the bird, slam on the horn, or turn around and go back to check on her).

The key to emotional intelligence, as we have already shown, is placing your attention on where you place your attention—referred to as *meta-attention.* Emotionally intelligent people (like you!) will be self-aware of their appraisal. They will notice as automatic thoughts arise and they will recognize the feelings that those thoughts evoke, and with that awareness, they will choose the best path forward.

By paying attention to their appraisals, emotionally intelligent people give themselves choices about how they feel in the moment and how they will respond. They are also able to tap their mental brakes. They notice their immediate appraisal and then consider alternatives. This is the point at which they move from intrapersonal processes (those internal processes of a leader) to interpersonal processes—where *empathy* emerges as an option.

Did you consider what might be going on with the middle-aged female driver? What might be causing her to drive that way? What was causing her distress? Self-awareness is what guides the flow from agitated thoughts (e.g., "What the hell is she doing?") to empathic thoughts (e.g., "Is she OK? I wonder what is happening with her. She must be overwhelmed."). In this chapter, you will see that empathy is a critical skill in a multitude of leadership scenarios as it is strongly associated with trust, teamwork, and other key organizational metrics.

Lawyer scenarios. You can take this erratic driving scenario and apply it to a team meeting at work. Often we are quickly agitated or annoyed by others and their different approaches to tasks. Self-aware lawyers recognize these automatic thoughts, then manage them by redirecting their attention to empathic thoughts.

Let's up the ante a bit. Imagine you are grabbing coffee one Saturday morning and run into a legal colleague who is wearing a MAGA Trump hat.

Self-Awareness: What are you thinking? What is your initial appraisal? What emotions do you feel? What do these emotional and cognitive reactions make you want to do?

Self-Management: How do you manage the tide of positive or negative emotional reactions that ensue? Do you pause to notice your appraisal, or do you continue without giving much thought to it?

This single article of clothing carries so much weight, without a doubt. Would anything have been different if your colleague had also been wearing a Grateful Dead T-shirt?

Emotionally intelligent people notice where their attention goes. In the context of this example, they would be able to reflect on their immediate appraisal of their colleague and its influence. They would recognize the flood of emotional and behavioral reactions they were experiencing based on their associations and appraisals of their colleague wearing a MAGA hat.

Let's imagine that a short time after running into this colleague, you meet him in a settlement conference as opposing counsel in a high-stakes case. If you have written off the lawyer in a negative manner based solely on what he wore and the associated politics, then you may approach the negotiation defensively, agitatedly, and maybe even with preconceived judgments about your colleague's interests and intentions. Without practicing emotional intelligence, you might have settled on a harsh appraisal of the opposing attorney, feel activated and angry in his presence, and be quicker to react negatively to his legal moves, potentially missing key aspects of the negotiation that could have helped your client's interests. On the flip side, emotionally intelligent leaders are able to recognize their initial appraisals of and associations about the colleague, use mindful awareness to take stock of what those appraisals and associations suggest, and focus on doing the work to really understand the colleague beyond what he wears outside of the office. The point here is that emotional intelligence allows you to be aware of the myriad factors influencing how you approach working with others. Without awareness of the appraisals you make or biases you have, you are prone to fall under their influence. But with emotional intelligence, you are able to consider and explore the individual free from bias.

Let's continue with this scenario. Imagine that you invited this colleague out for coffee as the legal work unfolded. Over coffee, you learn that this colleague was raised in a working-class, rural, Midwestern, small town with few financial and career opportunities. He struggled to get out of the situation through hard work and grit. In getting to know him, you learn that he overcame an abusive stepfather, paid his way through college and law school while caring for his younger sisters and mother, and, during this time, developed strong conservative ideals. He has found that Donald Trump's conservative economics resonate with him.

Exercising empathy at this point in the scenario does not mean that you have to agree with him. Rather, it means that you now understand his story and can put yourself in his shoes enough to see how he got to where he is. With this newfound understanding, you are able to maintain rapport, and your colleague will likely feel validated and understood, which will lower his reactiveness to you. When you get to the negotiation stage, he is more likely to be agreeable, respectful, professional, and open to listening to and possibly understanding your client's interests. In this way, emotional intelligence can help make legal work more humanistic and less adversarial, benefitting all parties involved. The key here is to understand that having "other" awareness, that is, how we think about people and events in our life, allows for conscious and mindful emotional and behavioral outcomes. With that new understanding, we are primed to be our best and most effective selves.

2. Overcoming Mental Heuristics

We all survive in this fast-paced, tech-heavy, media-driven world using *mental heuristics*—that is, shortcuts to organize and make sense of the torrent of data coming at us every minute. The human brain is a master at carrying out this process, which is an essential survival feature. Simplifying the complex world that we live in feels good and gives us a sense of control. We do this naturally when we meet new people. When faced with groups or individuals who are different from us, it is easy to judge them quickly, then categorize them into groups: red or blue, old or young, liberal or conservative, nerd or jock, and so on. We oversimplify appraisals of others to give us a sense of understanding and control (think on/off thinking here).

We have all seen how these oversimplified appraisals can easily lead to divisiveness and erode our natural sense of trust. Yet many of us have had the experience of initially disliking someone, say a coworker, because of differences—initially labeling her as different based on shortcuts or heuristics. But over time, as you got to know the coworker and learned how similar you really are, you learned to appreciate who she is and her unique differences. That is empathy creeping in. You start to be able to put yourself in someone else's shoes, and your understanding and even affinity for that person grows with that understanding.

Expanding your empathy requires self-awareness of your current level of capacity, a desire to expand that level, and a willingness to do the work involved in that expansion. In *I Thought It Was Just Me (but it isn't)*, Brené Brown references nursing scholar Theresa Wiseman's four attributes of empathy, which highlight what is involved in this expansive work:

- *To be able to see the world as others see it.* This requires putting your own "stuff" aside to see the situation through another's eyes.
- *To be nonjudgmental.* Judgment or prejudgment (amygdala-driven judgment) of another person's situation discounts the experience and is an attempt to protect ourselves from the pain of the situation.
- *To understand another person's feelings.* We have to be in touch with our own feelings in order to understand someone else's. Again, this requires putting your own "stuff" aside to focus on your loved one.
- *To communicate your understanding of that person's feelings.* Rather than saying, "At least you . . . " or "It could be worse . . . ," try saying, "I've been there, and that really hurts" or (to quote an example from Brown) "It sounds like you are in a hard place now. Tell me more about it."[1]

Taken together, these steps start inside oneself (self-awareness and growth) and extend to and connect with the other person (relationship or social awareness). Sympathy lacks this kind of recognition, involving just a judgment of the other person's condition.

Getting empathy right is important. According to Brown, empathy brings people together, while sympathy can lead to isolation and disconnection.[2] This happens because sympathy, although usually coming from a good place, can create an uneven power dynamic. When we show empathy, we make ourselves vulnerable to others while recalling painful or frustrating experiences. Sympathy is disengaged from these challenging feelings and can be seen as looking down on the other person and the situation in which that person finds herself.[3]

3. Embracing Social Awareness

The third domain of Daniel Goleman's social and emotional competency framework (see Figure 8), social awareness (of which empathy is an important part), holds the power to truly change the landscape culturally. Chade-Meng Tan, one of Google's original engineers who later changed his job title to Google's Jolly Good Fellow, wrote the leadership book *Search Inside Yourself*. He famously added the subtitle *The Unexpected Path to Achieving Success, Happiness (and World Peace)* in recognition of the powerful impact of more empathy in the world.[4] Since the publication of *Search Inside Yourself* in 2012, the need for more empathy has grown exponentially as a result of increased racial tension, alternative facts, political polarization, divisive leadership, and loss of trust in democracy. As we move into the domain of social awareness, we see how self-awareness and self-management allow for greater empathy and more effective interpersonal functioning.

Broadly speaking, social awareness is about tuning in to others and, more specifically, exercising empathy and organizational awareness.

Empathy. Empathy is about understanding other people's feelings and perspectives and using that understanding to inform your actions. It is the ability to hear and understand accurately the unspoken thoughts, feelings, and concerns of others, but not to necessarily agree or disagree with them. Highly empathic leaders can accurately read people's moods or emotional cues, understand others' perceptions when they are different from their own, and accurately understand the reasons behind another's actions. As a result of leading empathically, these leaders are often able to listen attentively and make people feel heard and understood. Empathic leaders can bring about less defensive, more open and vulner-

FIGURE 8

THE EMOTIONAL AND SOCIAL COMPETENCY FRAMEWORK

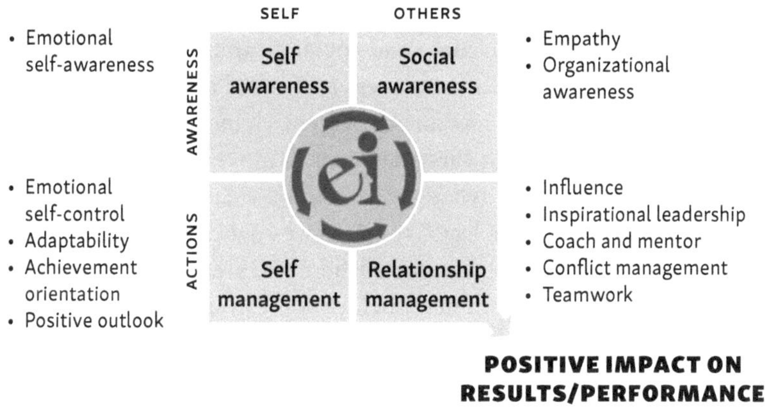

able communication, and have the ability to respect and relate well to people of diverse backgrounds.[5]

Remember, do not assume that everybody does things or values things in the same way, or in the same way that you do. We learn about differences by observing and asking, and by noticing when others respond to things differently than we do. Being open to others' opinions, viewpoints, and ways—but not necessarily agreeing with them—is key to understanding others and embodying empathy. "It is the mark of an educated mind to be able to entertain a thought without accepting it."*

Organizational awareness. Organizational awareness, which takes empathy from the personal level to the organizational level, is the ability to understand the "power" relationships in one's own group or organization. This includes the ability to identify the real decision-makers, who can influence them, and how things get done. It is about knowing who to build relationships with to move an agenda forward or build a program. It is also about recognizing the unspoken values and cultures of organi-

* This quote is often attributed to Aristotle. Regardless, whoever said this understood empathy.

zations and how these affect the way that people act and behave.* When leaders shine with organizational awareness, they often understand the political forces at work, accurately read key power relationships, and know what relationships to invest in to accomplish their agenda.[6]

Link between self-awareness and social awareness. There is a real and direct link between self-awareness and social awareness. Without self-awareness, a person has an 83 percent chance of lacking social awareness as well.[7] Though this may seem intuitive, when you are self-aware you are more than twice as likely to be socially aware. You can think of this as "inside-out leadership." As we have discussed numerous times so far, you must first recognize where you are placing your attention (i.e., practice self-awareness) before you can choose an empathic lens. Emotionally intelligent leaders have an understanding of and appreciation for the role of empathy, and they value what that brings to their life. But having this value alone is not emotional intelligence. Emotional intelligence is recognizing when your attention is on other matters instead of on the interaction you are having with another person, and being able to use that awareness to shift your thinking toward forming an empathic understanding of the other person's position.

B. Clarifying Empathy

Now let's dive deeper into the core competency of social awareness: empathy.

1. Empathy versus Sympathy

When we first present the term *empathy*, there is usually some confusion because many people confuse *empathy* and *sympathy*.** Empathy is the ability to step into the shoes of another person, aiming to understand that person's feelings and perspectives, and use that understanding to guide your actions. Sympathy is a feeling—feeling sorry for the position

---

* Many legal organizations have mission statements and/or identify values on their websites. In practice, though, the values may differ.

** One of the best ways to understand this difference is in Brené Brown's masterful short video. *Brené Brown on Empathy*, YouTube, https://www.youtube.com/watch?v=1Evwgu369Jw (last visited Apr. 6, 2024).

in which someone finds himself. "[E]mpathy is not an emotion at all, but rather a capacity for assessing the internal life of another person."[8] Thus, in a client counseling setting, your clients may want some sympathy from you, but what your clients really need is your empathy—they need you to understand how they feel in their position so that you can better represent their interests and find solutions that match their needs.

Having empathy actually allows us to "feel what [another] person is feeling, appreciate what he or she values, and respond appropriately."[9] Empathy is "a necessary precondition to the experience of sympathy, compassion, guilt, and other emotions that push us to take into account the concerns of other people."[10] Empathy can "jar us out of thoughtlessness and indifference and focus our attention on the human consequences of our decisions."[11]

Not surprisingly, researchers study empathy as a measurable capacity and have identified two kinds of empathy:

- *Cognitive Empathy:* the ability to imagine someone's thoughts and feelings; and
- *Affective Empathy:* the drive to respond with an appropriate emotion.[12]

Stuck in a Hole until Empathy Arrives

A woman walks down the street, minding her own business, and falls into a hole. When she cannot climb out, she yells for help. Hearing her calls, a doctor walks up to the hole. The woman asks him to help her out of the hole. He says, "Sure," writes a prescription, throws it down to her, and walks on. She renews her calls for help. Hearing her, a priest walks up to the hole. The woman asks him to help her out of the hole. He says, "Certainly," writes a prayer on a piece of paper, throws it down to her, and continues on his way. The next to hear her calls is a friend. The woman asks her friend to help her out of the hole. Her friend says, "Absolutely," and jumps into the hole with her. The woman says, "Why did you do that? Now we are both stuck down here." Her friend says, "Don't worry. I've been down here before and can show you the way out."

Research also suggests that beyond being more generous and concerned with others' welfare, empathic people also tend to have happier relationships and greater personal well-being—a win-win for everyone.[13]

2. Empathy and Lawyers

In addition to nurturing sympathy, empathy can facilitate effective communication and improve leadership ability,[14] two skills critical in the legal profession. In terms of communication, empathy allows lawyers to better understand their clients' problems. This, in turn, allows a lawyer to improve the questions asked of the client—and thus, in further investigation of the facts, to reduce the degree of miscommunication and misunderstanding with the client,* and to explain and present the client's story in more effective and compelling ways.[15]

Empathy is also critical in leadership because leadership is all about managing the emotions of others so that team members are happy and work well together. In so many ways, empathy ends up being the most effective skill in achieving organizational goals. For example, let's say you want to develop a new practice area in your firm focused on cybersecurity and data protection. As the firm's managing partner, you decide that the firm's well-established securities practice group would be ideal to take the lead in this new initiative. Without first seeking to understand how the top lawyers in that practice area feel and where those feelings originate—which is empathy in leadership—it will be quite difficult to make progress. You can do it, but leading without empathy in this context often leads to unnecessary challenges related to unacknowledged or invalidated feelings and dynamics. Leaders have to first value empathy and see its purpose before they are able to practice it in real situations.

Empathy in the corporate legal world is becoming especially important for three main reasons: (1) the workforce is becoming more diverse at every level; (2) mergers are on the rise, which necessitates the blending of cultures; and (3) associates are leaving large law firms in record numbers. Pre-pandemic, John C. Coffee Jr. reported on the increasing number of law firms that employ over one thousand lawyers, the result of a rise in mergers, and predicted that the number of U.S. law firms with at least one thousand lawyers will rise from twenty-nine to over fifty in the next decade.[16] While the pandemic slowed down that trend, post-pandemic data show a return to pre-pandemic levels, with mergers during the first quarter of 2023 exceeding all law firm mergers in 2022.[17] While the reasons behind this trend are important, we are most inter-

* Remember the earlier-mentioned most common ethical violations (Chapter IV)? Lack of communication is way up there.

ested in how lawyer leaders can effectively manage the people experiencing these mergers. Empathy plays a key role.

Post-pandemic sources report a rise in lawyer attrition above pre-pandemic levels by as much as 18 percent in 2024 and predict lawyer attrition to continue at rates close to 25 percent above pre-pandemic levels for five years post-pandemic.[18] Reasons for this attrition vary by gender: male associates report burnout and well-being concerns, while female associates report lack of mobility, sexual harassment, and other reasons. In addition to being very concerned about the continue rate of sexual harassment, a report of executives and human resources professionals points out that while leaders believe they are more empathetic post-pandemic (67 percent said so), employees report the lowest levels ever of leader empathy.[19] Empathetic leaders matter for worker productivity, retention, and development. And they matter so much that a clear majority of Gen Z employees would choose an empathetic employer's job offer over another employer's offer of higher pay.[20] There is every reason to think, given the client-centered nature of legal work, that the numbers are similar among young associates in law firms.

ROB TAKING THE LEAD / KIM'S STORY → I was recently coaching a practice group partner (let's call her Kim). Kim was informed by C-suite leadership in the firm that her financial practice group would be merging with one of the corporate practice groups and that they would be announcing that she would eventually oversee both practice groups. As the lead partner from the corporate practice group was phased out, Kim started to see and experience toxic, divisive workplace behavior emerge in her newly merged group. There had evidently been a split within the corporate group over how they felt about the merger, which left several corporate group lawyers upset at the firm.

One lawyer from the other corporate group (let's call her Jaylynn) was particularly angry, directing her hostility at Kim, her new boss. Jaylynn reportedly started to recruit other lawyers in the group to demonstrate defiant and disruptive behaviors in an effort to derail the new group's progress.

Kim's approach to that particular lawyer became a focal point in my coaching sessions with her. In an effort to help build insight, Kim and I explored her reactions to the situation and quickly realized that her focus was on how egregiously Jaylynn was acting. Kim said that Jaylynn was difficult during meetings, often on her phone, and pushed back on every decision the group made. Kim had tried to address Jaylynn's disruptive behaviors by calling her out in meetings and holding performance reviews to discuss professionalism in the group. The more her leadership focused on Jaylynn's negative behaviors, the more distant the relationship grew. Her narrative was also eroding her own well-being. At one point, Kim even said, "If I didn't have to deal with all of these egos and difficult personalities, I could lead this, no problem."

What Kim had not thought about was empathy as a key tool in her leadership-skills bag. I asked her, "What do you think Jaylynn is going through?" Kim paused, pondered, and then told the story about what Jaylynn had been through over the past year. Kim explained that Jaylynn had actually been a rising star in the corporate group that was dissolving and was close friends with that group's lead partner, who was being phased out. They were still frequently seen out after work together. Jaylynn had a rapport with and allegiance to the former group leader. And when the corporate group merged with the finance group, some of Jaylynn's key practice areas were either completely dissolved or reassigned.

With these revelations, Kim was able to practice all branches of emotional intelligence herself in that single, hour-long coaching session:

- *Self-awareness:* recognizing that she was overfocusing on Jaylynn's negative behaviors as opposed to what Jaylynn was feeling and going through, and recognizing that she herself was annoyed and frustrated
- *Self-management:* managing her own frustration and anger, which were contributing to her being very direct and short with the team
- *Social awareness:* practicing both empathy and organizational awareness

Kim realized that she needed to talk with Jaylynn more about the year they had just been through, likely in a one-on-one setting, in order to identify Jaylynn's underlying fears and losses and to connect around shared purpose so that Jaylynn could feel validated, lower her defensiveness, and collaborate on how to move forward. It was a breakthrough moment made possible by the power of empathy.

↔

3. Empathy and Relationship Management

The value of high levels of empathy also extends into the fourth domain of emotional intelligence: relationship management. A high level of empathy enhances one's ability to read social cues and relate to others in team settings and in coaching or developing others (mentorship and inspiration). Research confirms the importance of empathy in teamwork, customer satisfaction, and leadership, and that it is a capacity that we can cultivate into a habit to improve the quality of our own lives.[21] More simply put, having a better understanding of others allows us to do things that are more helpful and less hurtful. When we feel empathy for coworkers and colleagues, we experience greater motivation to work with them.

Consider this simple example: Think about a situation in which a friend says something that hurts you. If you respond from that hurt position, then you will probably hurt that person back with a comment or action (or inaction, like brooding or distancing). The outcome is that two people are now a bit further apart. Now change the circumstance slightly and respond with empathy: A friend says something that hurts you. With self-awareness you ask yourself, what would make him say that? With insight, you then ask that friend, in a non-accusatory, non-judgmental way, where did that comment come from? In response, he says that he is having a bad day. You are no longer hurt by the comment and suggest you get coffee and talk about it. The friend's day (and yours) is better already.

Now extend this example into a team project with coworkers instead of friends. As your work deadline approaches, you meet to assess your ability to get the work done on time. Bob texts that he is running five minutes late and "will be there asap." When Bob walks in, Kelly says, "Well, I guess we can finally get started." Without hesitation, Bob responds, "You probably weren't going to get anything done without me anyway." Chances are good that the meeting will be less productive than it would have been had it started in a different, more empathic, way. Kelly had no idea why Bob was late: maybe the train was late because of track work; maybe there was an accident on the highway delaying Bob's commute; maybe Bob's mother called him with some bad news, and he took five minutes to console her. Certainly, Bob's text could have detailed why he was running late, and Kelly could have responded, "I hope everything is OK." Both messages would have shown high levels of self-awareness, self-management, and empathy—leading to everyone's remaining on task, caring for each other, and supporting the team's functioning. When members of a group feel cared for and understood, the intellectual and creative regions of the brain turn on so that work can be accomplished.

↑↓↑

SELF-DISCOVERY EXERCISE 14: THINKING ABOUT EMPATHY

Identify someone you find difficult to work with and practice being empathic. Then answer each of the following questions:

1. What is it about this person that is difficult?
2. Where might that come from in this person's life?
3. Can you relate to their experience in any meaningful ways?
4. What might you try to ask to learn more about them? Why?

As you answered the questions above, did you notice a shift in where you typically place your attention about the person you find difficult? Had you ever thought about where your attention goes in regard to the person who is difficult? Oftentimes, when we take a step back from our thinking—try to distance ourselves from it—we are able to see other perspectives, giving us the option to choose the best path forward, that is, the path that best promotes our own wellbeing and improves the relationship. Continue to notice how offering some empathic thoughts into your outlook about others changes your approach to working with them.

C. Building Empathy

Now that you understand the unique nature of empathy, both as a capacity to build and the power once in place, we turn to some additional challenges for empathy in the legal profession, then to how to build your capacity for empathy in your legal work and life.

1. Hurdles to Building Empathy That Are Unique to the Legal Field

We need to confront some potential impediments to building empathy that are unique to law students and lawyers.

Anti-change perspective. The first impediment is that legal education and the law are not about embracing change; rather, the law itself is anti-change. Think about it. What is the first principle, or one of the first principles, taught in law school? *Stare decisis.* This is Latin for "stand by things decided" or, in common parlance, "don't change." So we are taught to value great and lasting consistency and to change only when it is really important or necessary to do so.

But accepting that change happens and adapting to it is critical to building and exhibiting empathy. Our clients come to us not because everything is going along the same or swimmingly well but rather because something has happened, or because they want something to happen that will likely necessitate someone changing something. Thus, a key aspect of the lawyer's job is to effectuate change. As lawyers, we need to be able to shift away from the thinking and learning habits we were taught in law school in order to maximize our capacity to be empathetic with our clients and to the changes in their worlds.

Legal education encourages on-the-spot judgments. The second impediment to building empathy is students' desire to formulate an answer immediately upon hearing or before understanding the whole problem. Certain law teaching methods like the Socratic method and long, time-pressured exams focus on immediacy and speed in responsiveness, effectively elevating both above contemplative thinking. Lawyers need to be able to respond quickly and also to know when time is needed to think something through. With emotional intelligence you will be better positioned to respond correctly for your client in the moment.

More often than not in your work as a lawyer, you will need to work hard to quiet your mind, silence your initial impressions regarding the answer, and reserve judgment until you fully understand your client's facts, perspective, and core beliefs. This includes being willing to reconsider your initial assessment in light of a higher empathic understanding of your client's situation, as well as a readiness to reconsider assessments in light of any change in the facts from investigation, a new understanding (in your minds), or otherwise.

Most lawyers do not have enough fingers and toes to count the times when they thought they understood a case, only to have to reassess the entire situation upon learning new facts or perspectives. Often, lawyers ask, "Does this new fact change anything?" But this question is a bit reductive as it involves looking at only one fact and the law. A better approach would be to think of the new fact as a new puzzle piece that could change how the entire picture looks.

With empathy, you can step into your clients' shoes, a position that allows you to understand their thoughts and feelings (and view of the facts) and to relate more closely to their experiences. You can then utilize your training and skills to determine how best to represent your clients' experiences, thoughts, and feelings to others in such a way that they can understand and relate.

Adversarial nature of law. The last impediment to building empathy is that law is often presented as adversarial and zero-sum. In litigation, the sides are drawn and separated, only brought together by circumstances. What one side gets is what the other side does not get. This battle over limited resources can stifle curiosity about ways to make the outcome better match the needs and interests of the respective parties.

Curiosity can lead to creativity, which, in turn, can reveal additional opportunities. In any negotiation (litigation, a deal, or legislation), it is only zero-sum if you want it to be so limited. This is why students in negotiation courses are taught to consider the interests of both sides, an inherently empathetic task. With curiosity and the understanding and empathy that result from it, both sides are able to become more creative and flexible, which in turn can lead to solutions that meet more of what each party needs. Simply put, curiosity in negotiation allows parties to see past their differences and reach solutions that courts or arbiters could not or would not reach. Thinking so creatively is a direct function of one's empathy and creativity—EQ and IQ together.

2. Steps to Building Empathy

Now that you understand the hurdles to building empathy, we will turn our attention to how to build empathy. The simple first step in building empathy is to get to know your colleagues genuinely. Sometimes we refer to people as icebergs—a wee bit on top for all to see and a great deal below the surface, unseen unless actively explored. Getting below the surface is what enables you to really understand your colleagues.

What lies below the waterline are matters of the heart: values, motivations, and interests that are not necessarily visible unless they relate to the current project or work. Often, we hold these below the waterline because they are valuable and sharing them makes us vulnerable. When trying to build empathy, it is not enough to dive below the surface in an effort to better understanding your colleagues—to really make connections, you will need to share parts of yourself that lie below the surface. Sharing and making these connections with others can lead to building strong(er) interpersonal connections. Once you see shared values or a shared purpose, mission, or passion, you will want to know what others think.

The second step in building empathy is to focus on fulfilling the collective purpose of creating something meaningful rather than just acting to achieve goals. Whether you call this *mission* or *passion*, it is about understanding why you are doing something and not just that you are doing it.

The third step is to try to understand your colleagues' motives, values, and interests and how they align with the organizational mission. Both people and organizations have values that make up their mission or passion, which must be understood to build empathy. This connection links the first two steps; see this connection yourself and help others to see it as well.

3. Five Practices of Empathy Empowerment

Several researchers/authors have made particularly useful contributions to the field of empathy. Roman Krznaric identified six habits of highly empathic people (HEPs), many of which focus on the first step in building empathy: getting to know others (see previous subsection).[22] HEPs expand their empathy by actively gaining direct experience with other people's lives, putting into practice the Indigenous proverb "Walk a mile in another man's moccasins before you criticize him." Building empathy in this manner is also core to Chade-Meng Tan's exploration of the power of mindfulness when applied to your relationships with others.[23] Finally, Marshall Rosenberg developed the concept of radical listening.[24] Combined, all three make a powerful case for the notion that empathy can be developed and for how to do so.

To maximize your leadership potential through the development, use, and sharing of empathy, we distill the methods of these researchers/ authors into five practices of empathy empowerment:*

- Cultivate curiosity in others;
- Challenge your biases;
- Think beyond your reactions and step into another's shoes;
- Engage in radical listening and make yourself vulnerable; and
- Inspire others through ambitious imagination and empathic meetings.

These practices involve activating high levels self-awareness and self-management as well as the ability to shift your focus away from yourself so that you can focus on another. As we elaborate on these practices, we will link these empowerment tools to the legal profession and to leadership.

Cultivate curiosity in others. Cultivating curiosity in others involves more than having a brief chat with someone about the weather or another mundane topic. It extends beyond asking someone how his weekend was. It is about asking someone how he is feeling while actually caring about and trying to understand the world inside the head of this person.

Doing this with people we know or with whom we have a professional relationship is actually the easy scenario. Daily, we are confronted by strangers, like the woman who delivers your mail or the new entry-level employee who always eats his lunch alone. Set yourself the challenge of having a revealing conversation with one stranger every week. All it requires is a bit of courage. Think about the things in the world that are on your mind and ask a stranger what she thinks about those matters. Then think about how to have that conversation and be curious, at greater depth, with people you actually know.

The exercise of starting a conversation with a stranger every week and challenging yourself to understand them is a great place to start cultivating curiosity. Our clients are strangers when we first meet them and we have to engage them in this same way. In a client setting, this means

* These categories are adapted from Krznaric's *Six Habits of Highly Empathic People*. We consolidated several and supplemented them with material from additional sources, as mentioned.

setting aside the agenda for as long as necessary to ask clients or potential clients what is going on with them today—really—because you never know how that insight might alter, impact, or benefit your understanding of the underlying issues that they came to you to address.

This is equally true of everyone else in a legal workplace. At the start, everyone is new. Be curious about them, ask questions, and listen to the answers. For example, if you work in a relatively large law firm, then you probably work for a number of partners. Each one is unique, with his or her own style. One gives you assignments in writing with detail. Another sends you cryptic emails as assignments. Another wants to meet in person and just give you the insular question without explaining the larger context. Another tells you about the case, eventually standing and delivering the closing argument or convincing rebuttal in negotiations, without ever telling you who else is working on the matter and what parts need to be researched. How do you listen to and engage with each? Your task is to gather sufficient detail to understand what their expectations are of you. This requires you to be curious and ask questions, then listen closely to all they say. And you will benefit from doing this in advance of getting the assignment!

At the same time, you must not treat the client as a novelty. Doing so is not practicing empathy, and it can be seen as inauthentic or demeaning. To represent clients, you need to hear and learn everything about their situation so that, ultimately, you can see it from their perspective. Only then can you determine what is important in representing them, what is important to understanding their motivations, and, perhaps, what obstacles or weaknesses may prevent them from obtaining what they seek.

CLIFF TAKING THE LEAD → One day, new clients came into my office: a Black family of three (parents and a preteen son), all who had been abused by the police. The son got the worst of the treatment; thus, his testimony would be particularly important.

I was assigned to interview the son. He was a sweet kid with a tough exterior who rarely made eye contact when talking. I recognized even at this early stage that while his lack of eye contact might not be a problem initially (like in a deposition that was not video recorded), it could be very problematic at trial if he could not look at the jury members and tell them what happened.

After talking a bit and trying subtly to get him to make eye contact with me (you know, moving my head to be in front of his face when he looked away), I took a more direct approach. I asked him why he would not look at me. He got silent. I told him that he needed to look at the police, opposing counsel, and the jurors. If he could not, then that would be interpreted by some people as a lack of truthfulness. He got even quieter. Again, I asked him why he would not look at me when he spoke. Slowly, he talked about how he was raised to respect elders—that is, the adults at school, church, and lots of other places. He said that his grandma and his parents had taught him to look down as a sign of respect for those who were older or in positions of authority. He added that he was taught to look down and never look a police officer in the eye.

I had thought this might be the reason, but only now, after his confirmation in response to my curiosity, could I fully empathize with him and truly understand his perspective and the challenge we had to surmount in representing him. This is also how curiosity and empathy open the door for cultural competency (which we will discuss in more detail in Chapter VI). With this cultural awareness in mind, we could then have, with his parents present, frank discussions about how to persuade others, particularly others who were raised differently than we were.

I became a better lawyer because of my empathy for him, and he became a very compelling witness by learning empathy for those who were going to judge him. Although clearly greater cultural sensitivity in the legal profession would have avoided his having to explain his initial lack of eye contact, the point is that I would not have been able to understand what was going on with him without being curious and asking questions in a culturally competent and compassionate manner—a necessary component of effective practice and humanistic legal work.

↔

The practice of cultivating curiosity is also essential in leading team meetings, as we see in the next example.

ROB TAKING THE LEAD → I was recently working with a managing attorney (let's call her Hannah) who was charged with building a new cybersecurity practice group in a large corporate law firm. She requested coaching because she was struggling to be seen as approachable and relatable.

After a few coaching sessions, it became clear that her strengths were in data and task orientation. She was a taskmaster and prized efficiency over relationships. She valued short and efficient meetings, which, of course, we all appreciate, but it was clearly coming at the expense of building trust and rapport with her team.

She told me that she did not appreciate when people waste her time by starting meetings with "unnecessary conversations" or small talk. Through our conversations, we realized that her task orientation made it hard for her to get to know her team because she was essentially uninterested in learning their stories. Her strengths in task orientation, achievement, and optimization had become *overstrengths*, and the consequence was a deficit in morale and connection with the people whom she led. It was no surprise, then, that she was struggling to build trust and garner engagement, she found herself doing most of the work, and no one was talking or sharing ideas during team meetings. She had even earned a reputation for being unapproachable.

Hannah and I also identified that she did not like sharing her personal information at work. Her cultural and family values led her to believe that such sharing was unprofessional. She had also gotten feedback early in her life that small talk and social skills were not an area of strength, so she had decided the best way for her to lead was by capitalizing on her strengths in efficiency. Her approach had actually carried her quite far in her career, and she was seen by the managing partners as an effective leader. However, in more advanced leadership roles with other high-powered lawyers, she was finding that her task-focused approach had limitations.

We spent time exploring who she viewed as highly professional, top leaders. Through this exercise, Hannah recognized that she appreciated leaders that shared an appropriate amount of personal information about themselves, got to know her on a deeper level, and created collaborative, person-centered teams. So Hannah and I worked to identify specific parts of herself to share at work and how she could share them in a way that aligned with her cultural and family values. She also started to practice vulnerability.

Through coaching, Hannah became much more self-aware: she recognized that she did not value exploring other people's feelings, and then she worked to gain deeper insight into the origins of this. After incorporating my recommendations to begin each team meeting by checking in on how the team members were doing, to master the art of small talk, and to identify key team members to build rapport with, she learned more about her team, and empathy grew throughout the group. She eagerly came to her weekly coaching sessions and was excited to tell me how much more she had learned about each team member. The increased value that Hannah placed on making time for colleagues to share and explore their personal stories during team meetings led to greater connection. Her reputation for being unapproachable changed over time. She built trust and became more relatable. This is because empathy increases when we cultivate a curiosity in those we work with and when we value understanding who they are and how they got there. This, in turn, leads to the emergence of other essential factors in team functions, like trust, support, and open communication, to name a few.

↔

Cultivating a curiosity in others is a first step that naturally leads to thinking more deeply about why we need to ask these questions and why we are not immediately aware of these differences that, once known, make us more empathetic. Why is the client or the partner like you or different from you? How do you make sure you ask questions about what you want or need to know (below the waterline) versus what you already know (above the waterline)? There is certainly value in asking how a client's world is like your own, despite the obvious differences, or in asking how a partner's role in the law firm is like yours, setting aside their ownership interest, their greater wealth, and their higher position and greater authority. We need to be able to shift to questions that take us into potentially less-comfortable areas.

↑ ↓ ↑

SELF-DISCOVERY EXERCISE 15: BEING CURIOUS

1. As you think about colleagues at work, who would you like to learn more about?
2. What will you ask them to learn their story?
3. How can leading with curiosity bring about greater empathy?
4. How does this relate, for you, to client interactions?

[**STOP and COMPLETE before reading further.**]

↑↓↑

REFLECTION ON SELF-DISCOVERY EXERCISE 15

→ On an intellectual level, how did that feel—comfortable or uncomfortable?
→ Did your mind play out the conversation?
→ Did you think about particular client relations where you might or might not have done this?
→ Would it have made a difference?

Now try to apply this self-discovery exercise. Go out and talk to someone or be more curious with a client. Then return to these debrief questions.

[**STOP and COMPLETE before reading further.**]

□ □ □

Challenge your biases. We all have biases, and all biases are not inherently bad. We tend to like ourselves and people who are like us. Why? Because we are a known quantity, and being around people who are like us is self-affirming. The goal here is to be aware of what your biases are so that you can be conscious of their impact. This way, when we see people who are different from us, we can draw on knowledge, experience, and even unconscious lessons learned in life to "understand" these differences.

Empathy, though, requires that we challenge any inherent narrowing of our willingness to understand and appreciate another person without preconceptions. Thus, to empower our empathy, we must be willing and able to notice our preconceptions and biases (or prejudices). This highlights the role that self-awareness plays in building empathy. Metaphorically speaking, you should take a deep breath, dive below the waterline, and be open to discovering differences between you and others that were previously unknown to you. And you will find more than just previously unknown differences beneath the waterline—perhaps surprisingly, you may discover that you share much in common. Either way, your understanding and empathy will grow. In this spirit, we can see why Tan called empathy the "recipe for world peace."[25] When we cultivate curiosity and challenge our biases, we are able to learn about and understand each other better.

In our legal work, biases and the opportunity to challenge them can arise in myriad ways. For example, many of your clients might not look like you, might not have similar life experiences, and might be in situations that you cannot imagine being in yourself (let alone having to get out of). Often, such clients will quickly bring to your mind biases, stereotypes, and prejudices that need to be acknowledged; this acknowledgment opens the door for true understanding of those clients, where they are at, and how they got there. Of course, these biases can arise just as easily and carry the same judgmental dangers even when encountering clients who look just like you. Despite looking like you, they may not be like you—or at least they may not seem to be like you—and so you will have to go through the same process of challenging your biases to truly understand them.

This all leads us to one of the biggest obstacles to broadening one's thinking: confirmation bias. Confirmation bias is the tendency to seek out or favor information that reinforces or confirms our existing beliefs, and it is a topic that comes up a lot in discussions about society and politics today. For example, many people react to social policy issues by doubling down on their current thinking, seeking information that confirms their existing views, engaging only with people and sources that share their views, and avoiding information and views that are inconsistent with their thinking. Generally, reaffirmation and confirmation feel good, and we want to believe that we are correct and that those who disagree with us are wrong. Compromise can make everyone feel bad.

Law students typically do not like having their views questioned or challenged, and they feel good when their perspectives are complimented.

Thus, all bias, whether weak or strong, originates with that feeling of comfort we find in the initial thought or conclusion. Building empathy necessitates acknowledging confirmation bias, *getting comfortable with our discomfort*, and actively seeking thoughts and ideas beyond our own. When we see an expression from someone who we don't understand fully or agree with, we need to think of at least two possible interpretations before jumping to a conclusion. For example, if your friend is not returning your call, you may be tempted to think that he is ignoring you—but you could also consider the possibility that he is very busy. When we avoid personalizing other people's behaviors, we can perceive their expressions more objectively. People's behaviors have more to do with them than with us. Well-known psychologist and researcher Daniel Amen said that "[a] negative look from someone else may mean nothing more than they're constipated!"[26] Widening your perspective on the situation and accepting some discomfort reduces the possibility of misunderstanding. There is no space for empathy when confirmation bias fills the room.

In some respects, the challenging-biases empowerment tool is not unlike the general manner of teaching in law school. The key to strong legal analysis is the ability to see all sides of the issue. The best lawyers are able to set aside their preconceived notions of "the answer" and *really* consider other possibilities, particularly what and how the lawyers on the other side of the deal, case, or policy debate are thinking.

Yet, whether admitted or not, all law students and lawyers have preconceived notions about everything, and the best lawyers recognize theirs and adjust. They build empathy through the exercise of self-awareness and self-management. And, to be sure, the benefits of being able to set aside biases and see and explore other views extend beyond personal empowerment—they will make you more valuable to your organization and cause others to see you as having wisdom.

This is relevant to the fact that lawyers never really work alone. On a team, everyone should contribute, and those contributions should complement each other.* By challenging your biases, you will increase your receptiveness to others and reap the benefits that flow from working with

* See Chapter VI.

team members who bring differences to bear on the task and who question your thoughts and ideas. You create endless possibilities when you learn and understand others better, even if you do not agree with them.

↑↓↑

REFLECTIVE WRITING 13

Think of an opposing counsel with whom you inherently disagreed on some matter and in whom you see little that you like (just the tip of the iceberg!). This person can be someone on the other side of litigation, someone on the other side of a transaction, or someone opposing legislation or regulations that you favor.

- → What is the conflict about? Describe it.
- → Now ask yourself where this person is coming from.
- → What motivates this person?
- → What do you and this person have in common or agree on?
- → If you really were a big fan of this person, how might you view him or her?

[**STOP and COMPLETE before reading further.**]

☐ ☐ ☐

When you recognize your biases, another higher-level benefit of empathy results: strong levels of mindfulness and empathy open an element of understanding that expands kindness. But the challenge is whether you can develop empathy for those you dislike: enemies; people with whom we disagree, perhaps fundamentally; or lawyers on the other side of a very contentious matter. We will turn back to this topic after completing our discussion of the five practices of empathy empowerment.

Think beyond your reactions and step into another's shoes. Once they have awareness of their preconceived notions, challenge them (if necessary), and then set them aside, highly empathic people move forward and step into the other person's shoes. This requires actively trying to think what the other person is thinking and trying to actually do what the other person is doing.

This practice aligns with a lawyer's core duty and function: to investigate the facts. If your client wants you to develop guidelines for a particular employment practice, such as a nondiscrimination policy, you need to understand why your client wants that. You can easily say to yourself, "I know why I think that is important and why someone accused of discrimination might want to do that." But that may not reflect what your client is thinking or why your client is thinking about this now. Beyond talking with your client, getting into your client's shoes may entail going to their place of business, seeing their employees and how they interact, and seeing how your client engages with their work and employees. All of these steps require doing more than just reviewing policy statements, examining emails the client received from others that detail concerns about the policies or its deficiencies, and researching legal obligations. Only by taking these additional measures will you really be able to step in the client's shoes with curiosity and without judgment.

CLIFF TAKING THE LEAD → I once had two clients who were legally blind—the degree of one's visual ability will vary within the definition of *legally blind*—and who alleged that they were beaten by the police. They were very young and not so savvy. When deposed, they fell into the trap of embellishing their blindness.

As teens, they did not feel that their condition should limit their ability to do what others their age were doing. So, just like their friends, they wanted to ride bikes and drive cars. They did not realize the devastating extent to which riding bikes and driving cars contrasted with their descriptions of blindness. And so the day came when opposing counsel sent me a video recording of my clients skateboarding and driving cars. Counsel planned to introduce the video at trial to show that my clients were lying about their visual impairment and, by extension, lying about what happened to them or who did it. I watched the recording and saw what opposing counsel wanted the viewer to see: two people acting like everyone else, sighted and mobile.

My clients did not have much to say on the matter. It was them. They wanted to be like everyone else their age. Their friends described the lay of the land to them, and off they went (just like the scene in the movie *Scent of a Woman* where the blind Lt. Col. Frank Slade (Al Pacino) is driving fast around southern Manhattan, making sharp turns at the direction of Charlie Simms (Chris O'Donnell)).

I "understood" what they were saying but simply could not relate to it. As a fully sighted person, I was only thinking "Wow, that was pretty stupid." I had zero empathy or curiosity, but I needed to somehow step into their shoes. To build that empathy, I consulted with an expert on the mobility of visually impaired persons. She was able to walk me through the recording and show me the telltale signs—in how my clients moved, stepped, and leaned, as well as many other indicia—of the existence and extent of their visual impairment. That explanation allowed me to relate to my clients' thoughts and tap into our common experience of being young and wanting to do what everyone else is doing, such as riding bikes and driving cars. Only then could I build my empathy and connect their conduct with my job of representing them.

Stepping into their shoes also allowed me to see more clearly the gap between what I knew and what the typical juror would know and understand (even after hearing the expert's testimony). Empathy gave me the ability not only to understand my clients but also to better represent them.

↔

What this story describes took place over the course of months, a fact that demonstrates the challenge of building empathy within a shorter time frame. In movies, however, we are used to seeing empathy growth happen quickly. Because movies are relatively short, they naturally struggle to depict the actual, often laborious process of empathy growth in individuals. Consequently, they show an empathy-growth-on-fast-forward version of events, sometimes quite literally. For example, in the movie *Trading Places*, two men with more time and money than they need place a bet and agree to conduct an experiment in which a successful trader (Dan Aykroyd) and a homeless man (Eddie Murphy) switch places, and this situation leads to empathic learning. In *What Women Want*, the main character (Mel Gibson), who is very chauvinistic and sexist, finds himself suddenly able to hear what women are thinking and ends up developing empathy for an entire gender. And there are a slew of movies—*Big*, *Freaky Friday*, *13 Going on 30*, and *Face/Off*, and so on—in which characters literally become each other to gain this understanding. In real life, however, we cannot complete the hard work of growing our empathy in two hours, give or take, and so we have to be patient and persistent in building it. There is no quick fix as in the movies.

↑↓↑

REFLECTIVE WRITING 14

Think of a time when a team you were on adopted a course of action that you, in whole or in part, opposed or were hesitant about.

- → Was it difficult to let go of your original position?
- → Did you try to understand where the others were coming from with their idea(s) or approach(es)?
- → Did you try to cultivate your curiosity? If not, why not?
- → Did you have any preconceived notions or biases about or against the path taken?
- → Did you try to challenge your notions or biases? If not, why not?
- → Did you try to really think beyond your reactions?
- → Did you try to step into the shoes of the other team members? If so, how did you do so?
- → Did you support the action in the end? If so, how did you get to that position?

[**STOP and COMPLETE before reading further.**]

□ □ □

In an adversarial setting, you know your side, think you know the opposition's interests and arguments, and want to get to the next level with the highest net gain. Do you completely understand the opposing client, the opposing counsel, and the neutral arbiter who seems to always rule against you? Adversarial settings present a higher empathy challenge. This is particularly true in law practice, where you will repeatedly encounter people who have strong personalities, use aggressive and sometimes questionable tactics, and exhibit high levels of opposition and intransigence. You need to be able to empathize with people whose beliefs you do not share or who may be "enemies" in some way. In the deliberation moment, you must choose between taking a humanistic (empathic) approach or an adversarial one; the empathic approach is usually the better choice as it lowers the opposing lawyers' defenses, allowing them to become more agreeable.

Again, empathy does not mean agreement. It means understanding another's perspective. For example, assume you are a strong believer in climate change and want to devise the most effective strategy to change an oil company executive's views on developing clean, renewable energy. Here, the ultimate empathic challenge would be to step into the shoes of that executive to understand her thinking and motivations. A little of this "instrumental empathy" can go a long way and bring high rewards.

Can you use your curiosity and step into another's shoes to challenge preconceived notions by being creative and finding linkages? Recall the iceberg metaphor. We all need to get below the waterline one way or another, either by lowering the waterline or strapping on scuba gear and diving below the surface. This leads us to the next empowerment tool.

Engage in radical listening and make yourself vulnerable. To really know how to step into someone's shoes, you have to be able to listen hard (closely) and be willing to open up even if that means being vulnerable. In this respect, two things are required for being an empathic conversationalist: radical listening and vulnerability.

Radical listening. The first step to becoming an empathic conversationalist is to master the art of radical listening. "What is essential," said Marshall Rosenberg, psychologist and founder of the Center for Nonviolent Communication (NVC), "is our ability to be present to what's really going on within—to the unique feelings and needs a person is experiencing in that very moment."[27] This kind of listening draws directly on mindfulness training and the ability to focus your attention in the moment, gently acknowledging any other thoughts, sensations, or emotions that arise and then bringing your attention back to the conversation. This is not easy to do because your mind is actively processing the information you receive, looking for similarities and biases as noted above, and thinking about everything else going on in your professional and personal life.

Where necessary, you can exercise curiosity and ask the other person to clarify why they are behaving the way they are. To do this, ask open-ended questions ("I'm just curious, can you tell me why ...?")

and avoid accusations and judgments ("Every day I see you doing this. Do you really need to do that all the time?"). Compare that person's words with their body language and behavior to check for congruency. In the example where a friend is not returning your call, you could withhold judgment until you have a chance to ask, "What was going on with you that you did not return my call?" The basis of any good relationship is to understand the needs of the other person, and one can only do so by listening closely. This is why lawyers need to listen closely to their clients.

Good listening means taking in verbal and nonverbal cues, as well as listening for changes in intonation, words, and feelings over time. Listen for what is meant behind the literal words. Listen for the underlying emotion. For instance, think about a telephone conversation where the words you hear might be less important than the emotional feelings below and behind those words. You must be nonjudgmental and silence your internal reactions and responses (recall Herm's story in Chapter II). Listening closely to the other person's story will make you better able to help the that person revise and retell. In this sense, you are the recorder/interpreter for the other person.

Does everyone say exactly what they mean? Of course not. Close listening involves taking in another's words and unpacking what is behind them. As dean of students, Cliff often spoke to students who either did not know what they wanted when they came to speak to him or knew what they wanted but could not voice that desire. He needed not only to unpack the request but also to decipher it. As a practicing lawyer, Cliff often had clients who told him exactly what they wanted, but he could tell that there was something else behind the words. In whatever role you are in, it is essential to listen to what is being requested and to think about the multitude of implications that are behind, flowing from, and following the words.

Finally, listening once or only initially is not enough. The only constant is change—assignments change, a client's story will change, the facts can change, and the law will change (albeit slowly). So we need to continue listening, beyond what we first hear, for changes in the story—changing needs, changing desires, and changing reactions. If our job is to help our clients navigate a change, then we have to look for it to happen as we represent them. And we must be willing to change ourselves as well. This is close listening.

Close listening is radical in the sense that you are actively working hard to keep your focus and understand the other person's emotional state and needs, often across multiple conversations. This is true both personally and professionally. Personal examples might include a situation where a friend has just been diagnosed with cancer or where a partner/spouse is upset at you for working late yet again. A legal example is even clearer: as lawyers, we are expected to have legal solutions at hand, so we tend to mentally comb through our legal knowledge and experience for applicable material as our mind is absorbing and processing what our client is saying. But can you do both simultaneously, such that you truly understand the facts and the client's perspective? Probably not, and certainly not well. Listening to your client while meeting together is far more important than trying to mentally find applicable legal knowledge. All that legal knowledge and experience is not going anywhere—you can tap into it later. Keep your focus in the moment.

Radical listening is also a key leadership skill. Think about a meeting you have been in where the leader weighs in. What happens next? Typically, not much. The same is true if you weigh in before a client is finished telling you the whole story. In such situations, people think that you have heard all you need (or want to hear), and so they stop sharing. To engage in radical listening as a leader, you must be willing to make and maintain space in which you can listen and gather as much information as possible.

↑ ↓ ↑

REFLECTIVE WRITING 15

→ When I listen, am I really paying attention to what the other person is saying? Or do I lose concentration or think about what I can say next?

→ Do I pay attention to both verbal cues (tone of voice, speed, loudness, nature of language) and nonverbal cues (hand gestures, head gestures, direction of eye gaze, leaning forward or backward) in order to identify what is really being said?

- → Do I "mind read" and make assumptions, correct or incorrect?
- → Do I ask questions to understand what the other person is really saying, feeling, or needing?
- → Do I provide feedback—verbal or nonverbal—so that others know that I am interested and listening?

[STOP and COMPLETE before reading further.]

□ □ □

Vulnerability. Radical, or close, listening is just the first step in being an empathic conversationalist. The second step is making ourselves vulnerable. Empathy is a two-way street that, at its best, is built upon a mutual understanding. The mutuality could mean an exchange of our most important beliefs and experiences, even if those do not match. The mutuality can also mean sharing that you have no basis for appreciating what your client is sharing and acknowledging that you need the client's help to build your understanding (and that you will reciprocate when it comes to the law and legal systems by being equally open and sharing with the client). Whether you are sharing common points, contrasting points, or a lack of a starting point, you are making yourself vulnerable to the client's judgment. In doing so, you are building your empathic capacity and modeling how they can do the same.

The act of making yourself vulnerable relates to a lawyer's professional responsibility of zealous advocacy. Where does that zeal come from? You like to think that it comes from within. You are a smart, creative, and nimble advocate who can develop arguments, respond to counterarguments, and thread the needle to get your clients whatever they came to you for! Sure, that's partly true. But it mostly sounds like ego stroking. Your zeal actually comes from your clients. Their cause and concern empower you to exert it on their behalf. And only when you fully embrace empathy (through cultivating curiosity, eliminating your biases, stepping into another's shoes, radical listening, and being vulnerable) will a client's story and cause align with your education and experience—allowing you to advocate on their behalf truly and zealously.

CLIFF TAKING THE LEAD → When I was in clinic in law school, I was as dedicated as one could be. I enrolled in the Women's Rights Litigation Clinic but found that in early discussions of our cases, I was limited in what I could bring to the conversation. I understood the issues, such as sexual harassment and reproductive rights, and I knew the law; thus, my head and heart were in the right place. But something was missing.

While I could not put my finger on it, my mentor in the clinic knew exactly what I was feeling and how to address it. Within a week of starting in the clinic, a client came in for an interview, and my mentor asked me to join. The client had been sexually harassed in her employment.* The client described what happened to her, how it made her feel at the time, and how it affected her ability to work and her personal relationships. As I sat and listened closely, I could feel the palpable shift in my thinking and motivation as she told us what happened to her. What I felt but could not properly label at the time was a growing empathy within me, a key complement to the skills and dedication I already had. A million thoughts (a bit of an exaggeration, but you get the idea) bounced around in my head. After the interview, I met with my mentor, and she asked me what I was thinking. I surprised myself with the flow of creative ideas that I had about how to pursue the facts, the law, the defendants, the causes of action, and the relief. She smiled and said, "Get organized," and then left me to create a plan of action.

What I did not realize until later was the empathy that my mentor had for me. Rather than tell me what I was missing, she understood what I needed and found a setting in which her empathy for me turned into an expansion of my own empathy.

At the same time, I was not only willing to listen closely to the client but also to be vulnerable and to acknowledge what I did not know and did not understand—the combination of which created the motivation necessary for me to do the best work for our client.

Once in practice, I also embraced vulnerability as a natural part of empathy. My firm had a particularly tough police brutality case in the

* The year was 1983, when sexual harassment in the workplace was neither commonly spoken about nor commonly litigated. My mentor was one of the first to argue and prevail in getting recognition that antidiscrimination laws included sexual harassment cases.

office. The legal issues were pretty straightforward, but the medical issues were not. We needed help, and not just the kind of help one gets from hiring experts. We reached out to opposing counsel from a prior suit (in which we had prevailed) because their preparation of the medical issues had struck us as particularly thorough and creative. They were intrigued to be seen as not just a defense firm and, once we described the legal issues, jumped at the chance to work with us on the case. Our respective vulnerabilities in deciding to work together were the product of having gone through many of the empathy-building steps mentioned above.

↔

Initially, empathy may aid you in finding commonalities that bring you both closer to a satisfactory resolution of the matter. Secondarily, it may allow you to resolve the issues and establish an amicable relationship. Finally, that amicable relationship might allow you to reach out to the other party in the future for help, or to resolve a matter in advance of spending a great deal of attorney time (and client money!).

Let's come at vulnerability from another related angle: *narrative humility.*

Many of the EI foundations involve reaching inside ourselves for awareness, values, and emotions and then extending those learned lessons as we connect with others. As lawyers, we do this on a regular basis with our clients—listening to their stories, engaging their narratives, and learning their underlying values and needs. We are trained to step forward in that representative capacity fully armed with the law in an effort to share their voice and needs to seek the relief that they need or want. Described this way, it sounds easy, right? Not really. As law is taught, many lawyers do not appreciate the full power that comes from that client connection and instead jump ahead to infer what the client needs, how to present it, and how to get it.[28] This is particularly difficult when our clients differ from us in fundamental ways—their business, culture, race, religion, gender, gender identity, perspective, and so on. Lawyers' EI skills, a key part of which is relationship awareness, need to include narrative humility to bridge this chasm.

Narrative humility gained credence in medicine some years back as a way to identify this gap. An example is the doctor who knows what the patient needs and quickly sends the patient on her way with modern medicine, never having fully understood the problem or fully explained the solution. In a TED Talk, Sayantani DasGupta described—with deep humility—how she gave a mother an oral antibiotic for her daughter's ear infection without telling the mother how to administer it, only to learn later that the daughter's lack of recovery was due to the mother's injecting the liquid into her daughter's ear—but it was really due to DasGupta's own failure to engage with narrative humility.[29]

In a short piece in the *Lancet*, DasGupta described the concept (adjusted here for clients, not patients):

> One very literal aspect of narrative humility is the fact that the [client's] story, at least initially, belongs entirely to him [or her or them]. Unlike the [lawyer] of mine who, during a recent [visit], interrupted me to say, "You don't have to say any more. I know exactly how your story ends", [professionals] cannot, of course, ever *exactly* know how any [client] story begins or ends. As careful interviewers and witnesses, we become invested in, wrapped up with, and, yes, coauthors of our [client's] narratives, but we cannot ever claim to comprehend the totality of another's story, which is only ever an approximation for the totality of another's self. . . .
>
> Narrative humility acknowledges that our [clients'] stories are not objects that we can comprehend or master, but rather dynamic entities that we can approach and engage with, while simultaneously remaining open to their ambiguity and contradiction, and engaging in constant self-evaluation and self-critique about issues such as our own role in the story, our expectations of the story, our responsibilities to the story, and our identifications with the story—how the story attracts or repels us because it reminds us of any number of personal stories. Also by thinking about it as *narrative* humility . . . , we recognise that this is a perspective we take with *all* the stories with which we engage—not just something we do when those "other" people walk into our office, whatever that may mean to us—while simultaneously not losing the idea, the parallel sociopolitical narrative, that there are larger forces that enable the telling of certain sorts of stories and silence other stories.

> Narrative humility allows [practitioners] to recognise that each story we hear holds elements that are unfamiliar—be they cultural, socioeconomic, sexual, religious, or idiosyncratically personal. Assuming that our reading of any [client's] story is the definitive interpretation of that story is to risk closing ourselves off to its most valuable nuances and particularities.[30]

Hopefully, at this point, you are not saying, "Great, so doctors and lawyers can be really clueless, but what does this mean for leaders?" If so, the answer lies in the question itself. Lawyer leaders can be just as clueless by failing to see beyond the obvious possibilities with emotional intelligence to the absolute possibility of putting this all together and allowing a culture of social responsibility to emerge. Twenty-first-century leaders leverage the essential EI characteristics in the first instance to increase their relationship awareness and relationship management. And in the second instance, they leverage these EI characteristics to bring about a socially just culture around them, which starts with socially or culturally responsible leadership and a humanistic level of leading. (More on that later in this chapter.)

You can have ambition in your career, in your research, in your writing, and in brainstorming meetings. You can imagine the success you seek and the success that your client wants. But sometimes this includes admitting your weaknesses. You often will not know who your client is, what your client does, or what is important to your client. And if you think you know these answers, you will want to set those aside as potentially bias-laden. The starting point is your client and her facts and situation, and your ambition should focus on her. Only then will empathy empower you and your representation.

Inspire others through ambitious imagination and empathic meetings. And yet there is another step that you can take in building empathy—the final practice of empathy empowerment: inspiring others through ambitious imagination and empathic meetings. To do so, you need to pool all available resources to have the greatest degree of empathy possible.

As a foundation to discussing this final empathy empowerment practice, we must note that our discussion of building empathy necessarily bridges the EI domains of social awareness and relationship management, which highlights the integral relationship between the two. Rela-

FIGURE 9
THE EMOTIONAL AND SOCIAL COMPETENCY FRAMEWORK

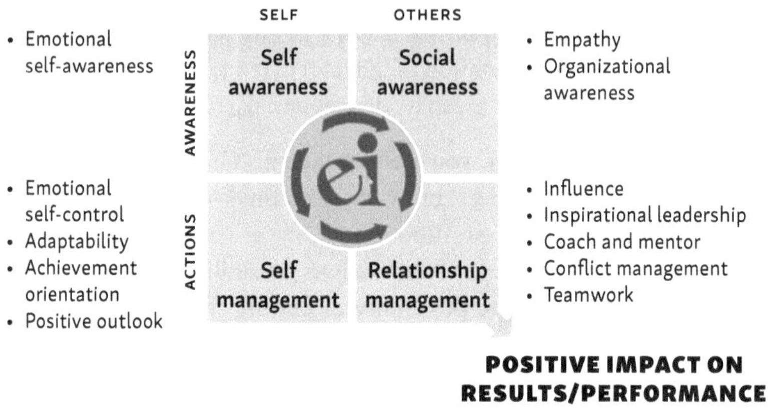

tionship management has several competencies, including inspiration, influence, mentoring, conflict management, and teamwork, as seen again in Figure 9.

Truly understanding people and organizations opens the path to being readily recognized as a potential leader in the organization. Listening and connecting, and being authentic in the process, are key to convincing people that they should follow your lead. Thus, it is not surprising that highly empathic people take their understanding of people and organizations to the next level: inspiring mass action and social change. While empathy is typically assumed to happen at the individual level, the strength of your empathy can also result in a mass phenomenon that brings about fundamental social change. Barack Obama is a recent and prime example of a highly empathic person whose empathy brought about fundamental social change. Other examples include Cesar Chavez, Winston Churchill, and Eleanor Roosevelt.

Inherent in inspiring mass action and social change is the ability to develop and appreciate ambitious imagination. With empathic capacity built, one can do far more than empathize on a one-to-one level. While we tend to think of empathy as reserved for those living on the social margins or who are suffering, which is quite important and necessary, it is hardly a complete picture. Everyone deserves empathy, and with deep empathy comes fresh ideas. Empathy in meetings, on teams, and in other instances when you engage with others necessarily creates space for and builds creativity. Invention is a social act.[31] This theme will pervade the remaining chapters of this book.

A small-scale view of this is the meeting setting. Ronald Adler and Russell Proctor wrote about honing the accuracy of reading social cues through thinking beyond your reaction, seeking clarification when needed, and, ultimately, facilitating empathic meetings.[32] We have already discussed the first two. So what is involved in an empathic meeting? Or, to build on the question, can you be an empathic leader of a meeting that develops empathy in others? Certainly. According to Chade-Meng Tan, here is the tone to set for everyone entering that meeting:

1. Assume that everybody in this room is here to serve the greater good, until proven otherwise.
2. Given the above assumption, we therefore assume that none of us has any hidden agenda, until proven otherwise.
3. Given the above assumption, we therefore assume that we are all reasonable even when we disagree, until proven otherwise.[33]

Underlying inspiring others and holding an empathic meeting is the idea that if you are going to lead, you need to lead everyone. And to lead a large group, you need to find connections that bring the group together. These connections can arise from shared, or complementary, experiences, perspectives, and competencies. But if everyone you work with is alike, then you will be limited in what you can do. The challenge is to have a workforce of diverse members with complementary skills who can find mutual connection (beyond "we all work here").

Empathic leaders are more inclusive than not because they see possibility where others do not. This requires the level of self-awareness that you now have. Empathic leaders pay attention to the dynamics during the meeting, not just the content. They notice nonverbal signals and the interpersonal process between team members, and they try to understand who they are leading. For example, in trying to schedule a group meeting where one of the key attendees is a Muslim man, an empathic leader will be sure to schedule the meeting at a time that does not conflict with daily prayers to ensure his presence. If one of the key attendees is a single mother, an empathic leader will be sure to schedule it at a time that does not conflict with her child-care responsibilities.

But what if a certain team member's presence is not key to the meeting, and you are thinking of not including this person? Then you should ask yourself some questions:

- Are you thinking in the same mindful manner as you would for those of other religions or with other responsibilities in scheduling?*
- Are you that mindful for everyone else?
- Do you want everyone possible to attend the meeting?
- Do you really know that this person is not key to the meeting?

D. Applying Empathy

Much of "applying" empathy is in using it. It is up to you to decide if you value empathy. Once you make that decision and model it in your organization, you can create a positive ripple effect that leads to empathic meetings and, ultimately, to an empathic organizational culture. As we share scenarios and questions, continue to think about how leaders might model empathy for their team. Applying empathy entails leading a movement from the content (substance) to the dynamic, which will result in stronger connection and team function. (The next chapter discusses the domain of relationship management, which involves applying empathy in terms of teamwork, inspiring others, mentoring, influence, and conflict management.)

* We use these examples because, as a society, we are much more aware of Christian and Jewish holidays than Muslim holidays (to put it more bluntly, no employer expects you to work on Christmas Day; and if it did, you would expect to be well compensated for the imposition), and because, as a society, we presume that a parent has made all arrangements to allow full commitment to work.

1. From the Content to the Dynamic

Empathic meetings really come about from emotionally intelligent leaders who are self-aware and know when to shift the group's focus from the content to the dynamic. As an emotionally intelligent lawyer leader, your goal is to constantly be paying attention to not only the *content* but also the *dynamic*, or the *interpersonal and emotional processes*, that will inevitably be unfolding in any work with more than one person.

By *content*, we simply mean the actual agenda items. People love to be task-driven and solution-focused. Recall the leader that Rob coached, who was a cherished taskmaster of the organization but lacked rapport. Leaders with low emotional intelligence do not value the emotional and interpersonal dynamics happening as the content is being discussed and therefore miss key aspects at work, such as how people feel, that will ultimately determine if goals are attained. Low-EI leaders stay focused on task completion when what often really matters is how the individuals they are leading and working with think and feel about what is being discussed.

Prioritize making room for that discussion in your meetings, and they will be empathic meetings. In other words, as we have mentioned previously in this book, there are always two conversations unfolding when people work together: (1) the content being discussed and (2) the emotional and social processes taking place. The latter conversation that is happening in any meeting is the dynamic. Shifting your attention from the content to the dynamic is how you lead empathically, and it requires self-awareness.

When you shift your attention from the content to the dynamic, you notice others' reactions and can then make empathic comments, which will allow those around you to feel heard and validated and will open up key discussions about the motivations and reactions of the group. Having empathy for a team member or colleague allows you to continue to understand that person and where she is coming from, genuinely. All team members have something valuable to share, and if you write them off without empathy, you will miss their contributions. Equally important, if your team members do not feel empathy from you, they will feel misunderstood, and there will be a slow disengagement from their work. To put it differently, this is an example of reading the room.

2. From Empathy to Loving-Kindness

From empathy and the understanding that it brings, you will gain insight into others that naturally leads to a general growth in feeling kindness toward others. As you work on the five practices of empathy empowerment, you may find that your empathy reveals similarities between you and others that you could not have predicted. Seeing that other people are like you in many ways leads to a growth in kindness.

Working on the five practices of empathy empowerment helps you to develop mental habits that enhance empathy—and thus kindness. As the Buddha suggests, "Whatever one frequently thinks and ponders upon, that will become the inclination of his mind." And you are now thinking about things that you had not been thinking about before. What you think often, you become. Luckily for us, this type of leadership helps reduce burnout, improves wellbeing, and brings out the best in others, allowing for effective organizational performance.

Empathy does not just breed kindness—it also increases with kindness. Kindness motivates you to care, and it makes you more receptive to others—and them to you. The more kindness you can offer to people, the better you can empathize with them. It all begins with mental habits. Look at any human being and think "I want this person to be happy." Imagine going into any class or meeting and saying, "I want these people to be happy; they are just like me." We readily acknowledge that doing this is very challenging when it comes to those you do not like or think very little of or those who have very different interests from you. However, these habits can change everything—from how you see and interact with others and vice versa to, most importantly, what you can do for your respective clients.

This high level of empathy allows you to disagree in a civil or perhaps kind way, which could help get parties to a solution beyond a zero-sum division of an arbitrarily limited pool of resources. Through such a high level of empathy, you may also find points of similarity. And the more you perceive someone to be just like you, the more you can empathize with that person. When you can look at another human being, your thought should be "This person is just like me." This should remind you of the iceberg—that "just like me" part may very well be below the waterline. Over time, looking for this will become a habit.

↑↓↑

SELF-DISCOVERY EXERCISE 16: JUST LIKE ME AND LOVING-KINDNESS MINDFULNESS

Using a mindfulness app, website, or other like resource,* find a guided meditation on each of the following:

1. Just like me
2. Loving-kindness meditation

After each mindfulness session, write how you felt in the practice. For example, the prompt may be to think of someone you know and like or someone you know and dislike. Repeat this meditation with different prompts and continue to record your feelings.

[**STOP and COMPLETE before reading further.**]

↑ ↓ ↑

You might recognize this chapter's self-discovery exercise as an adaptation of an earlier self-discovery exercise. With your newfound knowledge about empathy, see if your perspectives have changed.

SELF-DISCOVERY EXERCISE 17: WHAT'S THEIR PROBLEM?

Identify one person you find very difficult to work with, and answer the following questions:

1. What is so difficult about this person?
2. When does this come up for you? What's the situation?
3. What do you want from this person?

Now, put yourself in this person's shoes. Try to describe the following:

4. What is this person feeling?
5. What drives this person? What's this person's agenda?

* There is one on the Northwestern Law Wellness page: https://www.law.northwestern.edu/student-life/student-services/wellness/.

6. What does this person bring out in you? And how do you react?
7. What positive aspects does this person bring to the situation or work?

[STOP and COMPLETE before reading further.]

□ □ □

The following reflective writing exercises are designed to enable you to deeply explore aspects of relationship awareness (and some organizational awareness) in a variety of ways. The first is about seeing relationship (and organizational) awareness in people and institutions. The second asks you to step back and think about the legal profession more generally. The third exercise is a tool to use in thinking about your day-to-day experiences.

↑↓↑

REFLECTIVE WRITING 16

Each of the following scenarios is based on Cliff's real-life experiences. Read each scenario. Think about each character. What was his or her level of self-awareness and self-management? How did that impact the outcome? What was his or her level of empathy? Use the five practices of empathy empowerment to evaluate. (These prompts will repeat after each scenario.)

- **Scenario 1: The Happy Student.** The day before graduation one year, I was walking down the hall to the café, thinking about whether everything was ready for the next day. Approaching me was a student with a wide grin on his face. We had worked on many issues together—substance abuse, anger management, and academic performance—and thus I was never sure if an encounter was going to be a high point or a low one. I took the lead from his grin and asked him what he was so happy about. He then looked shy and flustered. He said that he was hoping not to run into me until tomorrow, on the stage at graduation—because then he would tell me that he had just won a case that freed a juvenile from custody. He was walking on air, gave me a big hug, and said, "Thanks! I could not have done it without your support." Then, as he walked away, he said, grinning, "See you on the stage!"

For each character, what was his or her level of self-awareness and self-management? How did that impact the outcome? What was his or her level of empathy? Be sure to use the five practices of empathy empowerment to evaluate.

- **Scenario 2: The Plunger.** Many years back, a clinician called me to talk about a student. He came to my office and said that he was concerned about this student because of something that she did while they were with a client at court. I thought, *What did she say? Was she not prepared?* The clinician said that the client (a woman) had gone to the bathroom and not come back, so the clinician sent the student to find the client in the bathroom. The student came back with the client, but the student was disheveled and a bit wet. The clinician learned that the client was in the bathroom so long because after she used the toilet, it clogged and would not flush (who hasn't had that awful experience?). The client did not know what to do, so she stayed there. The student, coming on the scene, took matters into her own hands.

  After this conversation with the clinician, I called in the student, whom I knew, and asked what happened. She very calmly described the same situation: stuck toilet, client wouldn't leave, she (the student) unstuck it. She told me that there was no plunger in the bathroom, and the client would not leave the toilet like that. The student saw no other path to getting the client back in the courtroom—which was her job—than to unstop the toilet by whatever means necessary. So, she rolled up her sleeve, put her arm in the toilet, and unclogged it. Then she washed up and brought the client to the courtroom.

  I stared at her, not sure whether to say "You did what?!?" or "Bravo!" Finding a janitor might have been more sanitary but certainly not as quick. Not many lawyers, maybe one in a thousand, would have thought of doing that—and fewer would have actually done it.

For each character, what was his or her level of self-awareness and self-management? How did that impact the outcome? What was his or her level of empathy? Be sure to use the five practices of empathy empowerment to evaluate.

- **Scenario 3: The Lazarus Student.** One August, I received a voicemail from the mother of a student entering one of our smaller programs. She said that her daughter was on her deathbed and would not be coming to school. I quickly contacted the director of the program, he came to my office, and we called the mother. She told us that her daughter suffered from a chronic condition. Unexpectedly, she lost consciousness, fell into a coma, and was now on life support. The doctors told her that there was permanent brain damage. Her daughter's husband was on his way, and they were removing the life support that afternoon.

  We were heartbroken for them. We searched in silence for the right words to express our sorrow. When someone older or infirm passes, the conversation is far easier. This conversation could not go in that direction. We tried to express empathy, to console. Ultimately, I asked what, if anything, we could do for her. "No bills, no nothing," she said. The mother did not want to see anything from us that would remind her of what her daughter would not be able to do. I agreed—although in the back of my mind, I was worried about whether a bureaucratic institution was up to meeting the request. We expressed our sorrow again and hung up.

  When we got off the phone, I was itching to call the registrar, student accounts, financial aid, and any other office that occurred to me in an effort to remove the student's presence from our system and cut off any mailings. The faculty member, though, did not immediately leave. He asked me what to tell the other students in the program. I said, "Tell them nothing." He said that even though classes had not yet started, all the students had been talking with and expecting to see each other. They would want to know where she was. I repeated, "Tell them nothing. This is a private matter." They had no real need to know, and it was not our place to share the information. He left, and I made my calls.

Two days later, I received a call from the mother. Before they could remove the tubes, her daughter started breathing on her own. She was quite alive but weak, and had suffered no permanent brain damage. She wanted to come to school and start her studies. After some time talking with the student and working through the joy, the logistics, and the necessary medical clearance, I called the program director and told him the good news. There was a deep penetrating silence on the phone. I thought the line had gone dead, and so I said, "Hello?"

He let out a long exhale. "I need to know what to do," he said.

"What do you mean?" I asked.

"I told the other students that she died."

"Well, you need to tell them that she didn't."

"Will you tell them?" he asked.

"No," I said. "You told them she passed. Now you need to fix it."

"I will send them an email."

"I think this is the kind of thing you want to talk about with them in person."

"But that will be so much harder."

"And so much more effective."

For each character, what was his or her level of self-awareness and self-management? How did that impact the outcome? What was his or her level of empathy? Be sure to use the five practices of empathy empowerment to evaluate.

[STOP and COMPLETE before reading further.]

↑ ↓ ↑

REFLECTIVE WRITING 17

- → What are your thoughts about being an empathic lawyer?
- → What are the benefits of leading with empathy? Do you see any consequences?
- → What is your biggest concern about being empathic?
- → Given that empathy is critical at times, how do you plan to develop your empathy?

[**STOP and COMPLETE before reading further.**]

↑↓↑

REFLECTIVE WRITING 18

Over the next two weeks, think carefully about your interactions with others. With respect to those interactions, ask yourself these questions:

- → When I listen, am I really paying attention to what the other person is saying? Or do I lose concentration or think about what I can say next?
- → Do I pay attention to both verbal cues (tone of voice, speed, loudness, nature of language) and nonverbal cues (hand gestures, head gestures, direction of eye gaze, leaning forward or backward) in order to identify what is really being said?
- → Do I "mind read" and make assumptions, correctly or incorrectly?
- → Do I ask questions to understand what the other person is really saying, feeling, or needing?
- → Do I provide feedback, verbal or nonverbal, so that others know that I am interested and listening?
- → Make time to network. Try to get to know people across your organization. Develop these relationships slowly and with sincerity. How do others' experiences of the organization compare with yours?

→ Find out more about the history of your organization or department. What, and who, has been influential?

□ □ □

You have now completed a very tough chapter. As we said at the start, empathy is a challenge, particularly in the law. With your newfound capacity and growth potential, you are ready to move into even greater applications.

CHAPTER VI

Relationship Management

THROUGHOUT THIS BOOK, we have asked you to ponder some big questions: Who are you? What makes an effective leader? What determines success? And others. We have given you a recipe for what we see (and what the mounting body of research on leadership over the past century suggests) as the most essential ingredients in leadership: self-awareness, self-management, and social awareness (empathy and organizational awareness), which collectively make up emotional intelligence. Now let's turn with greater precision to even more pressing questions: What are you doing when you are leading? And what exactly are you trying to accomplish as a leader in the law?

While your level of emotional intelligence determines whether you are an effective leader, leadership itself is really all about *relationships*. At the end of the day, your success as a leader hinges on how effective you are at building relationships, nurturing them, collaborating in them, and maintaining them. Leadership is about seeing potential in others, finding points of connection, building trust, and inspiring others to join your mission. Leadership is about helping others find their best self and reach their own potential so that they can lead with authenticity and find happiness. Thus, Daniel Goleman and his group coined *relationship management* as the fourth domain of emotional intelligence. At its core, this final piece of emotional intelligence is about how leaders help others maximize their potential.

Effective leadership is about how you make others feel. Most metrics used to gauge leadership are really based on the leader's efficacy in bringing out the best in those around them to accomplish a shared goal.

Your success as a leader depends on others taking ownership, being healthy, feeling good about themselves and the organization, feeling valued and respected, staying motivated, living with integrity, and staying focused on the purpose of their work. Thus, a leader's guidance in helping members achieve autonomy in their work and a leader's perceived support for members' work are key metrics for gauging how well a leader is supporting team performance. You want members to feel that they are a part of the organization and its mission. Maya Angelou once said, "At the end of the day people won't remember what you said or did, they will remember how you made them feel."[1]

The notion that successful leadership is about dominance and power, with minimal emphasis on rapport, has repeatedly been proven to be outdated. In the "Best Boss" self-discovery exercise (Exercise 1 in the Introduction), we asked you to reflect on the best leaders that you have ever had. Chances are good that the person who came to mind saw your greatest attributes and helped you realize your full potential. This leader inspired you to become your best self through their strong EI skills. With *self-awareness*, this leader maintained their focus on seeing your strengths even when you might have been struggling and kept the focus on building a connection with you. This leader practiced *self-management* when times got tough by remaining cool and levelheaded in a storm. Using *empathy*, this leader put herself in your shoes and, with awareness of your developmental level in mind, sought to understand how you were approaching tasks.

CLIFF TAKING THE LEAD → When I was dean of students, I worked for a dean who shared some of these leadership qualities.

I had spent eighteen months training for my first marathon. I was not a runner and had committed to the challenge to motivate my daughter through a very difficult time in her life.

The night before that race, I learned that several of our law students had been in a terrible automobile accident. I knew that this incident would reverberate throughout the community. After learning the news, I quickly worked to get information about informing relatives, was in communication with the police, and had a good idea of how to communicate with the various constituencies in the law school community.

Then I called the dean to inform him of the accident and its seriousness, share what I had already done, and share my plans. He listened intently, acknowledged my work and plans, and then asked what I was going to do. I paused, not understanding the question. I said, "What do you mean? I just told you what I was doing and would do." He said, "No, I get that. But are you going to run tomorrow?"

In that moment, I realized how much of a leader he was. He did not say it directly, but he trusted me implicitly. He did not heap praise on me for what I had done—he simply acknowledged it, and that was enough. The matter was quite serious, but he was no more of an expert than I, so he did not ask questions that might undermine his other messages. And he cared for me—so much so that while he was very concerned for his student population, once he was comfortable that they would be attended to, he could then express his concern for how this was affecting me personally.

Great leaders know how to bring together these disparate skills and exhibit them with a facility that often goes unnoticed and can be awe-inspiring in its depth and tact. I had not thought about whether or not to run (the news of the accident rocked me to my core), but his concern let me know that I should be thinking about that also. I did run. Not well, mind you. But I did have five hours to think about leadership, humility, knowing our limits, life's challenges, and, most of all, gratitude for being able to run, achieve, and wake up healthy the next day.

↔

The relationships that you have in your professional life are a most prized asset, and how you maintain them and care for them should be center stage in your work leading in the law. The ability to build high-functioning relationships is also an essential part of your well-being and happiness.[2] Thus, your ability to build, develop, and maintain relationships is also key to leading yourself and will extend to those you love and with whom you want to collaborate beyond the office. This chapter is divided into six sections, each building pieces that are inherently about relationships, at work and beyond. The same skills are needed in both spaces. Section A explores our social nature as humans and the current state of post-pandemic loneliness. Section B connects emotional intelligence to social intelligence. Section C presents a four-stage model of relationship development. The final sections add the layers of building trust, working on teams, and managing conflict—all key components of exceptional leadership. A conclusory section rounds out the chapter with a discussion about the two faces of empathy in relationship management.

A. The Social Nature of Humans and Loneliness

1. Social Capital and the American Deficit

Research suggests that leaders' *social capital* is a key differentiating factor in their success.[3] *Social capital* is defined as "the networks of relationships among people who live and work in a particular society, enabling that society to function effectively."[4]

First written about specifically in the early twentieth century and later popularized in the writings of Robert Putnam, the concept of social capital captures the notion of the power of connection.[5] Putnam highlighted the decline of social capital in the United States since the 1950s, which was due in large part to a dwindling civic engagement and social connection stemming from the erosion of institutions like marriage and organized religion. Unfortunately, the trends that Putnam noted just prior to the turn of the century appear to be growing today as many Americans find themselves siloed at work and making their way through life alone on screens and personal devices.

American society faces an increasing challenge with social connection. Current societal patterns do not make it easy to connect. For example, if you were to look around in a restaurant or coffee shop, you would see people are glued to their phone, tablet, or laptop screen. Rob was recently out to dinner with his family and could not help but notice a younger couple who were not engaging with each other in direct conversation and connection but rather were focused on their respective smartphones. Are we losing the skill to sit through a meal with a loved one and converse? Are we losing the ability to connect? Is our addiction to technology and thirst for screen-based information updates eroding our social abilities?

Ironically, while technology kept many of us "connected" through the COVID-19 pandemic, it simultaneously pushes us further into isolation. Technology brings many benefits, but our ability to navigate socially dwindles with each tweet and each notification. While electronic platforms allow for connection, we must consider the nature of the relationship that technology creates and supports.

An additional consideration regarding technology is generational comfort and discomfort. Rob was born twenty-seven days into 1980, has always identified as a late Gen Xer (those born between the mid-1960s and the early 1980s), and was uniquely situated as the youngest of fifteen cousins to see clearly the older, less tech-savvy of those who essentially grew up without technology. To them, technology was beautiful. They were lucky if they had the original Nintendo. No one worried about making sure they would look good in online pictures or making sure their phone was charged. They and their parents were more present without a smartphone addiction. Rob's childhood was one of the last to be relatively free of technology dominance in every corner of life. Nowadays, children are lucky to get their parents' attention for one minute without a phone interruption, and social exchanges progressively happen through apps and online formats.

In light of this, think about technology and interpersonal connection. How does technology fit into your personal life? How is technology used in your office and during meetings? How does it impact your workspace? How does it impact the culture of your workplace and colleagues?

ROB TAKING THE LEAD → I was coaching a midcareer vice president in health care, and she wanted to talk about challenges she is facing as she attempts to bring back in-person meetings for a team of thirty-plus physician leaders who collectively focus on quality in health care. They used to meet in person and work across two different sites in a major metro area. In recent years, she has noticed waning engagement, increased burnout and turnover, and difficulties building team morale.

We came up with some solutions to help reunite the team, and one was to start having some meetings in person again, to allow the staff to reconnect and support one another. She decided that she wanted to have their monthly meeting in person again, but first she wanted their input on this decision, as opposed to just making it mandatory—a good idea in theory.

She was shocked when the poll results found that 83 percent wanted to stay in a virtual format. When I asked her how she had worded the question, she told me that her message read "What do you want to do, virtual or in person?"—not "What do you think we need to do?"

So she did a new poll with different wording and was amazed to see that roughly the same proportion (80 percent) felt they "needed" to meet in person.

↔

Why share this story now? The poll results highlight where people are more comfortable at this point in time—and that their social comfort does not always equate with what they think is best socially. The point is that while many of us have grown more comfortable alone in our rooms on screens than we are in person connecting, we recognize that in-person interaction is ideal. While people dislike fighting traffic, find working from home to be much more comfortable, are more anxious socially now than ever, and maybe think they are less comfortable or more irritated (or both!) being around people, we are social creatures with social needs. And we all know it.

There is a joy in human connection, and the research supports it.[6] People need people. We have a need for human connection, now more than ever—not just for leadership success but also for human survival.

2. Social Isolation and the Pandemic

Relationships are essential for human existence. In this respect, let's take a closer look at the impact of social isolation during the coronavirus pandemic.

Data from the World Health Organization reveals that depression and anxiety rates skyrocketed during the pandemic.[7] Psychologists saw the highest demand for services ever. Work productivity and efficiency metrics plummeted.[8] The importance of human connection and collaboration took center stage.

Loneliness. The pinnacle of another epidemic that had been brewing below the surface for years was occurring at the same time as the COVID-19 pandemic: loneliness. Prior to the COVID-19 pandemic, the world had been slowly creeping toward the worst rates of loneliness ever seen.[9] Lack of trust was one factor. As the social fabric of American life has diminished, trust in each other and institutions have dropped to historically low levels.[10] According to research on the topic of trust, the percentage of Americans who feel that they can trust other Americans has declined by approximately 15 percent over the past fifty years.[11] Without trust, there is no connection; and without connection, there is loneliness. Men are particularly vulnerable to loneliness; women have done a much better job of buffering themselves from it.[12] Nonetheless, loneliness cuts across all demographics, including socioeconomic status, race, ethnicity, gender, and age. The data is clear that we have a fundamental need for belonging but collectively have been coming up short, even prior to the COVID-19 pandemic.

Much has been written over the past five years about mental health, the pandemic, and the contributing factors of loneliness and social isolation, pointing to key factors such as increased use of technology,[13] shrinking social networks, and decreased community involvement.[14] Psychologists like Rob had been talking about expansive loneliness for decades, especially as they saw the growing impact of technology on work and social life. The COVID-19 pandemic accentuated loneliness particularly among young people, playing a central role in the increasingly concerning pediatric mental health crisis. Indeed, recent research has identified loneliness and disconnection as key carryover impacts of the pandemic.[15]

Recent studies have found that the ability to discuss challenges and the shared plight of the impacts of the pandemic with close friends can reduce and reverse loneliness and generate increased satisfaction in individuals, even if done via electronic mediums.[16] Beyond this level of virtual contact and despite the benefits of electronic communication in keeping us connected throughout and past the COVID-19 pandemic, studies have shown, unsurprisingly, that it is vital for individual well-being to gather physically with others.[17] "[In-person gathering] is fundamental to a human need for intimate touch, physical comfort, reinforcing interactional norms and providing practical support."[18] Thus, to effectively address loneliness, individuals have to embrace both virtual and in-person contact—a so-called "intelligent balance"—to most effectively build and cultivate individual relationships.[19] Key to success in doing so is one's adaptability,[20] a core aspect of EI self-management.

An example of intelligent balance is ensuring that everyone is in the office on the same day on a regular basis, whether that is once a week or less often. Another example is holding regular virtual meetings that are usually substantive but can sometimes be just check-ins. Encouraging and cultivating out-of-office gatherings is crucial as well, creating more localized communities among colleagues who work remotely. Leveraging neighborhood coffee shops for regular meetups and engaging in community volunteer efforts with local coworkers can help build community and social networks.[21] As a leader, supporting the creation of and being present at these gatherings is imperative. Your presence communicates that your time with your team members is as valuable as it is when spent on other tasks, and it should empower your team members to exercise the initiative to build community resilience as well.[22]

Additionally, leaders should exercise their empathy and be curious about whether these methods are working, or whether other methods are needed to make these interpersonal connections. Leaders with high levels of empathy not only will recognize the benefits of interpersonal connections but also will understand why the physical and emotional costs of loneliness and separation undermine an organization's core mission and values.

Loss of social capital. Another casualty of the separation that happened during the pandemic was social capital. Just as finding ways to meet in person is the first step in addressing loneliness, building social capital has been found to mitigate fear and stress in individuals and better enable individuals and communities to cope with crises.[23] Social capital is a product of trust, respect, and effective communication among members of an organization or community, and the process of building it generates better cooperation, teamwork, and coordination, among other outcomes.[24] Both personal and professional engagement with one's local community strengthens social capital.

Think of social capital as a by-product of connections, which are particularly gained by people with high levels of empathy. Thus, building social capital is directly related to building empathy. If you felt some loneliness during the pandemic or in remote work or have fewer person-to-person contacts of late, revisit the empathy-building skills discussed in the last chapter. Are you curious about what others are doing? Are there now more people to learn about? How can you work on your empathy in such a way as to break out of isolation, overcome any loneliness, and build social capital? Answering these questions will increase your emotional intelligence.

3. Link Between Relationships and Happiness/Health/Success

The research linking healthy relationships to happiness and success is unequivocal. In *The Good Life*, Robert Waldinger and Marc Schulz summarize research from the longest scientific study ever conducted on happiness.[25] This incredible longitudinal study had a very clear finding: positive relationships are at the core of happiness. Individual accomplishment alone will only take you so far. Living a good life is really all about shared experience. Relationships are the nutrients for the plants in the gardens where we find meaningful lives.

ROB TAKING THE LEAD → My teenage daughters, like most adolescent girls today, worship Taylor Swift. And I mean *worship*. Their walls and water bottles are covered with Swiftie slogans and images. Things could be worse. As I have come to learn more about her, I am very grateful that she is the idol they strive to emulate. One of my daughters and I were recently watching her documentary, *Miss Americana*, in which Swift quite eloquently made the point that relationships are needed for a meaningful life. She shared her experience of winning yet another Grammy and recognizing that she had no one in her life except for her mother to call and share in the joy. In that moment, she realized that winning an award, even as significant as a Grammy, has limited value if there is no one to share the joy with.

↔

Clearly, the real prize in life comes from our connections with others and the joy of sharing in our accomplishments. We all know that this is true on some deep level from our own experiences.

In case you need more support for the core value of human connection and its synchronicity with addressing loneliness, one other fascinating body of research magnifies the importance of taking a relationship-centered approach to life and leadership. The research on centenarians, those who live to be 100, found that relationships, especially with family, tend to be a differentiating factor in longevity.[26] Literally, relationships allow us to live longer, healthier lives. While diet and movement are key as well, those who live longest (and, by that definition, have the best health) have regular contact with community.[27]

Connecting with others is not only good for happiness and health but also for leadership success. Leadership is about how you carry yourself on a regular basis, in a more expansive, day-to-day sense. The next time you are in the coffee shop waiting in line, put your phone in your pocket, look around, and wonder with curiosity about the people around you—maybe introduce yourself or converse with them. Building the skill of connecting on a personal level makes us more comfortable doing so in the work context (rather than always moving directly into the task of the day or meeting). We each need relationships to keep learning, stay inspired, and accomplish our personal and professional goals. Time and again, this has proven true with respect to the busy leaders we (the authors) have coached and worked with. Our collaboration on this book is another example. If we had not made our relationship the focus of our work over the past decade, this text would not exist.

The point is simply that relationships matter a lot, and they take work. At our jobs and in our communities, we have to build a culture focused on strong and healthy relationship patterns—a culture that is grounded in valuing those relationships, opportunities for social connection, habits centered on connecting beyond the business, and empathy and compassion as the norm. Creating a sense of belonging is not only a key part of being an effective leader but also something that we should all care about for our own health and for the well-being of others. We can do this by monitoring our use of technology, placing value in spending time with the ones we love, and developing the skills and habits necessary for relationship success, which we will share with you throughout the remainder of this chapter.

B. From Emotional Intelligence to Social Intelligence

1. Self-Awareness of Your Beliefs about Relationships

A common goal in coaching is to improve relationships. People often come to these engagements motivated to learn relationship skills so that they can overcome some conflict and improve the relationships in their life, whether with a sibling, spouse, or colleague. They are often surprised (and at times frustrated) when they learn that the first step to enhanced relationship management is exploring and working on what is happening internally for them. Indeed, the first stage in relationship management is developing greater self-awareness—that is, gaining insight about your mental, interpersonal, and coping habits and the utility of each in relationship outcomes. The beliefs that you have about relationships generally and the beliefs that you hold about your ability to build relationships in particular are key to your relationship success.

↑↓↑

SELF-DISCOVERY EXERCISE 18: YOUR RELATIONSHIP WITH RELATIONSHIPS

1. Are relationships important in your life? Professionally? Personally? Why or why not?
2. Are you good at building relationships? Why or why not?
3. Do you like building relationships?
4. Where did you learn about the importance of relationships?

[**STOP and COMPLETE before reading further.**]

↑↓↑

REFLECTION ON SELF-DISCOVERY EXERCISE 18

You know that without self-awareness of your narrative, the other EI skills are essentially impossible to achieve, including relationship management. With greater awareness of what your beliefs are about relationships and how you feel about your abilities to develop them, you can adjust accordingly.

→ As you answered the questions above, what did you notice regarding your beliefs about relationships and about your social skills?

→ Have you traditionally valued the importance of relationships?
→ In what context did these beliefs originate?

Be sure to take time to journal and explore what your beliefs are about the importance of relationships and where you learned those beliefs.

[STOP and COMPLETE before reading further.]

□ □ □

As a starting point, these questions emanate from our work with busy, high-achieving leaders in various industries over the past two decades. We have time and again heard leaders express a narrative marked by the belief that they wish they did not have to tend to the "drama," deal with team dynamics, and put up with their colleagues' annoying behaviors in meetings. Do you fall into this camp? Do you find yourself saying, "Wow, he talks nonstop," "She just goes on and on," "He says one thing and does another," or "I wish we could just get this done"? If so, you are human! We all fall into negative beliefs about the people we work with and the time it takes to manage and lead people. While this is human nature, you have to be able to identify these faulty, negative beliefs because they influence how you feel and act.

Your mindset about relationships is a good place to start because it influences virtually everything else that you do. You know that now because you have already read the chapters on self-awareness and self-management, which deepened your understanding. Take a minute to write down what comes up for you cognitively, your beliefs and thoughts, in team meetings and work with your closest colleagues. Are your thoughts sounding productive and healthy? Once you get in touch with negative thoughts about your colleagues and about the need to tend to the relationships, you can reframe them, and your motivation will improve. With awareness of your outlook on relationships, you can adjust accordingly. With a positive cognitive reframe, you can reorient your leadership toward collaboration.

To do this well, you need to not only recognize the value of the relationship but also utilize your newly improved self-awareness skills to pay continuing attention to where you are placing your attention. That's right.

Keep focusing on what you are paying attention to in the relationships in your life. We find that many busy leaders are focused on the work and on getting the colleagues they are in a relationship with to do the things that they want the colleagues to do, or they are focused on what characteristics the colleagues have that drive them crazy, and not on empathic statements or cultivating curiosity about how their colleagues are doing. Effective leaders know how to keep their attention on empathy for the other person and on empathic thoughts such as "I wonder what this is like for him?" or "I wonder what he is feeling today?" This awareness practice of what might be going on for the other person, what the other person is good at doing, what you appreciate about the other person, and points of connection with the other person is the most effective method for building a relationship that moves the work forward.

↑↓↑

SELF-DISCOVERY EXERCISE 19: SELF-AWARENESS OF SOCIAL SAVVY

1. What are your beliefs about your social abilities?
2. How do you do socially? At networking events?
3. Do you see yourself as someone who is savvy socially? Skilled at connecting with others?
4. In what areas do you think you are effective interpersonally, and what tendencies do you think make you ineffective?

[**STOP and COMPLETE before reading further.**]

↑↓↑

REFLECTION ON SELF-DISCOVERY EXERCISE 19

Your answers, which will vary, are key insights into what makes you more socially savvy. For example, maybe you are good at convincing others but struggle with developing deeper connections. Your thoughts here are important enough that you should transform them into lists or journal entries so that you can revisit and revise them.

Beyond your beliefs, have people given you feedback about what they find difficult about you? What was that feedback, and do you believe it? Have you worked to stay self-aware of these tendencies and try out new ways of interacting with them?

If you notice that your beliefs about relationships in general, the importance of relationships, and/or your social skills tend to be negative, then take some time to explore if that has changed as you just read about the importance of relationships for successful leadership, well-being, and longevity. Think of some positive reframes based on the literature we presented. Later in this chapter, we revisit the Myers-Briggs Type Indicator (MBTI®) (*see* Chapter III), which can help you learn more about your interpersonal and coping style and how those patterns play out for you, both positively and negatively, in relationships. Take time to have self-awareness of your thoughts about your social efficacy.

Strong leaders recognize the importance of relationships, and they place a premium on them. In reframing, you may want to create mantras on this specifically: "Leadership is all about relationships," "Leadership is about how you make others feel," or "I know I get frustrated with her when she does X, but I know she is great at X, and I am motivated to support her in this work."

You may also want to practice seeing yourself as skilled in relationship building and social life. For example, you might want to tell yourself, "People will enjoy interacting with me because of ..." or "My colleagues want me there." Then give reasons for these positive beliefs. Why do your teammates want/need you there? What is good about you, and what do others typically enjoy about being with you? Add these to your lists or journal entries.

2. Self-Awareness of Your Personality Traits

Now that you have focused on what you are telling yourself about relationships, let's gain insight into how self-awareness of your interpersonal and coping patterns plays a role in your relationships.

↑↓↑

SELF-DISCOVERY EXERCISE 20: SELF-AWARENESS OF PERSONALITY TRAITS

1. How would you describe your personality?
2. How do others tend to describe you?
3. What is your default mode under pressure? (You answered this in an earlier chapter.)

[STOP and COMPLETE before reading further.]

□ □ □

ROB TAKING THE LEAD → For the past five years, I have been coaching a partner in a large corporate law firm who is one of the most driven, intelligent, and skilled lawyers I have ever worked with. She came to coaching with a CV that would catch anyone's eye, with degrees from top undergrad and law schools as well as prestigious clerkships and associate positions, and now she was on a partner track at a top corporate firm. She explained that she had been struggling with burnout and anxiety for the past few years due to feeling that she was being overlooked for leadership positions in key practice areas. She noted that she was struggling with some of the leaders in the firm so much that their relationships had become divisive and conflicted. She also noted that she had already worked with a coach in the past and focused on "professionalism" and "demeanor," with little progress.

As we explored her background and upbringing, I learned that she was from a high-achieving family and that she had been struggling with anxiety for most of her life as she pushed herself to meet both family and professional expectations. She was intense and individually driven.

It also became evident that she had decided that others did not like working with her because of her personality. She was often left out of key leadership meetings and passed over for opportunities and had assumed that this was because others did not like her. As we explored what was happening, it became progressively apparent that she was resorting to more assertive, direct, and taskmaster patterns when stressful situations arose at work. Her default mode under stress was to be snippy, direct, abrasive, and controlling. She could go months without letting these underlying patterns surface, but then they would bubble up to the surface once a heated work situation arose, and others would judge her for it, reinforcing her negative reputation in the office. When she was calm, she was clearly a compassionate, kind, and considerate colleague; but under pressure, she was direct, opinionated, and controlling. While some colleagues appreciated her decisiveness in difficult situations, others found her off-putting and unprofessional.

Through practicing mindfulness, doing self-awareness exercises, and exploring her interpersonal and coping patterns when anxiety and stress kick in, she was able to gain self-awareness of her default mode under pressure and better understand how that was impacting relationships. She was eventually able to name her persona during these episodes and thus could catch these tendencies more easily as they emerged. She learned what situations were most triggering so that she could be prepared to practice anxiety-reduction strategies prior to and during the engagements. She learned to recognize what it felt like when stress and anxiety were entering her body; this knowledge enabled her to practice awareness of how she wanted to present interpersonally. With a deep level of self-acceptance, she eventually learned to harness her take-charge nature and soften her engagements through new ways of interacting. Even when the iron was hot, she learned to practice empathy and compassion, hear others' perspectives, and soften her responses. Even though she still gets hot at times, she now has done the work to be able to turn down the heat most of the time. And even when the heat rises, she is able to quickly recognize it and do the repair work with others through self-acceptance and self-compassion.

↔

Paying attention to your personality tendencies and how they come across to others is a key relationship strategy. In this way, self-awareness is a relationship management skill. When we recognize our personality patterns and interpersonal tendencies, we can catch them in real time with gentle awareness and then practice more effective strategies (i.e., self-management). There is a direct and correlating flow from one into the other:

Self-awareness → Self-management → Relationship management

However, the interaction is more cyclical than linear, as shown in Figure 10.

FIGURE 10
CYCLICAL NATURE OF EI DOMAIN INTERACTIONS

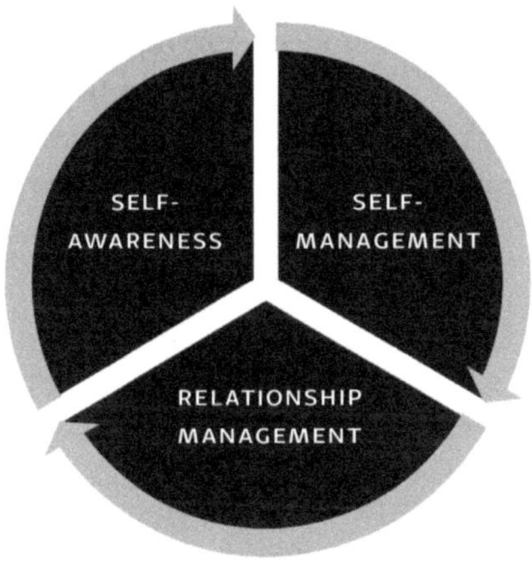

When most of us think about emotional intelligence, we think of people in our life who are able to respond in various emotionally charged situations with grace and composure. That is how the second domain of emotional intelligence, self-management, interacts with self-awareness to allow for leadership excellence. Because you have put in the effort and completed the exercises in this book up to this point, you should now have high a level of self-awareness. In most relationships, you will also experience strong emotional currents as colleagues exhibit their own emotional responses. In those moments, you need to take stock of what emotions you are feeling when you are with them. What are you telling yourself at a cognitive level? In other words, what are your thoughts, interpretations, impressions, biases, and judgments about those colleagues and their actions? Think about what emotions are arising in you. With awareness of your emotions, think about how that emotional response influences your actions and behaviors toward these colleagues. In doing this, you are moving from self-awareness to self-management, which naturally implicates relationship management.

For example, after having removed you from a case with a difficult but important client, your law partner says, "I'd like for you to take on that case again, if you don't mind." What do you think? How do you feel? Do you think "Great, what an opportunity" or "You should not have taken the case away from me to begin with"? This is where emotionally intelligent leaders shine. They notice their interpretations and thoughts, how those lead to emotional responses, and how those emotional responses influence their reactions and behavior. They recognize that their reaction in a moment such as this is just that—a default reaction. If you practice awareness of what you are feeling—really tune in—you will bring your default reaction and underlying tendencies to conscious awareness and can choose how to respond. In that space between your default reaction and your response, you can self-manage for the betterment of the relationship, be it with a partner, a client, or the firm.

C. The Four-Stage Model of Relationship Management

Now that you have a better understanding of the human need for connection, the societal circumstances challenging that human need, and the natural and cyclical flow from self-awareness to self-management to relationship management, let's look at a model to clarify the relationship-management skill.

The four central steps of relationship management that we have identified in our work are *identifying* key people with whom to build relationships, *initiating* those relationships, *developing* sustainable and healthy relationships, and *collaborating* in those relationships to achieve some desired outcome. This model is practice-based, has proven successful with busy leaders, and provides a framework and language for thinking about how to activate EI skills over the course of relationship development: identify, initiate, develop, collaborate.

In this chapter, we have pointed out how your skills in self-awareness, self-management, and empathy form the base for strong social skills, moving from intra- to interpersonal. We will now walk through the four stages of relationship management so that you can see how to bring these EI skills together and apply them to effectively lead others in the law.

1. Identifying Stage

By *identifying*, we simply mean identifying the people you would like to build relationships with, whether because of what they bring out in you or how they make you feel (e.g., excited) or because you see the

FIGURE 11
FOUR STAGES OF RELATIONSHIP DEVELOPMENT

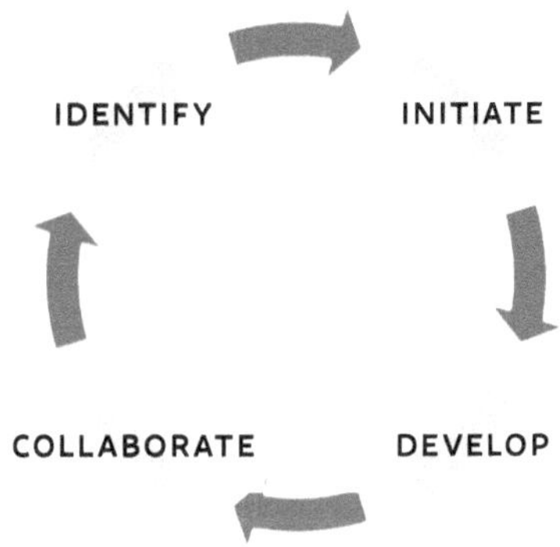

potential to collaborate with them on something (e.g., you both like to play music or you share an interest in real estate law).

The first step in building strong relationships is—you guessed it!—tuning in to how you are feeling as you identify with people around you. The time that you spend paying attention to what you are feeling and thinking sets the stage for you to tune in to how others make you feel and the emotions they bring out in you. When you pay attention to what others bring out in you, you can consciously choose how to respond as you interact with them. Great leaders tune in to how others make them feel and what those others bring out in them so that they can respond in a way that is both appropriate to the circumstance and includes an empathic element geared toward future interaction. Utilizing your EI skills in the identifying stage allows you to assess how to proceed in order to be effective. This will allow you to have an open mind toward and dedicate appropriate time and energy toward those relationships.

Self-awareness of your interests and values also plays a key role in the identifying stage. Through the self-awareness exercises you completed earlier in this book you learned more about your values and interests, and we hope you dedicate time to enjoying your interests through hobbies and recreation. So what do you enjoy doing? Whether it is running, canoeing, camping, or crafting, keep dedicating time to what you enjoy and developing activities around your interests. Make this a habit. You can then identify others who also enjoy spending time doing that activity. Self-awareness of what you like doing allows you to know where to spend your time, while self-management provides the motivation and dedication to build those interests and then identify others who also enjoy doing it. Relationships will come about through that shared interest.

Leaders who are high in emotional intelligence are able to resonate with others in terms of this identifying stage. They practice empathy to put themselves in others' shoes, really understand where they are in life and what they might need, and then recognize points of connection with themselves or potentially with someone else. Indeed, great leaders connect others who share mutual interests or who might benefit one another. Because great leaders approach life with a curiosity about the people around them, these similarities and opportunities emerge, and great leaders notice these potential opportunities for collaboration and pursue them with enthusiasm.

Hopefully, you recognize that this does not mean that you should only choose to identify others who will help you in some way or make you feel happy. Quite the opposite. Emotionally intelligent lawyers have an open mind about others' experiences and interests and a curiosity and appreciation for diverse lifestyles, and they choose to have relationships with others regardless of whether those relationships will benefit themselves or not. When they notice a connection with someone, emotionally intelligent lawyers identify that point of connection and act on it.

2. Initiating Stage

This brings us to the initiating stage. By *initiating*, we mean establishing relationships with the people you identified in the previous stage.

You are now moving forward by initiating contact with curiosity. Emotionally intelligent leaders explore the world with openness and inquisitiveness, with an appreciation for diverse lifestyles, backgrounds, cultural traditions, and rituals. They are aware of how exploring and appreciating others' stories expands their worldview and helps them grow. They explore and adventure in their daily lives, curiously pursuing their interests, people, and opportunities. They follow their curiosities with passion. When you lead others, you want to have a genuine curiosity about their stories. How did they get to where they are? What are their defining moments and who are their influencers? (Note the connection to your own passion mapping.) How does that story relate to their goals? How do those goals align with what you are setting out to accomplish? What are they getting into? Is that something you are curious about? Exploring your curiosities in others will lead to points of connection, and the relationship will begin.

Whether at work or outside of work, we all have the choice of talking with others—or not. How often do you seek space around you when you eat at a restaurant? It is no surprise, then, that when you pick airplane seats, the window and aisle seats go first (yes, comfort is a factor, but isn't that about space as well?). In writing about interactions between people, Waldinger and Schulz reported on a study of people's feelings about talking to others on a commuter train: most people do not want to engage in those types of conversations for a variety of good, though self-focused, reasons (e.g., they want to read a book or listen to a podcast or they do not want to talk to a random stranger).[28] However, Waldinger and Schulz also reported on research on "affective forecasting"—that is, predicting what will make us most happy in situations like riding a commuter train—and the results suggested that when forced to start a conversation, the result is a positive experience.[29] In other words, interacting with others has core benefits.

CLIFF TAKING THE LEAD → I recently had a rough day of flying—boarding, plane maintenance, deboarding, gate change, extended delay, and more. We've all been there. No fun! It was fascinating to watch, though, as the air travel circumstances broke down that initial hesitancy barrier such that everyone was talking with others; groups of otherwise strangers had dinner together; and the level of chatter, or informal conversations, among the passengers predominated over the usual isolation one sees at an airport gate.

↔

Leaders understand the benefit of random interactions such as those that Cliff observed and readily seek out others for that positive relationship and the benefit of connection, whether known or unknown, that will flow from identifying others with whom to build relationships and the subsequent initiation of contact.

The "talking to strangers when traveling" scenario has a work parallel in the silos found in most work settings. The silos separate us both horizontally (different areas or departments) and vertically (management and nonmanagement, skilled and unskilled, etc.). Thus, initiating a relationship requires significant effort that is beyond coincidence (such as who is seated next to you) and is empowered by your emotional intelligence. Your EI skills are at work when you walk down a hall where you do not work, see an open door, knock, smile, and say hello. That initiation of conversation (and a relationship)—the question you ask—is self-awareness and self-management plus empathy in action.

In law practice, initiating is important for mutually beneficial relationships—but, admittedly, it is not easy. We work in an inherently adversarial system, whether in litigation, transactional work, or the regulatory space. You and your legal team are forced together with another legal team, often where the respective interests press to compete for limited resources.

CLIFF TAKING THE LEAD → I often found that building relationships with opposing counsel—through self-awareness of what they brought out in me and self-management to make sure that I never lost sight of my client's interests—would make the work on that case flow better and more completely. In one case in particular, opposing counsel were good lawyers, and their work on damages was quite impressive. After the case was completed, we maintained a relationship with the lawyers even though we were typically on opposing sides of issues. Then, when we had a client with particularly challenging damages issues, we reached out to those lawyers, asking if they would join our representation team. They leapt at the opportunity.

↔

Maintaining such relationships is not easy in a highly competitive space, but leaders refrain from hasty judgment because building relationships without expectation is key. In short, while identification and initiation can be uncomfortable and even difficult, they can increase positive emotions and lead to a positive relationship.

3. Developing Stage

Once initiated, a relationship needs to be developed. By *developing*, we mean growing sustainable and healthy relationships, in particular by being vulnerable.

ROB TAKING THE LEAD → When I was a postdoc at the health center at Northwestern University, one of my supervisors was Wei-Jen Huang, PhD, a wonderfully talented emotional intelligence master. Northwestern students referred to him as—no joke!—"Dr. Love," and he facilitated standing-room-only training sessions on relationships. One of the particularly profound things that he taught me was that relationships are about giving and receiving in a genuine way. Wei-Jen would say that there are two parts to relationship success. The first is that we should ask questions from a place of empathy and exploration and receive responses in a heartwarming and compassionate way, with added curiosity. Second, and at the same time, we should open up and share in a real and vulnerable way, even when that means feeling discomfort. Wei-Jen referred to the act of confiding in someone else as "giving a gift." He recognized the significance of giving the gift of something real and genuine about yourself to another person.

↔

Quite obviously, vulnerability in the workplace requires care, thought, and intentionality that are not present in other spaces. Strong emotional intelligence allows you to recognize the context to decide what is appropriate to share. Leaders make themselves vulnerable, which builds trust in those with whom they share—and that trust is crucial to establishing and maintaining relationships. Strong emotional intelligence, your self-awareness and self-management in particular, allows you to accept your discomfort—or, as we like to say, get comfortable with your discomfort. This requires self-awareness of what to share, self-management of the anxieties and emotions that come up when you give the gift of authenticity, social awareness of context, and empathy with regard to putting yourself in the listener's shoes to know if the listener is ready to receive. When you practice vulnerability during the initiation and development stages, real and lasting relationships start and flourish. Brené Brown's research on vulnerability shows that vulnerability allows positive emotions to flourish—emotions like belonging and empathy in the other person, which are particularly desirable for both leaders and the people with whom they work. Likewise, her research shows that vulnerability is the "birthplace of creativity and innovation."[30] Thus, using vulnerability to develop relationships not only builds trust but also, as Wei-Jen would say, results in gifts.

4. Collaborating Stage

The final stage in relationship management is continual nurturing of the relationship. Beyond trust and vulnerability, building a collaborative relationship requires time and effort. We call this final stage *collaborating* because it is all about bringing the relationship to fruition around some shared purpose, which expands the developing stage to actually working together. Collaboration may be enjoying a round of (disc) golf together, as an informal example, or developing a new legal practice area or jointly landing a new client, as more formal examples. The collaboration stage involves capitalizing on the solid foundation of trust and vulnerability established between two or more people to bring their shared visions to fruition.

To reach collaboration, you have to practice self-awareness to know how you feel about the relationship and how that is influencing your motivation. With self-awareness, you notice as motivation waxes and wanes and then can recommit to spending time nourishing the connection.

Self-management in this phase often entails making the choice to continually connect, that is, to not take the connection for granted. This can be as simple as sending the other person the text that you considered sending or popping into the person's office really quickly just to say hello. It is about recognizing that even though you may be busy or distracted with other things, it is important to stay connected—and then taking that extra step. Revisiting original points of connection can help reignite motivation to see the other person in person.

Finally, with empathy as the driver, you can continue to practice attempting to understand what the other party might be going through and then use that as a source of connection. You can think of this as attunement, that is, our ability to be aware of and respond to others' emotional needs. Only through a high level of self-awareness and self-management can leaders be humble enough to allow collaboration through ups and downs or as projects wax and wane, maintaining those relationships necessary to work as a team with trust.

ROB TAKING THE LEAD → When we were first developing this course at Northwestern in the early 2010s, I worked hard to learn the landscape of legal education and the legal profession, particularly as each related to mental health and leadership. I wanted to *identify* the primary drivers who were conducting research and working with law students and lawyers, across the globe, to boost mental health and well-being in the field. After identifying the key law faculty, consultants, and practicing attorneys, I *initiated* contact with them, typically by email, introducing myself and the programs we had established at Northwestern, to see if we could meet. After an initial connection by Zoom or phone, I often followed up over the years that followed to *develop* a relationship with them. It was helpful during that development stage to find points of connection, such as mutual interests, shared experiences, or values. Those relationships have provided numerous opportunities for *collaboration* over the years that would not have been possible or come to fruition without those first three stages of relationship development. I walked through the steps, continually gauging my self-awareness and self-management and utilizing empathy.

To drive home the importance of collaboration in developing relationships, I will share a story about one of my most rewarding relationships. I met Michael Colatrella, a law professor at the University of the Pacific, McGeorge School of Law, at a legal conference in Las Vegas focused on lawyer well-being. Michael and I quickly identified shared interests in helping law students be successful via enhanced emotional intelligence and psychological science. After engaging in lengthy conversations together, we followed up with emails and phone calls over the next year, sharing insights and getting to know each other (developing!). Michael then invited me to the law school to give an orientation talk on law-student well-being. Over the course of the following year, I continued to have conversations with Michael about law school, wellness in the legal profession, and deeper topics such as the meaning of life and careers, and eventually, we decided to offer a leadership course for law students at McGeorge. Michael and I taught the course for several years

(I served as an adjunct faculty member) up until the pandemic. It was an exciting time to be in California's capital and to work with eager and enthusiastic future lawyer leaders, many of whom would go on to serve in state and national government roles.

I share this story because it highlights the collaborating phase that flows from having heartfelt, meaningful connections. I have often joked with clients and students over the years that you can build an entire career on the shoulders of a few relationships, especially if you choose them wisely, stay humble, practice empathy, remain vulnerable throughout the process, and invest in them.

↔

It is important to point out that collaborating will not always end up being as formal and rewarding as getting the opportunity to teach a for-credit leadership course in a law school. Most of the time, collaborating in relationships, as we mentioned earlier, can be as simple as sharing an article or podcast of interest, meeting up for coffee, or connecting one another with colleagues.

Relationships like the one just described, and the time spent in them, can ingrain in you a deep and lasting sense of appreciation for the power of relationships as well as highlight their role in successful leadership. Relationships pave the way for success and meaningful work. When you lead with curiosity (as Rob did in the story above), find the courage to initiate, and take risks to share your story with vulnerability and courage, you create the opportunity to establish and nurture your own decade-long partnership and the personal satisfaction and rewards that come with it.

5. Recap of the Stages

Again, the four stages in effective relationship management are *identifying* key people to build relationships with, *initiating* those relationships, *developing* sustainable and healthy relationships, and *collaborating* in those relationships to achieve some desired outcome. Take some time to think through how your EI skills come to life to assist you in each of these stages.

Are there people you want to connect with but have hesitated to out of fear? Maybe you have prioritized other pursuits above making these connections? What would it take for you to send that email or make a phone call?

↑↓↑

SELF-DISCOVERY EXERCISE 21: EXPLORING THE FOUR STAGES

1. Think about the four stages and lasting relationships you have had. Do any fit the four stages?
2. Identify a short list of new people to build relationships with. Practice self-awareness as you make the list.
3. What anxieties or fears come up for you? Are your anxieties or fears related to the person or the process?
4. If related to the process, which stages are you more or less comfortable with? How will you address that discomfort to move through those stages?
5. If related to the person, what are your preconceived notions about them and what they might think if you reach out?
6. What is your natural style of initiating?

[**STOP and COMPLETE before reading further.**]

☐ ☐ ☐

In Rob's practice alone, he has coached thousands of clients through this process and has never had one come back and say they wished they had not reached out. He cannot say the opposite is true.

D. Building Trust

In the developing stage, trust is crucial to establishing and maintaining relationships. Meanwhile, law students and lawyers are taught to maintain a critical eye (in a highly competitive culture, no less), and we often turn this critical eye on each other in a way that can undo relationships. This behavior can appear in the simplest of circumstances, like in a conversation with several people where a friend expresses doubt about something that you say. Your first reaction might be to doubt the trust that you had placed in that friend. Likewise, at work, leaders want everyone to be able to express ideas openly to find the best solutions, but doubt or critique can challenge that notion. Strong EI skills, particularly self-awareness of what you are feeling and self-management in reconsidering the appropriateness of your response, certainly help to restrain this doubt (or the way it is expressed) and maintain existing trust. Leaders know the value of trust, the close connection between mistrust and dysfunction, and how to maintain trust in the face of challenges.

CLIFF TAKING THE LEAD → Once when I was teaching, I had the students self-select into pairs for a research and writing assignment. Four students were left unpaired: two domestic JD students and two international JD students who already had a law degree in their home countries. Though not purely volitional, the two domestic students gravitated toward each other, as did the international students.

I sensed that a lack of trust in each other's skills, maybe rooted mainly in language issues, was driving their decisions. Given my sense of the source of their initial hesitation, I suggested that they pair the other way: one domestic and one international. I asked them to trust me and to trust each other's strengths in the process. When they looked at me quizzically, I explained that the benefit in my pairing, if they trusted each other, was that each team would have complementary strengths: one person skilled in the English language to ensure good writing and one person who was already a lawyer skilled in the profession. They agreed, and all had a great experience when they trusted each other and built on that trust to use their respective strengths.

↔

Trust is a key factor in relationship management and thus in a productive work environment—and emotional intelligence is the foundation of trust. Leaders can most effectively build trust by showing trust in others, exhibiting a high level of empathy, fostering growth in others, and maintaining open lines of communication.[31] Strong emotional intelligence in leaders, such as mindfulness, the key to a high level of self-awareness, builds trust,[32] which is the cornerstone of all teamwork success. A close connection exists between EI strength and work performance and trust[33] and between EI leadership (authenticity) and employee trust.[34] "[N]euroscience experiments ... show that when people intentionally build social ties at work, their performance improves."[35]

Conversely, the Deloitte survey found that employee migration can largely be attributed to trust issues: of employees looking for new work, approximately 50 percent do so because of "loss of trust."[36]

To help you understand how building trust is key to relationship management, we present some trust models; examine multicultural leadership, the heart of building trust; discuss trust and virtual teams; and offer insight into building community and relationships post-pandemic.

1. Trust Models

Five dysfunctions of a team. When it comes to teams, trust is the cornerstone of strength and success, and lack of trust is the seed of dysfunction. Organizational cultures built on trust have a significant advantage over those that are not. In this section, we present a few of the most widely recognized models on trust and explore how to use them, in the framework of EI, to build trust.

In *The Five Dysfunctions of a Team*, Patrick Lencioni paired the dysfunctions with five cures. Most notably, the foundation of his pyramid on dysfunction is lack of trust, and the cure is building trust with vulnerability. While this pyramid is presented in the context of a team, it is really about trust and distrust in general and their impact in relationships.

Lencioni's pyramid model for teamwork illustrates that for a team to function effectively, it must address each of these layers, and vulnerability-based trust creates the foundation. As you can see from Figure 12, lack of trust closes down the willingness to communicate, raises concerns about others, and results in both individual disengagement and lack of accountability to others. Alternatively, with trust we are open to other ideas even if they embody conflict; the line of communication is open to share ideas, concerns, and disagreement; and all of that results in unified commitment, accountability, and measurable results. The pyramid highlights the fact that for teams to function effectively, everyone must be willing to be vulnerable to each other. So the question becomes, how do we practice vulnerability? As you reflect back over this text and the self-discovery exercises you have completed, what will allow you to be vulnerable in your work groups? Capitalizing on your enhanced

FIGURE 12
THE FIVE DYSFUNCTIONS OF A TEAM

© 2002 by Patrick Lencioni. Adapted with permission from Patrick Lencioni, *The Five Dysfunctions of a Team: A Leadership Fable* 188–189 (Jossey-Bass 2002).

self-awareness allows you to notice as fear surfaces, to recognize the underlying beliefs driving that fear and uncertainty, and then to rework your thinking to open up and share.

The ABCD Model. In Ken Blanchard, Cynthia Olmstead, and Martha Lawrence's 2013 book, *Trust Work! Four Keys to Building Lasting Relationships,* they present one of the most widely accepted frameworks to build trust—the ABCD Trust Model: Able, Believable, Connected, and Dependable.[37] In the context of a team, when individuals are willing and able to engage in each element, these elements build trust among the team members. The model highlights the four behaviors that need to be present in order to build trust and suggests that without even one, trust begins to erode. We believe in this model and see it grounded in EI. As we review the four key elements, think about how your training in and development of EI through will come to fruition in each of these essential features.

The A is for *able* and means that when team members can demonstrate their competence in key areas of work, they begin to gain the trust of others. Consistent, high-quality results shows that you are knowledgeable and skillful, and that you can be trusted to deliver. Being able entails knowing your strengths and limits, scope of practice, and a willingness to speak up and share when you have technical knowledge and skill to offer.

The B is for *believable* and means that you act with integrity. In order to be believable, you must be willing to admit when you are wrong and own your mistakes and insecurities, and be honest and up-front with colleagues. Trust comes from admitting when you do not know something or make a mistake and learn from your failures.

The C is for *connected* and means that the team members care for each other, which inherently builds connection. When team members are connected, they care deeply for each other beyond strategic goals and results. They show interest in one another and practice empathy!

And finally, the D is for *dependable* and means that the team members will maintain their reliability. The 'D' reminds us of *fire* in the self-management domain of EI. When you're dependable, you follow through and do what you say you will do. You are accountable and see projects and commitments through to completion. This requires self-management of motivation. It also requires continuing to see yourself accomplishing the goal with optimism and vision.

Acting in these ways communicates both a desire to be trusted and a willingness to trust others if they act the same. While the ABCD model for building trust leans into substantive skills, leaders build the strong relationships through strong emotional intelligence, which provides the foundational support for others to flourish in the model.

2. Multicultural Leadership

When you follow the ABCD Trust Model, maintain curiosity, and aim to build trust, you will necessarily be developing relationships with many people who are not like you. This will require another skill—*multicultural leadership*—to support how relationship management fits into your leadership. Multicultural leadership necessarily implicates *multicultural competency*—that is, understanding your own and others' cultural identities and effectively utilizing cultural skills with diverse groups, which is a natural product of strong EI skills.

Need for multicultural leadership. As the population changes, so does America's workforce. And so, ideally, does the way we lead in that workforce.

More specifically, the legal profession has acknowledged both the need to diversify and the challenge in maintaining diversification achievements.[38] The problem is that while law schools have improved diversity in admissions and graduation, law firms have not improved diversity in advancement and retention.[39] Why is it that attempts at diversification have changed neither who advances in a firm nor the discomfort of those who are perceived as different? Why is it that even though efforts have been made at the admission, training/education, and graduation levels, law firms have not effectively embraced those efforts? The simple answer is that the law itself, which is deeply rooted in English common law, changes quite slowly. Thus, efforts to change too dramatically are shunned and seen as destabilizing, in the sense that they undermine the certainty that law is supposed to bring to society.

Thus, multicultural leadership, like emotional intelligence generally, is a challenge to ingrained aspects of the law. Multicultural leadership enables an organization that professes to value difference in its employees to actually do so—because organizational ethos matters. In short, the solution lies in stepping back and looking at how we need to be as twenty-first-century leaders.

You'd be hard-pressed to find an organization in American society today that is not embracing some form of multicultural competency or understanding, whether this is called diversity, equity, inclusion, and engagement (DEIE) or is known by some other label. Even successful small businesses are thinking about creating more equitable and diverse workplaces. And it is about time. Not only is multicultural competency socially and morally responsible, as history has taught us time and again, but also the research is abundant that more equitable employers outpace their competitors by creating respectful, accepting, supportive, and productive workplaces and teams.[40] Diversity in skills, worldviews, and perspectives allows for creativity, wealth of knowledge and skills, and innovation.[41] And diverse and inclusive organizations benefit from not only happier employees[42] but also deeper trust and greater commitment from their employees.[43]

Nonetheless, DEIE programs have largely failed to live up to their promise in the legal profession (and in other professions).[44] We say this because traditionally defined diversity in hiring far exceeds the diversity in who makes partner.[45] Despite recognition of the need for greater diversity at all levels of management, there has been little growth in such diversity for the past thirty years.[46] Furthermore, most leadership initiatives have been reactive as opposed to value-based. These trainings are often well-intentioned and provide employees with knowledge about diversity concepts such as implicit bias and microaggressions, as well as data on the lack of diversity, especially in leadership.[47] And many businesses have added grievance or reporting systems so that employees can report managers and colleagues who discriminate in the workplace.[48] However, while these systems give limited control and power to minority members, they have not led to creating thriving multicultural organizations.

Again, multicultural leadership is the key. As a leader, your newly developed emotional intelligence will help you value and lead diverse work groups while advancing social justice.

Multicultural leadership and EI skills. Emotionally intelligent leaders cherish multicultural diversity and strive to create socially responsible cultures. They recognize the importance of heterogeneous perspectives and the exchange of diverse ideas. Great leaders capitalize on diversity in their work groups through a culture of empathy and equity. At this point in time, it should be obvious to anyone studying leadership that a central mission is being able to bring people from diverse backgrounds together around a shared purpose. Indeed, one of the lessons to be drawn from American history is the importance of celebrating diversity in all of its forms. Strong EI-based leadership makes this a reality. As leaders and lawyers who want to create flourishing multicultural organizations, we must be able to work with diverse clients and colleagues and want them to thrive and feel heard. Not surprisingly, the EI skills laid out in this book are the vehicle for achieving successful diversity, equity, inclusion, and engagement.

What we mean by a "socially responsible" culture is a multicultural organization in which the leader values equity, awareness, and respect; leads with sensitivity and vulnerability; understands and appreciates difference; creates a trusting, psychologically safe space; and appreciates awareness of biases. This is the essence of multicultural leadership. We must not only overcome interpersonal differences and intergenerational disconnect but also value the benefits that flow from them. A twenty-first-century leader needs to be acutely aware of how to bring together all types of workers and keep them together in an ever-fracturing world. Core EI skills are the foundation for this, and narrative humility shows us the value of layering on multicultural competency.

Having a high level of self-awareness (both at the deep level of personal narrative and in the present moment) and building a high level of empathy (particularly with regard to curiosity about others, challenging one's own biases, thinking beyond one's reactions, and wanting to inspire others) naturally lead people not only to value multicultural competency but also to continually strengthen it. A high degree of multicultural competency is both the natural outgrowth of the EI domains and competencies discussed so far and part of the natural bridge from them to relationship management. A primary goal of many DEIE programs is to help people recognize their biases so that they are more aware of the impact those biases can have on decision-making and actions in the workplace. Leaders high in emotional intelligence value taking time to assess their biases. They work to understand what is triggered in them when working with people different from themselves. We also know that multicultural leaders recognize that multicultural competency is not about having no biases, as that is virtually impossible; rather, multicultural competency is about trying to see and be aware of those biases, manage our responses to them, and recognize their impact. Through self-awareness, leaders see their limitations, their biases, and the value in other perspectives.

↑↓↑

SELF-DISCOVERY EXERCISE 22: RATING SELF-AWARENESS

1. Rate your level of self-awareness (scale of 1–10).
2. Think about what you need to do to increase your self-awareness. (Feel free to review your responses to earlier reflection prompts.)
3. What are your limitations?
4. What are your biases?
5. What do you value in others' perspectives?

6. How do others' perspectives complement your own?

[STOP and COMPLETE before reading further.]

□ □ □

Self-Discovery Exercise 22 should have helped you to establish a baseline of strengths and weaknesses in your self-awareness. An ever-expanding and expansive level of self-awareness and humility (narrative or otherwise) allows you to constantly improve your EI skills. This is important because multicultural leadership requires acute awareness of various situations, contexts, and assumptions. To deal with the challenges in managing a multicultural organization, leaders must increase their ability to appreciate differences and adopt inclusive approaches.

Leaders must also constantly remind themselves that although there are universal values that most cultures (and thus most people) appreciate—such as politeness, kindness, honor, and acceptance—"universality" is relative across cultures and subcultures. This concept is known as *cultural relativity*. Rather than trying to define every culture's approach, narrative humility in combination with cultural relativity means that multicultural leadership is based on an exceptional level of open-mindedness from which one can understand the value added from all team members and their cultures—that is, the skill of multicultural competency.

Multicultural competency and EI skills. The concept of multicultural competency has evolved over the years such that it is now based on a human rights framework whose foundation is EI skills.[49]

There are both internal and external aspects of multicultural competency. For example, multicultural competency viewed internally is "the acquisition and maintenance of culture-specific skills required to (a) function effectively within a new cultural context and/or (b) interact effectively with people from different cultural backgrounds."[50] Shifting to the external aspect, multicultural competency is "the ability to communicate effectively and appropriately in intercultural situations based on one's intercultural knowledge, skills, and attitudes."[51] Viewed together, then, multicultural competency is having knowledge and awareness of one's own culture and that of the client or others in a workspace and actively acknowledging and addressing how that would affect treatment.[52]

This duality highlights the alignment and development of EI skills with those of multicultural competency. The basis of multicultural competency skill development lies in building self-awareness and empathy. As with building self-awareness generally, researchers have observed a connection between mindfulness and multicultural counseling competency.[53] Mindfulness focused particularly on loving-kindness practice reduces implicit race-based bias.[54] Similarly, this practice of mindfulness leads to greater acceptance of and dedication to racial justice.[55]

Many people misunderstand the concept of multicultural competency by limiting it to racial awareness as opposed to recognition of the underlying truth that we genuinely accept those who are like us at the expense of those who are not. We fail to recognize that we have much more in common with each other than we have differences, yet we often first see the differences and act on them before even considering the similarities. To a great extent, not exercising multicultural competency will undermine efforts to bring diverse and divergent people together. By exhibiting multicultural competency, leaders message to others the importance and value of empathic understanding and the depth of their willingness to lead a diverse group through the resolution of any issue.

The success of using multicultural competency skills in counseling has been replicated within the medical field with both doctors and nurses. Including an emphasis on multicultural competency and its training in nursing yielded a reduction in health-care inequity.[56] The successful use of multicultural competency within both counseling and the medical field can and should lend credence to its extension to the legal profession: attorneys provide essential legal counseling services in their representation, and multiculturally competent attorneys can relate to and advocate better for their clients, leading to better outcomes.[57]

Three competencies of multicultural leadership. Researchers have not settled on a primary way to accomplish multicultural competency, particularly given the vast differences among cultures.[58] Still, the research by Patricia Arredondo (who was on Rob's master's thesis committee) and others gives us a nice framework to build the skills necessary to become a multicultural leader. These researchers identified three competencies of multicultural leadership:

- Competency 1: Awareness of one's own cultural values and biases
- Competency 2: Awareness of others' worldview

- Competency 3: Culturally appropriate leadership strategies[59]

Competency 1: Competency 1 is about having an even stronger level of self-awareness. The key to understanding those you are working with continues to be awareness of yourself, your emotions, and your reactions. Understanding what is arising in you or how you feel is the first step and can only happen if you have deep awareness of your own cultural values and how they have shaped your worldview. Learning about your own culture provides insight into the biases that you may hold. More specifically, as an emotionally intelligent leader, you are directing your attention not only to those differences that you sense but also to your judgments of those differences and how your own cultural upbringing has led to those judgments—in other words, you are noticing those judgments with accurate awareness. It might be helpful here to try to think about your own heritage and culture as an outsider would. What are the core values and beliefs inherent in the culture in which you were raised? Maybe some of these themes arose in your passion mapping work completed earlier in this book.

Competency 2: Competency 2 neatly divides into two parts: (1) "other" awareness and (2) knowledge of other groups and their experiences.

"Other" awareness begins with awareness of our own biases and stereotypes from Competency 1. Culturally skilled leaders are aware of their negative and positive emotional reactions toward other groups (racial, ethnic, religious, sexual orientation, gender identity, or other) that may prove detrimental to the mentoring or inspiring relationship. They are willing to contrast their own beliefs and attitudes with those of their culturally different peers in a nonjudgmental fashion. Culturally skilled leaders work hard to be aware of their stereotypes and preconceived notions that they may hold toward other racial and ethnic minority groups. This can be a difficult process for many. It is challenging to accept the reality that we all hold cultural biases about those different from us. The leadership challenge is not to never have biases but rather to recognize your biases with self-awareness, explore them with vulnerability and humility, and work through challenging them so that they do not lead to unconscious bias.

The next self-discovery exercise and related reflective writing are geared toward Competency 1 and its connection to Competency 2.

↑↓↑

SELF-DISCOVERY EXERCISE 23: KNOW YOUR BIASES

Step 1: Thinking about Yourself, Generally

1. Reflect for a minute on some of your automatic responses.
2. What are your biases?

If it helps, think about what you value in others, and then think about what things you find unappealing and whether you associate those with any particular group. For example, if you value achievement orientation, do you tend to judge others who live a more balanced and easy-going lifestyle? How do these biases show up for you in your perception of colleagues and/or clients?

[**STOP and COMPLETE Step 1 before moving on to Step 2.**]

Step 2: Thinking about Your Experiences: Negative Biases

1. Reflect for a minute on your work experiences.
2. What is one type of person or group with whom you find it very difficult to work? It might also be helpful to think of a subculture that you dislike.
3. Why do you dislike them? What bothers you about that type of person or group? What are your beliefs about them? (This may remind you of the exercises that you did with empathy! Do you see the connection between empathy (EI) training and multicultural competency?)
4. What assumptions do you hold about that type of person or group?

[**STOP and COMPLETE Step 2 before moving on to Step 3.**]

Step 3: Thinking about Your Experiences: Positive Biases

1. Reflect for a minute on your work experiences.
2. What is one type of person or group with which you find it very easy to work?
3. What attracts you to that type of person or group?
4. What favorable biases do you hold about that type of person or group?

[STOP and COMPLETE Step 3 before moving on to Step 4.]

Step 4: Thinking about Your Legal Experiences in Particular

1. Reflect for a minute on your work with lawyers, clients, and others in the legal profession.
2. What is one type of person or group with which you find it very difficult to work?
3. What bothers you about that type of person or group?
4. What negative biases do you hold about that type of person or group?

[STOP and COMPLETE before reading further.]

↑ ↓ ↑

REFLECTIVE WRITING 19

→ Do a guided loving-kindness meditation, thinking about that one type of person or group with which you find it very difficult to work.

→ Now write about how you feel and how you can work better with that type of person or group.

[STOP and COMPLETE before reading further.]

□ □ □

The second part of Competency 2 is having knowledge of other groups and their experiences, kind of like the exercise of empathy in the domain of relationship awareness but a bit deeper. You might have to do some research. Culturally skilled leaders possess specific knowledge and information about the particular group with which they are working. They are aware of the life experiences, cultural heritage, and historical background of their culturally different clients. Or they recognize that deficiency, decide to address it, and educate themselves to fill the gap. They do so because culturally skilled leaders understand how race, culture, ethnicity, and differences may affect them.

If you think about this in the converse, how often have you thought "If someone understood my culture, race, or ethnicity better, then they would understand where I am coming from or why I did something in a certain way"? Or how often have you written a personal statement, essentially seeking to allow the evaluator to better understand your identity, culture, and values? If you would tout these aspects of yourself as reasons to hire you (and we all do), then as a leader you should be equally desirous of wanting to truly understand such aspects of those who work with and for you.

Competency 3: Having a balance of understanding from the first two competencies enables the growth necessary for Competency 3—that is, developing culturally appropriate leadership strategies. Culturally skilled leaders understand and have knowledge about sociopolitical influences that impinge upon the life of racial, ethnic, and other minorities. Immigration issues, poverty, racism, stereotyping, and powerlessness impact self-esteem and self-concept in interpersonal settings.[60] In other words, as you gather news and information, you typically think about how this affects you and those close to you, as well as what you are doing and want to do—but how often do you stop and think about how this same news and information is processed by those who differ from you? As a leader, you cannot be limited in your perspective of events locally, statewide, nationally, or globally. The multicultural nature of the workforce, combined with the speed of communication and access to information, makes this crucial.

↑↓↑

SELF-DISCOVERY EXERCISE 24: KNOWLEDGE OF OTHERS

Think about Competency 3 and how you would go about this process. Take some time to think deeply about the various forms of diversity in the people who you will be leading and working alongside. As we mentioned, fight the urge to only think in terms of race. After you identify specific cultural groups that you might be working with, ask yourself the following questions:

1. Let's start simple. As you think about your legal career, what groups or cultures will you be leading and working with?

What culturally specific information do you need to actively seek so that you can implement culturally appropriate leadership strategies? How will you do so in a way that gives you a firm, unbiased foundation?

2. Pick one cultural group to consider learning more about their customs, worldview, and traditions.
3. Now that you have a specific group in mind, consider their experience in your law firm and how their perceptions and path have been different from your own.
4. How will you go about learning more about that specific cultural group without your own biases influencing where you look and what you think about what you find? How will you do so without singling out the members of that specific group or putting them on the spot to be the educator for the majority?
5. What EI skills will you need to muster to counter unconscious bias creeping in at this level?

[**STOP and COMPLETE before reading further.**]

↑↓↑

REFLECTIVE WRITING 20

→ Reflecting on Self-Discovery Exercise 24, what is coming up for you in this process? What emotions are evoked from doing this work?

→ How do the emotions you are experiencing impact your motivation, one way or the other?

→ Do you value this exercise and the importance of multicultural leadership? Why or why not?

→ Reflect on your current habits and patterns of multicultural leadership. Write about both your strengths and weaknesses in this area.

→ How will you apply these leadership lessons? Be specific.

□ □ □

Reverse mentoring. A discussion about multicultural leadership would be incomplete without a discussion of the related concept of reverse mentoring. Traditional mentorship involves a seasoned employee providing guidance and supervision to a new or young and inexperienced employee. Reverse mentoring flips this concept. There are documented benefits to using reverse mentoring, one of which is that it allows more seasoned employees and leaders to learn from their new hires, particularly in the context of learning about differences.[61] With reverse mentoring, traditional leaders are encouraged to expand their acceptance of input from younger employees, though not necessarily those they supervise.[62] Reverse mentoring pairs are typically people who are seen, on a surface level, as quite different from each other in many of the ways described in this chapter. For purposes of multicultural competency, reverse mentoring recognizes the value in young leaders and creates a space and opportunity for older leaders to accept this input.[63] The reverse mentoring process provides the opportunity for leaders, both young and older, to build and strengthen the core EI skills of self-awareness and empathy. With reverse mentorship, it is easy to see the inextricably complementary nature of strong EI skills and multicultural competency and leadership—one cannot exist without consideration and inclusion of the others.

3. Trust and Virtual Teams

Prior to the pandemic, research on virtual teams explored the benefits and challenges of creating and managing virtual teams, revealing best practices for team effectiveness.[64] Not surprisingly, trust was identified as the key ingredient necessary for virtual teams to operate with the highest degree of function.[65] The research showed that an early in-person meeting allowed a team to build trust in ways that virtual-only meetings could not match.[66]

Before the pandemic, teams could always decide to meet in person when necessary to support their work needs (communication, trust building, sharing of ideas, etc.) So what happens after a multiyear pandemic during which teams formed without any in-person contact; meeting in person was neither possible nor desirable; virtual meetings became the norm; and everyone felt a strain on their interpersonal skills, a struggle to build community, and the loss of traditional friendships

("Let's go hang out!")? The pandemic provided researchers with a unique opportunity to study the operation and functioning of virtual teams as revealed under these unforeseen and unforgiving circumstances, to validate and update prior best practices, and to provide key insights into the use of virtual teams in the future.

Trust-related challenges. Trust continues to be crucial to virtually all aspects of team collaboration. In the 2021 study *Virtual Teams in Times of Pandemic: Factors That Influence Performance*, trust was found to be the most significant variable for the performance of virtual teams.[67] Trust "helps build a collective identity between geographically dispersed team members" and is a key component of successful team collaboration and effectiveness.[68] Thus, trust can determine whether team members ask each other for help, share feedback, and discuss issues and conflict—all of which have significant effects on team performance.[69]

Studies also, not surprisingly, found communication to be one of the fundamental challenges of pandemic virtual teams. In-office work enables spontaneous, unplanned exchanges between coworkers before or after meetings, in office common areas, or around the proverbial water cooler. The elimination of these interactions can reduce employee feelings of connectedness and belonging to a cohesive team, as well as trust in that team and its leaders.[70]

In addition to building trust and effective communication, remote teams face additional challenges to productivity and satisfaction in their work arising from barriers in geography, time, cultural difference, and technology. In conjunction, these barriers hinder the sharing of information, the effectiveness of collaboration, and the ease of spontaneous and social interactions between team members. For example, geographic distance has been shown to create challenges for workers regarding their awareness of other colleagues, the motivation that the presence of others brings, the establishment of trust in coworkers, and the alignment of incentives and goals, to name a few.[71] This is amplified by virtual teams becoming even more culturally diverse.[72] At their core, these challenges can erode employees' trust in their team leaders and their organization, which in turn threatens employee and team productivity.

Seemingly, the studies are right back at the base of the Lencioni pyramid—absence of trust—which is where the core EI skills of self-awareness and self-management can make the difference between the path of distrust and dysfunction and the path of trust and success.

EI skills as a way to address challenges. Fortunately, pandemic-based research on remote work revealed new and modified best practices for remote teams—and their leaders. These best practices are focused on filling the communication gaps left by the loss of in-person interactions and on fostering trust between employees. Filling these gaps means using EI skills—self-awareness and empathy in particular—that translate into taking the time and energy and being vulnerable enough to engage directly with others. During the pandemic, when it was so easy to stay home alone, effective and authentic leaders reached out, listened, and shared with others in order to sustain motivation, inspiration, and the joint mission.

Addressing both challenges (trust and communication) can help improve outcomes in employee productivity, satisfaction, and psychological health. On the last point, team leaders should commit to ensuring that their team members feel psychologically safe—meaning included and comfortable enough to learn, contribute, and challenge the status quo.[73] Employees who feel psychologically safe will take appropriate risks, speak up with concerns, and take more initiative on projects and opportunities.

Team leaders play a critical role in promoting and facilitating communication among the members of virtual teams and need to compensate for the elements of communication lost in a virtual environment, such as spontaneous communication and nonverbal cues.[74] Effective team leaders establish seamless communication within their teams, which in turn fosters trust among team members.[75] Spontaneous and informal communication also fosters feelings of belonging on teams and helps facilitate feedback sharing.[76] Positive perceptions of leadership communication have been found to result in positive perceptions of performance by team members.[77]

Leaders can work to build trust within their virtual teams by engaging in activities such as one-on-one meetings, facilitating the use of communication channels, and promoting synchronous information exchange. "High levels of consistent communication between leaders and team members [are] positively related to trust and engagement within virtual teams."[78] Key examples of how leaders can build trust through communication in virtual settings include sharing the team vision and goals, delegating responsibility (promoting self-leadership), and increasing the frequency of communication.[79]

The use of technology is integral to facilitating communication and promoting trust among virtual teams. Technologies that facilitate rich discourse, spontaneous and informal communication, and face-to-face communication are necessary, such as videoconferencing, virtual breakout rooms, and instant messaging programs.[80] This is facilitated by technology designed to provide transparency, allowing workers to feel more aware of their teammates and boost visibility.[81] Virtual team performance is positively impacted by the deliberate leveraging of technology to the virtual setting.[82] To effectuate this, institutional and infrastructure tech support, policies, and procedures need to be keyed to support the needs of virtual employees and leaders to facilitate building trust. Sean Newman and Robert Ford outlined five steps that leaders can take to ensure successful culture and productivity for their virtual teams:

1. Establish and explain the new reality.
2. Sustain the corporate culture and reinforce the perception of leader trustworthiness.
3. Upgrade leadership communication tools and techniques.
4. Encourage shared leadership among team members.
5. Create and periodically perform alignment audits to ensure that virtual employees are aligned with the organization's cultural values.[83]

4. Building Community and Relationships Post-Pandemic

Earlier in this chapter, we discussed the pandemic's effects on individuals: isolation, degradation of interpersonal skills, breakdown of friendships, and a loss of value in social capital. Rebuilding trust and a belief in the value of trust in virtual and in-person settings alike are keys to reversing these impacts. Leaders with strong emotional intelligence naturally build trust between themselves and others through relationship management, which in turn inspires others to do the same in their relations. A great deal of this building and rebuilding happens through working together—on teams.

In addition, we know from pre-pandemic research that many people in powerful roles—that is, leaders—tend to have low empathy. They are less likely "to 'adopt another person's visual perspective,' less likely to 'take into account that other people [do] not possess their privileged knowledge,' and are less accurate in identifying emotions in others.'"[84] The obvious conclusion is that lawyers and leaders in such positions need to build this skill. We see this gap as an opportunity. In a post-pandemic world, those leaders who cannot recognize the need for change and fail to step up their own empathy and apply it in teams to inspire others will not be seen and employed as leaders for long. The opportunity can be fully gained through understanding the connections between emotional intelligence and teamwork. Through understanding the core aspects of teamwork and its benefits, the importance of trust, and the interpersonal needs of others, leaders in this post-pandemic environment who effectively draw on strong levels of self-awareness and empathy to rebuild their communities and relationships in light of the impact of the pandemic will thrive. You are in a new world order here and poised to apply your skills and experiences to effectively lead others in this space.

E. Working on Teams

We have been taught, and our society thrives on, the concept of individual success. Think about any field or genre, real or fictional, and you will find the individual highlighted for success: George Washington, Frederick Douglass, Perry Mason, Abraham Lincoln, Amelia Earhart, Susan B. Anthony, Jane Addams, Alexander Graham Bell, Martin Luther King Jr., Cesar Chavez, Gloria Steinem, Steve Jobs, Sitting Bull, Bill Gates, Serena Williams, Michael Jordan. But behind or with every individual, there is at least one lesser-known partner, and usually an entire team. The partner or team members are essential to the success of the endeavor.

There is no escaping working on teams in the law, even though legal education and the law value individualism over collective and collaborative efforts. Over two decades ago, Cliff wrote about how certain aspects of legal education and the law devalue teams and cooperation or collaboration.[85] Cliff then coauthored a book devoted to understanding how law students and lawyers can work better on teams.[86] Obviously, we will not repeat here all that is written there, but suffice it to say that EI competencies and MBTI® preferences play a huge role in the success of teams, the success of individuals on teams, and the success of leaders who utilize teams (which is everyone!). Many of you experienced this during the pandemic when teamwork (and virtual teams) became an even more integral part of education and work.

Teams are the ultimate site for relationship awareness, specifically the development and application of empathy, and relationship management. Emotional intelligence teaches us not only how to manage ourselves but also, and most importantly, how to manage relationships on a team. How successful one is at that probably correlates to whether one is a team member (leading oneself), a lateral leader (taking on some responsibility role), or a team leader (acting as a recognized, elected, or assigned leader of the team).

In this section, we bring together these EI competencies in the context of teamwork by examining the benefits of working in groups, debunking concerns about teamwork, and explaining how a variety of MBTI® personality types can be leveraged for the good of the team—all of which implicates strengths in self-awareness, self-management, empathy, and building and maintaining relationships.

1. Benefits of Working in Groups

Lawyers must recognize the limitations of the seven blind men (*see* Chapter II) and must work with a team to the extent that they cannot cover all divergent views, all experiences, and all areas of the law by themselves. In this respect, having a team with members of divergent views and experiences and providing the space within which to understand, appreciate, and incorporate those views is vital to the team's success. This is true regardless of whether the success is perceived by the members themselves or recognized by the external evaluators of the team's product. Not only is this how lawyers work, irrespective of the work setting, but this is also how great things happen.[87] As David Chavkin wrote, teamwork "envisions a process in which respectful interaction brings the talents of all parties to bear on a problem."[88]

The myth of individual achievement. In our society, there is the stock story of the American Dream. It is a stock story because, when invoked, everyone understands its meaning: anyone can get ahead in America if they just work hard. "Work hard and you will succeed" is the message that regularly draws immigrants to our shores.

You may even categorize your journey to law school as fitting this individual achievement myth. Why is it a myth? The answer is partly because we do not hear or appreciate stories where someone works hard and fails (whatever the reason), and partly, perhaps even more so, because no one really does anything purely on their own. People are usually working with others: Could you have made it to or through law school so successfully without the support of others, whether that support was emotional, social, intellectual, or financial? In fact, the research also debunks the myth by showing, repeatedly, that team efforts actually exceed the efforts of individuals and that individuals perform better when working with others. This idea of cooperative and collaborative work is really the fundamental cornerstone of achievement.

Cooperative and collaborative work. To drive home your understanding that the individual achiever is not only a myth but also a bad conception of how one works in the law (and a really bad way for leaders to approach their work!), we take a quick dive into the deep research on cooperative and collaborative learning.[89] Research shows that both cognitive and substantive benefits come from working in groups.

The cognitive benefits include hearing other opinions, learning how others reason, and learning how others write and learn. This should resonate with law students and lawyers, who are always looking for ways to expand their ability to see things from different perspectives to ensure that they are considering all options and avenues for their clients.

Research at all levels of learning and in a variety of fields reveals key substantive benefits from working in groups—benefits that apply equally in education and employment—including the following:

- Higher level of individual achievement
- Greater analytical ability (a higher level of thinking)
- Increase in reflective thinking
- Development of problem-solving techniques
- Better grasp of the relationship between background information and tasks in carrying out the process
- Ready embrace of the task of learning
- Better retention of subject matter[90]

To be sure, in group work there is a trade-off: you sacrifice time for quality. Put more simply, working in a group takes more time, but it results in higher-level, longer-lasting individual and group achievement. In the EI context, a leader's investment of time in building and maintaining relationships will yield significant individual and group benefits.

And there is even more to gain from cooperative and collaborative efforts. Research also shows additional emotional and psychological benefits to working in a group. According to research on law students, team members get to know each other better, learn how to work together to overcome disagreements, receive support from and provide support to each other, have less anxiety, and gain self-esteem.[91] Who would not want to hire and work with revitalized and team-oriented employees who know the value of building trust and relationships, conflict management, mutual understanding, stress reduction, and confidence?

The value of a heterogeneous group. It is important to note that all groups are not created equal. When you bring together a homogenous group of individuals to solve a problem, you necessarily limit the possible outcomes to those within the knowledge and experiences of those like individuals. All may view the problem, strategies, and solutions in a fairly similar way. However, when you bring together a heterogenous group of individuals with different backgrounds, experiences, and cultures, you expand the realm of possible ways to look at the problem, strategies to address it, and solutions that might be both feasible and in the client's interest—and you will likely improve the individual quality of your workforce in the process. Relating this back to empathy, building such a diverse and inclusive team is the first step, but ensuring that everyone listens, understands, and considers other perspectives is equally necessary.

2. Concerns about Teamwork—Debunked

Particular challenges to teamwork in the law exist because many law students and lawyers have achieved their current station and status as a result of individual merit, for example, earning high test scores or accolades. Thus, many of us harbor some inherent fear that less-accomplished individuals will bring down our work product; slow our learning and advancement; and, in the cataclysmic view, derail our career. Nothing could be further from reality.

Working on a team is all about building and maintaining relationships, as previously discussed. Thus, your EI skills combined with the four stages of relationship development, the ABCD model of trust building, and insights on working together can alleviate many concerns from the start. Emotionally intelligent lawyers have awareness of their fears (beliefs) about group work and can reframe them into more positive and productive expectations. With awareness of your concerns about group work, you can work to prevent the fears from becoming reality. Without self-awareness of your beliefs about group work, you are at higher risk of entering the team in a negative space.

Negative expectations largely unmet. In the research on cooperative and collaborative work among law students, the students entered group work with significant negative expectations. They were concerned about disagreements in writing style and analytical processes, students not pulling their weight, building rapport and being able to work with someone else, and needing to compromise to the detriment of quality, as well as generalized negative expectations.[92] To be fair, a small amount of this was attributable to prior bad experience. To be even fairer, much of this was the result of prior education that failed to recognize and implement cooperative and collaborative learning, either from the start or at key times (such as the start of high school, college, etc.).

So, what did the students, post-teamwork, identify as actual negative experiences? The list was short and included nothing about loss of quality. The main negative experiences were that it was hard to write together (a truism if there ever was one) and that it took more time (also expected). Students did report a perception that their partner did not do enough, but the reporting percentage was significantly lower (10 percent) than what they anticipated prior to the teamwork (22 percent).[93]

Positive expectations exceeded. The researchers also asked students about their positive expectations and positive experiences.

Their expectations were as follows:[94]

Pre-Teamwork Expectation of Teamwork Experience	Percent of Students Expecting the Named Experience
Share/challenge/criticize each other's ideas/work	43%
Improve writing process/skills	20%
Opportunity to receive feedback	20%
Share workload	15%
General unspecified positive expectations	15%
Good/high quality of final product	12%
Improve research/research skills	11%

The actual teamwork experiences of the students affirmed the Teton Lakota Indian saying "Tell me and I'll listen. Show me and I'll understand. Involve me and I'll learn." Post-teamwork, the students' reported positive experiences were as follows:[95]

Post-Teamwork Report of Teamwork Experience	Percent of Students Reporting the Named Experience
Engaged in healthy/helpful disagreement/ debate/brainstorming	33%
Good rapport with partner	28%
Less able to procrastinate/kept to schedule	26%
Never felt frustrated	25%
Rewarding/positive writing process	21%
Better research than individual research product	15%
Saw different (partner's) approach	13%
Considered new ideas	12%
Better final product than individual product	11%

The positive experiences show gains in relationships (good rapport, no frustration), gains in methods (healthy debate, better research, new ideas, new approaches), and gains in the work product.

Productive collaboration and EI competencies. To better understand the interplay between relationships, teamwork, and EI competencies, let's look at the reported experience from one pairing:

> Andy and Steve were the odd couple.... Andy came to Northwestern University School of Law ("Northwestern") from Iowa, and Steve hailed from Louisiana. Andy was tall and quiet, while Steve effused Southern politeness. They did not know each other before their professor randomly assigned them to rewrite their open research office memorandum—together—and for a grade. Each came to the task with Bs on his own memo, but they received a grade of "A" on their joint rewrite. The difference was collaboration, which allowed them to draw on their complementary strengths and minimize their weaknesses.*

* Their joint paper showed strengths that neither student's prior work had shown. Both students reported to their professor that collaboration was the key factor in improving their work. They felt that they both performed at a higher level when each had to

> Together, they produced work of a quality that neither had been able to achieve alone. Steve had a knack for telling a compelling story with the facts. He knew which facts and points of law were most important, but his structure was not always clear. Andy, in contrast, had a strong grasp of organization. He understood how to arrange the law and facts in the most logical order, but his writing style needed improvement. By working together, they each learned about writing in a way that improved their later individual work.** As another benefit of working collaboratively, the former strangers became close friends.[96]

So why were Andy and Steve able to achieve such productive collaboration when so many other partnerships do not? Why were they able to capitalize on their differences and balance one another out? They brought the best out in one another. But how? What we are interested in is why they were able to "collaborate." What are the key differentiating factors that allowed them to work so productively together as a team when their cultural backgrounds, varying strengths, and personalities were so different?

When we really break down collaboration, we find the first three EI competencies on center stage: self-awareness, self-management, and empathy. Healthy team functioning comes about when each individual team member practices these EI competencies. Think about it for a minute. Successful teamwork requires the following:

- *Self-Awareness.* Team members invoke an ongoing process throughout the project of practicing awareness of their attitude about the project and about the other members and how those beliefs/expectations make them feel.
- *Self-Management.* Team members reframe negative expectations into a positive outlook. Bringing an optimistic outlook and challenging negative cognitive reactions as they arise are key to making relationships work.

---

defend his analysis to his partner. Both reported that when working as a team, each had to respond immediately to the other's comments. They felt that this practice forced them to consider their writing more carefully than if they had waited to receive the professor's comments days later.

** Both received higher individual grades on subsequent papers than on their individual pre-collaboration work.

- *Empathy.* Team members continuously monitor how other members are doing. Teams thrive when the individuals think about each other.

Clearly, Steve and Andy both practiced self-awareness of any potential negative expectations/feelings about the project, group work, and the other's cultural differences. With self-awareness of any negative expectations (cultural (implicit) biases), they were able to self-manage and shift their thinking toward how they could work together to capitalize on their unique strengths. By putting themselves in each other's shoes and thinking about the other person's perspective, trying to really understand it, and looking for ways to see if they could really get where the other person was coming from, they nurtured a healthy relationship.

As an emotionally intelligent lawyer leader of teams, your job is to bring these same competencies and also manage each team member's abilities and the execution of those abilities on the team, working to develop them when necessary.

↑↓↑

SELF-DISCOVERY EXERCISE 25: YOUR TEAM EXPERIENCE

1. Think about your last team project. (It is fine if it was just a partnership.) What was the project? Recall the specifics of the context and team goal.
2. What expectations did you bring to the teamwork? Reflect on how you felt about the assignment.
3. What were your expectations about collaboration? Did you enter the project with awareness of those beliefs?
4. What beliefs about your team members did you have at the beginning and at the end of the project?
5. Now reflect on how your beliefs and expectations played out for you positively and negatively in the group process.

↑↓↑

REFLECTIVE WRITING 21

Think about a time when you were on a team (regardless of your role or position) and there was disagreement among the team members about what to do, how to do it, who should do it, how your results should be presented, or another core aspect of the work.

→ What was your role in the disagreement?

→ What was the outcome, and how would you characterize it (positive, negative, best possible outcome)?

→ Given what you now know about empathy and teams, what could you have done or done differently to make the outcome better (*better* meaning better for the team, the team members, the organization, or the client—not necessarily in that priority order)?

→ What kept you from taking that action or a different action?

3. MBTI® and Team Relationships

One final note on teams and self-awareness involves the Myers-Briggs Type Indicator® (MBTI®), a personality tool that measures our unconscious preferences along four dimensions of complementary strengths, which can also be seen as default positions (see Chapter III). In the MBTI® system, each individual is assigned a personality type based on the particular combination of preferences that they exhibit. The MBTI® is like a personal barometer of how we will respond if we do not exercise self-awareness and self-management. In developing relationships, individuals need to be cognizant of these default positions, how each corresponds to strengths or weaknesses, and how each complements or complicates the process.

Let's unpack the subparts of the MBTI® and then discuss further its relation to teams and relationships.

MBTI® preferences. Here is a nutshell version of each preference and its dimensions:

- *Introverts* are needed for conceptualizing the problem and looking deeply into issues.
- *Extroverts* are needed for knowing the situational variables and for making the social contacts needed in taking action.

- *Sensing* types are needed for knowing the facts and realities necessary in the planning stages and for working out details in the implementation stage.
- *Intuitive* types are needed for seeing the big picture, forging into new areas, and coming up with new possibilities.
- *Thinking* types are needed for spotting the flaws and inconsistencies of a plan.
- *Feeling* types are needed for seeing the human side, and for persuasion.
- *Judging* types are needed for system, organization, and decisiveness.
- *Perceiving* types are needed for openness and understanding, and for flexibility when the system breaks down.[97]

Need for a variety of personality types—and for self-awareness. It seems clear that in order to operate optimally, teams need members with every preference—and thus a variety of personality types. They also need team members who recognize the value of their default strengths and those of others.

Similar personality types, and people with obvious similarities generally, are naturally drawn together, and the results can be disastrous. For instance, if a team ends up with all perceivers and no judgers, then who creates the agenda, and how will the team know when it is done?

While every team cannot have every personality type, self-awareness and relationship awareness are key to solving the problem. Once you know your personality type, you also know the complementary strengths needed and can either seek out others with those strengths or try to grow your strengths in those areas to fill the need.

↑↓↑

SELF-DISCOVERY EXERCISE 26: YOUR PERSONALITY TYPE AND TEAMS

Thinking about the strengths and weaknesses of your personality type and your current level of emotional intelligence, answer the following questions:

1. What strengths, abilities, skills, or perspectives do you bring to a team? Balance humility and self-doubt to build an accurate and authentic list.
2. What strengths, abilities, skills, or perspectives would you want in your other team members?
3. If not present in yourself or others, what strengths, abilities, skills, or perspectives would you have to work hard to bring to the team to fill those gaps and aid the team's overall functioning and performance?
4. In anticipation of the situation presented in the preceding question, what can or will you do to build those strengths, abilities, skills, or perspectives in yourself?

F. Managing Conflict

Thus far in this chapter, we have talked about relationships in a variety of ways, all of which center on utilizing your core EI skills of self-awareness, self-management, and empathy to create, establish, grow, and maintain relationships in your personal and professional lives. We have given you a variety of ways to think about this process as well. You can start with flexing those basic EI skills. You can think of relationships in a linear identify-initiate-develop-collaborate approach. Those same four stages can also be seen as a recursive cycle you go through as you build relationships all around you. Alternatively, you can start with concepts of vulnerability and trust to build relationships. Teamwork, too, is really all about relationships, and research has documented the benefits that flow from working within those team-based conditions. The fabric woven from these strands highlights the importance and value of strong relationships, which form the foundation to support ventures into areas where conflict might arise.

1. Positive Contribution of Conflict

Talking about relationship development and trying to navigate the world of working with others necessitates talking about conflict, which many people dread. But is conflict really bad? If as a leader you want to put together a successful team, then you need people who have different experiences, backgrounds, and views. The resulting discussion will hopefully reflect those differences, with the understanding that incorporation of those views has value. If these are the starting premises, then conflict is good.

Substantive conflict is good because it tests ideas and theories, allows for many voices to be heard and incorporated, and, quite simply, involves a robust and thorough discussion. Thus, the group avoids the main pitfalls of teamwork involving little or no conflicting discussion. These pitfalls include groupthink, where consensus is valued over judgment; the Abilene paradox, where everyone agrees to something just because one person suggested an idea and no one wants to question it; and group polarization, where the more extreme individual perspectives intensify the group opinion.

2. Conflict Management and EI Skills

Myriad approaches to conflict, conflict awareness, conflict management, conflict resolution, and conflict transformation exist.[98] However, we believe that the key to choosing an approach lies not so much in understanding a model and its modes or a style and its strengths but in looking at the core elements in each that bring you back to your EI skills.

Raising your level of self-awareness increases your ability to understand how you respond to the presence of conflict or disagreement. Raising your capacity for empathy increases your ability to understand the position of the person, persons, or organizations with which you are in discussion. From this, you understand the parties' interests and perspectives and can then better determine the viability of potential solutions.

To put this differently, self-awareness and empathy help you to understand levels of cooperativeness and assertiveness, and willingness to compromise, which are the core pieces of the five common conflict styles: competing, accommodating, avoiding, compromising, and problem-solving.[99] Self-awareness and empathy allow you to navigate difficult conversations, anticipate disagreement, foster open conversation, and reach solutions that then take those concerns into consideration.[100] When conflict overwhelms you, self-awareness, self-management, and empathy allow you to avoid unproductive modes like shutting down, agreeing with points just to move on, or unnecessarily interrogating persons with different perspectives—and instead share civility and vulnerability that evidences an open mind and receptivity that others will notice and reciprocate.[101] Self-awareness and empathy enable you to transcend cultural, gender, and other societal constructs, which often impede reaching a broader understanding that avoids and resolves conflict, and transform the conversation and conflict into a tool for enhanced outcomes.[102] Using and modeling your EI skills in this manner makes you a leader as others follow your approach.

3. Application of EI Skills as Conflict Management

While most readers will likely agree that self-awareness is necessary for successful conflict management, practicing it may not be as straightforward. So, let's take a minute to review how to use self-awareness in conflict management, including some simple steps to apply the next time you need it.

MATTHEW'S STORY → Rob recently worked with an estate lawyer (let's call him Matthew) who runs his own practice. Matthew built his practice from the ground up, and it had grown exponentially in the past ten years from just Matthew and one paralegal to multiple attorneys and a support staff of over twenty. He was constantly coming to coaching sessions upset at himself for how he was handling errors that his staff had committed. He had been in control of all operations for years, and so he was struggling with the letting go and delegating that was needed to support his firm's growth. As he grew his firm, he came to realize that his reputation was not entirely under his control but was affected by what others thought of him.

Matthew and his accounting team were engaged in an ongoing conflict stemming from errors the team had made that cost the firm money and had made them look bad with a judge. His bookkeeper of many years was on the team, and during one team meeting, it came to light that she had miscalculated an important figure. When he confronted her about the error in front of the team, she pushed back and defended her calculations and approach to the work. He lost control, yelled, and aggressively slid the calculator across the desk in her direction. He was actually correct in his calculation, and the miscalculation was an error on her part; however, who was right in the argument no longer mattered.

He had once again lost control of his emotions; embarrassed a longtime, valuable employee; and appeared (unreasonably) unsupportive in front of several key staff members.

When Rob and Matthew reflected on the meeting and Matthew's reaction, Matthew realized that he was stressed. He knew that his bookkeeper had sent the wrong figures to the judge and to the family involved in the case and that similar mistakes had happened before. However, by focusing on bona fide self-awareness during the coaching session, Matthew realized that he was experiencing stressful thoughts like "We won't get the work if we keep this up," "This will impact our reputation in town," and "Our systems aren't working." And he realized that these thoughts had escalated quickly to "I can't rely on her," "She's not doing her job," and "She's messed this up." His anxieties and fears (core emotional response) about referrals and reputation, which were rational, were manifesting as anger and frustration (secondary emotions). These blaming thoughts in the heat of conflict at a team meeting were triggering an aggressive response. As he gained self-awareness after the fact, he realized that his response to conflict and errors was to be frantic and reactive.

When we are *reactive*, we respond emotionally without mindful awareness of the impact of our words and actions; when we slow down to form a *response*, we are in our wise mind bringing the conscious and unconscious together to achieve our desired outcome. Matthew reworked his narrative in this particular conflict so that when an issue arose again, he could maintain a helpful outlook that would bring about desired actions and responses. Instead of attacking her, he reframed: "Okay, we are making some errors here. Let's figure out the issue and learn together so that we can correct the problem. The entire team will benefit from this." When he practices catching the negative, defensive, fear-based appraisals and reframes them to more productive thoughts, he achieves his desired outcome.

Most importantly, Matthew realized that with self-awareness in teamwork, he could catch his emotional reactions and the behaviors they lead to in time to really think about the impact. Once he recognized that his unconscious preference under stress is to snap and show agitation, Matthew became skilled at noticing any escalating thoughts and anxieties, taking some breaths, thinking about the most effective response, and moving forward mindfully.

With self-awareness came empathy, which moved Matthew even further along in his leadership. He explained that this bookkeeper had been with him for over twenty years and had progressively taken on more responsibility as the firm grew, even managing accountants who had more advanced training. The more we talked about her and his reactions, the more he realized that he had been placing his attention on her shortcomings and mistakes and then dwelling on his anxieties of losing business and status in town. He said, "She's doing an incredible job. She's got a lot on her plate and managing that team really well." He added, "I know she wants to do really good work. I know her well. She never made mistakes like this before having so much responsibility. It's probably too much." By stepping into her shoes and thinking about what her role had become, he was able to lead with compassion and bring about a collaborative and supportive environment.

↔

When faced with conflict on a team, the first step is to recognize that you are in a situation that will require a high degree of self-awareness, being more mindful. You have to know the warning signs and know what your default mode in conflict is. Do you talk more aggressively or shut down? Do you slide calculators across the desk or talk more quickly? The second step is to engage and deploy your self-management strategies (*see* Chapter IV), which allows you to catch those default responses and practice awareness of your thinking. Once you learn your personality tendencies and utilize them in the relation-management context, those around you will see how you respond and either adapt to your behavior or help you in this process, whichever might be most appropriate to the context.

G. Conclusion: The Two Faces of Empathy in Relationship Management

Leading with empathy is the cornerstone of relationship management. There are two keys to harnessing empathy in building successful and healthy relationships: feeling empathy and showing empathy. The first requires trying to put yourself in others' shoes, and the second requires sharing an empathic response with the other person.

Relationship development happens when you have a curiosity about someone. When someone piques your curiosity and you explore that, a relationship usually emerges. The first thing you may want to consider is finding a common interest with this person. When you recognize a connection around a mutual interest, start a conversation around that interest. Bring a curiosity about who this person is. It is often beneficial in this phase to have back-pocket conversation starters, for example, "What's your story?" "Who are you?" "What makes you tick?" and "How did you come to be interested in [the mutual interest]?" Self-awareness also comes in during these interchanges. You have to practice attentional control and keep the focus on maintaining an empathic lens. Why are you curious about this person?

Once you feel empathy for the person and recognize where this person is in life, and recognize that you are curious about this person, you should make some empathic statements. Doing so allows the person to feel seen, that is, to believe that you recognize who they are. When you use empathic statements in relationship management, you allow for the emergence of a feeling of connection. Research supports this notion. Placing highly empathic people on teams results in all team members feeling an increased amount of relationship closeness and positively correlates with team effectiveness.[103] This same study found that members of teams will reciprocate expressions of empathy, and that impulse to reciprocate rises dramatically with higher levels of trust and greater experiences of genuine interpersonal relationship.[104] Highly empathic lawyers and leaders can also help others through the natural and inevitable fluctuations—the ups and downs—of work.[105] In addition, teams with some highly empathic members can more effectively resolve conflict and more effectively communicate, both of which correlate with increased success.[106]

With your new relationship management skills, you hold the power to bring about significant and meaningful change in the institution you work in and the community you live in. Keep seeking opportunities to share these practices to build community within your profession and in your personal life. When you lead with self-awareness, manage your emotions, and seek to understand and appreciate differences in those around you with empathy, you will build and maintain relationships necessary to your success as a twenty-first-century leader in the law.

CHAPTER VII

Emotionally Intelligent Leadership

Filling the Gap in Twenty-First-Century Leadership

ROB TAKING THE LEAD → I was driving to work one winter morning in 2023 when my phone buzzed with a text from my wife. She sent me an article headlined "Is the United States Going to War with China?" I immediately thought to myself, "Stop it, just stop." My heart sunk, my breath disappeared, and my eyes welled up with tears thinking about my three daughters and the world in which they are growing up. My reaction was clearly not about this one article, but the seemingly endless barrage of disheartening global stories out of Asia, the Middle East, and Eastern Europe. The astonishing failure in leadership we are witnessing at such a critical time in history hit me particularly hard in that moment. As my fingers gripped the steering wheel even tighter, my vision went blurry, and I continued to drive to my office, I thought to myself, "How is this possible? What do you mean 'going to war with China'? Some of my colleagues, clients, and best friends are of Chinese descent. The clothes I'm wearing and bag I'm carrying were all made in China." As I drove on through the tears and anguish, distraught from what the title of this article and the seemingly relentless news of global conflict and oppression triggered in me, even not having read a line of it, my mind started to race about the day ahead of me and the state of the world, and specifically about the leadership I would be teaching and practicing all day, both in my role as a clinical psychologist for clients and in my consulting as an executive coach. I thought about my Chinese American client, whom I would see later that day, and what this must bring up for her. I quickly identified that I was scared, sad, and angry. These feelings were not because of China's massive military or because of their alliance with Russia and the potential for World War III, both of which are very concerning, but because of the collective trauma we are experiencing as a result of the lack of social and emotional intelligence in global leadership.

As I thought and drove with tears in my eyes, my mind was flooded with the reality of the limits of human interaction and healthy coping. How quickly we move into a state of fear and resort to physical retaliation or, in this case, military action. How hard it is for us to see what is really happening collectively, emotionally, below the surface. Pushing onward on my commute and nearing my office, where I was sure to be greeted by a staff member or maybe even a client, I wiped tears from my eyes, thinking about how ridiculous it is that we lack such basic skills in social and emotional intelligence in the twenty-first century, repeating mistakes and retaking paths that history has taught us how to avoid. The anger started to brew inside me. I thought, "How did we get here? How did we let this happen? We all want the same things: prosperity, peace, love, happiness, a thriving planet for our children, safety, and opportunities for freedom of choice and lifestyle."

With my background and professional training, I could not help but start thinking about the human brain. How it is wired for survival from the brainstem up and has evolved over time to keep us alive. How we are now in the third or fourth tier of a global pandemic and have all been through this collective trauma, so we are raw with emotion and in a state of hypervigilance to protect and control. The deep fear of loss of control and power and how that makes us uneasy—so that when brief attempts at diplomacy fail, we are quick to resort to military action. My heart sunk lower as I thought about how sad this is and how slim the difference is between any of our ideologies. For the most part, we all want the same thing with subtle differences in how to get there. We approach things differently and look different from one another, and maybe we talk differently, listen to different music, or pray to a different god or deity, but pretty much all of us align on most things on this planet. As a psychologist who has spent the last two decades trying to teach emotional intelligence, self-awareness, empathy, mindfulness, optimism, collaborative teamwork, and resilience in leadership, the thought of a mass war in 2023 was the biggest disappointment of my life. Our global leaders need these fundamental attributes in order to work through conflict and meet the twenty-first-century global challenges, and yet we are falling gravely short at various levels of leadership.

↔

Indeed, the need for strong leadership worldwide is greater than we have seen in generations. While this has been the case for some time, the need is even more pressing due to the advent of technology and social media, which bring with them an overwhelming stream of information and rapid, often unconscious, social influence and change. It is also due to the global pandemic and the growing recognition of systemic inequalities, which arose in part from the Black Lives Matter and #MeToo movements, threats to our planet, and potent cultural divisiveness around the globe. The potential for authoritarian rulers and dictators to rise into leadership roles has grown in the face of these complexities and the fears that come along with them. There are multiple examples of this happening internationally. As the world grapples with existential threats, such as environmental change and nuclear warfare, and with cultural and religious differences, the influence of social media, and as racial and gender equality inches closer in the U.S., the potential for leaders who choose to exploit their power through fearmongering rises.

Chances are high that you have felt the impact of these global challenges at some level in your life. Maybe you hesitate to bring up politics at the family or holiday dinner table now. Or perhaps you have retreated from watching the news because it all seems so overwhelming and negative. Maybe you recognize the reactivity in others and how quick people are to label one another without hearing their story and perspective. Maybe you notice that you have fallen into some of these patterns yourself. Are you quick to judge others for what they choose to wear or for whom they vote? Do you find yourself easily agitated by your neighbors' car bumper stickers or yard signs? Perhaps you feel more distant from coworkers than you have in a long time, believing that they are just "not like you"? Or maybe you notice that you are quicker than ever to react with anger to a colleague's behaviors? These trends are potent, and they are now cultural norms that arise from poor or weak leadership. History teaches us that authoritarian leaders emerge when fear is on the rise; divisiveness and aggression, adversarial tendencies, grandiosity, and fearmongering give the masses a sense of control. The greater problem is that these leadership tendencies exacerbate these trends and push us further away from one another, making it even more difficult to rise to the occasion with collaboration and respect to meet the needs of our times.

These and other challenges facing us as a global community require what we refer to as *twenty-first-century leadership*. The growing number of leaders who have readily abused their power and position reveals both the opportunity for and the qualities needed in twenty-first-century leadership. This leadership is found at the crossroads of self-awareness, self-management, empathy, and the way in which you bring them together into relationships through mentorship, social influence, and healthy teamwork. It is about understanding how you feel as well as how you make others feel. Now more than ever, we need leaders who not only entertain diverse perspectives but also champion the exercise of empathy as a means to collaborate in the process of solving the complexities facing our world today. Twenty-first-century leadership requires training the mind to stay focused on what matters, whether it is paying attention to your own cognitive or emotional reactions or to the experiences of those around you. It requires leading with curiosity and openness, and respecting diverse worldviews and opinions, in order to find common ground and bring out the best in those you lead. As you now know, without self-awareness and attention regulation at your core, it is virtually impossible to be the kind of leader needed today. Through their ideas and deeds, twenty-first-century leaders show the way. They influence the behavior of others in a positive way, for the betterment of all people, and can make change happen. What else does a twenty-first-century leader look like? Quite simply, a twenty-first-century leader looks like you with enhanced EI skills!

Thus far, we have introduced and discussed all four domains of emotional intelligence, focusing on key competencies within each and why they are important to the practice of law. Also, we have introduced deep self-awareness, MBTI® personality type, and unconscious preferences, as well as the need to build on this foundation in teamwork. We have introduced numerous exercises to build and develop the EI competencies, to identify personal values, to establish personal narratives, to explore formative events and influencers, and to articulate your mission in your career. And you have reflected on each. All of these pieces, in combination, form the foundation for and key aspects of leadership in the twenty-first century. Our theory of leadership, *twenty-first-century lead-*

ership, is distinct in its underpinnings (emotional intelligence) and in its *individuality*. You are your best leader—don't try to be someone else's best leader.

In this chapter, we discuss in greater detail what we mean by *twenty-first-century leadership*, first linking it to organizational culture and key metrics of success and briefly discussing two other essential leadership theories that provide some foundational aspects (authentic leadership and resonant leadership). We then provide detail on the *Twenty-First-Century Leadership Profile* and our model for twenty-first-century leadership. We close by highlighting the path forward for you as a *twenty-first-century leader*.

Figure 13 below illustrates the relationship among emotional intelligence, the two other essential leadership theories, authenticity, and other characteristics and how they culminate in the Twenty-First-Century Leadership Profile, which is necessary to address the complexities facing our world today.

FIGURE 13
TWENTY-FIRST-CENTURY LEADERSHIP PROFILE

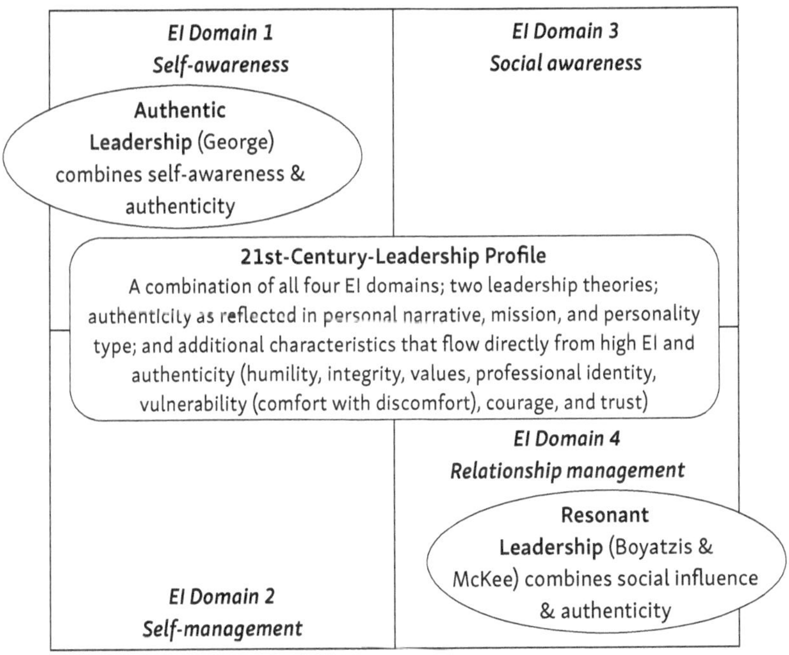

A. Clarifying What We Mean by *Leadership*

It is tempting to provide you with one specific leadership style—a set list of traits or an exact number of specific leadership practices that you could emulate to help you become an effective leader. This has been done time and again throughout the past century. A quick glance at most leadership consultants' bookshelves would show this to be true, with book titles such as *The Ten Best Leadership Practices*, *Five Essential Leadership Styles*, etc. While these texts do outline effective leadership practices, they often send an underlying message that there is a specific "right way" to be a leader. However, research over the past decade has suggested that outstanding leadership is not a one-size-fits-all model. Rather, great leadership emerges with deep self-understanding and a practice of staying true to your values. Leading with emotional intelligence means that you know who you are—that is, you know what you are good at doing and what you like doing, you recognize your shortcomings, and you tune in to the emotions within yourself and others to live out your values congruently.

1. Emotional Intelligence and Organizational Culture

ROB TAKING THE LEAD → In 2015, I was asked to develop a pediatric physician leadership development program for a large health system. Like law, health care has unique leadership challenges. Physician leaders are often charged with the task of balancing clinical roles, managing complex systems, leading their teams, and building new and innovative programs. Health-care organizations are constantly either being bought by larger entities or growing by purchasing smaller practices in order to have a seat at the table with powerful health-care insurance companies. Thus, the pace of change in the practice and systems of medicine and advancement is so fast that it can often lead to health professionals feeling overwhelmed, disenfranchised, and burned out. As health entities grow in size, they simultaneously grow more complex and run the risk of becoming bureaucratic nightmares contributing to physicians' moral injury.

Together with the president of the organization, I studied their leadership needs in the rapidly growing and changing health-care landscape. We quickly recognized that they needed leaders who could collaborate effectively with diverse personalities and backgrounds, connect deeply with the medical professionals they lead, inspire them to stay engaged with integrity, manage high-stress work environments, and stay resilient in the face of adversity. They needed emotional intelligence not only in the select few rising stars in the organization's leadership pipeline but also across the various levels of the organization.

Although the program was scheduled to meet once a month for a year, we fought the urge to choose twelve distinct leadership topics to organize around and instead focused on developing their leaders' emotional intelligence. This was no easy feat with a group of thirty high-achieving physician leaders entering the program. They had varying degrees of emotional intelligence, varying opinions of the value in this brand of leadership development, and varying amounts of motivation for self-growth. After I explained what emotional intelligence is and provided him with the research and theory supporting the importance of EI to leadership, the president of the organization readily agreed to this approach. Like most successful leaders, the more he learned about emotional intelligence and what it truly is, the more the concepts resonated with him, and the more he realized that EI training was exactly what company leadership needed in order to meet the challenges of the twenty-first century. Because he had already successfully led other major metropolitan pediatric hospitals through growth, he recognized that the organization's ability to meet the challenges of health care in the twenty-first century rested on developing self-aware and confident-yet-humble physician leaders who could resonate with patients and colleagues. More specifically, he recognized that by training emerging physician leaders in emotional intelligence and mindfulness, they would become more aware of their default interpersonal and coping tendencies and be able to successfully adjust to the diverse needs of patients, colleagues, and the organization.

I eventually moved into a leadership coaching role at the organization. Their in-house leadership team continues to run the program, which is still focused on developing emotional intelligence—the same cognitive and emotional habits that you have worked on throughout this book. As their leaders have developed greater self-awareness through the program and executive coaching, a culture of openness, humility, congeniality, autonomy, respect, and trust has emerged.

↔

Leadership practices lead to cultural norms, and when they are grounded in emotional intelligence, the organizational culture thrives. Research shows that organizations with emotionally intelligent leaders annually get the highest ratings for workplace culture.[1]

Organizational culture is how a group of people do things. It is the shared values, beliefs, and norms that shape the behavior and interactions of individuals within a company. Aristotle is attributed with the quote "We are what we repeatedly do." And culture matters. It has been found to account for a significant amount of a company's success. It is also progressively what young talent want to know about. In talking about their workplaces, we hear so many young lawyers ask, "What's their culture like?" In other words, they want to know if the workplace has a positive and collaborative atmosphere, or "vibe." They are interested in knowing not only what they will be doing but "how" they will do it. Do the behaviors and interpersonal norms reflect a healthy and positive culture? Healthy corporate culture breeds high levels of engagement, job satisfaction, and commitment.[2] The research is also clear that a company's culture often comes from the organization's leaders themselves. When the leadership is defined by healthy and positive interpersonal and team dynamics—such as optimism, recognition, humility, and empathy, to name a few, all of which come with emotional intelligence—employees feel a sense of belonging, trust, and meaningful connection to the purpose of the organization. All of this translates into performance and productivity.[3]

Leadership behaviors and practices together form an organization's culture; therefore, how you lead determines your company culture, and leadership-culture alignment is vital. Company leadership who possess high emotional intelligence know their purpose, believe in it, feel a sense of ownership and enthusiasm toward it, and pursue it with passion. As its EI-based leadership program has grown, the pediatric health-care organization's culture has become more collaborative and positive, marked by open and transparent communication, collaboration, and teamwork. Staff continue to feel inspired, safety metrics continue to improve, and the organization continues to inch closer to delivering exceptional care with happy doctors who are thriving.

↑↓↑

SELF-DISCOVERY EXERCISE 27: CULTURAL IDENTIFIERS

1. What's the culture like in the organization in which you work? Is there a sense of "how we do things around here"? Is that a positive, a negative, or a mix of the two? (If you are a law student, use your law school, a summer work experience, or a prior work experience to answer the questions in this exercise.)
2. Can you describe your company culture? Think about the norms and customs of the organization. For instance: Are people friendly? Is there open communication and a curiosity about one another? What are the behaviors and norms? Do people support one another when they make mistakes? Do they go out of their way to congratulate each other?
3. What is the purpose or mission of your company? Does the culture align with that purpose? If so, reflect on how it aligns. If not, what kind of culture do you want to develop in your company? What would you notice if the culture was what you desired? Can you describe what you would notice and see? How would it feel?
4. What leadership practices do you notice that really shape your company culture? How would you rate your leadership in terms of emotional intelligence, and how does that impact the culture? Try to draw parallels between leadership, emotional intelligence levels, and the culture.

[STOP and COMPLETE before reading further.]

2. The Ubiquity of Leadership

Leading with emotional intelligence in the law is not about being in a defined or traditional leadership role as much as it is about leading in whatever context you are in with self-awareness, mindfully attuned to your own and others' emotional experiences and how they impact you, and paying attention to others and how they are doing. It is about seeking resonance with the people you work with. It is also about reading the room, paying attention to all interpersonal and emotional dynamics in a given situation so that you can align your behaviors accordingly.

Through our work with lawyers and law students, we have realized that success and wellness come when you approach each day in a mindful, conscious manner. Leadership in this sense is leading every day, everywhere, in every role, and in every situation you find yourself in. Great leaders practice the EI habits that we have taught you in all areas of their life. They do not need to be in a specific, defined leadership role. Leading in the law with emotional intelligence is about staying in touch with yourself and others in a curious and genuine manner in every role in which you might find yourself. Great leadership emerges from emotionally intelligent people who play various roles in any organization or situation.

JEN'S STORY → International Team Projects (ITPs) are semester-long, student-organized comparative law courses. In 2004, the ITP involved two weeks of field research in the country being studied. That year, I (Cliff) went to Cuba with twenty-three students. One of our service goals coincided with two research projects and led us to a church in Havana. The students had made contact with this church because it held group sessions for HIV-positive men recently released from detention and trying to reintegrate into the community. One group of students was researching prostitution and AIDS, and another group was researching post-detention reintegration. Both groups planned to solicit information from the men.

We delivered clothing and supplies amid many thanks and much warm conversation. We were then shepherded into the meeting area, where we sat in the front of the room toward the sides (away from the main table facing the men). Many young men were seated in the pews, talking animatedly. Finally, the meeting started.

Before we had embarked on this trip, a student in our group who was born in Cuba and raised in the U.S. Cuban community briefed us on Cuban Spanish. She said that Cubans typically speak very quickly and drop the last letter or syllable of each word, such that one word runs into the next. Thus, *muchas gracias* becomes something like *muchagracia*. And indeed, the leader of the meeting (and others) spoke so quickly that I could not identify, let alone understand, any word, sentence, or concept that was being discussed between him and the men in attendance. To us, their words were a blur that left all of us looking to each other to see if anyone else understood any better.

After five to ten minutes of speaking at this pace, the man running the meeting introduced one of the students, Jen, and turned the meeting over to her. He stepped aside, indicating that he was not going to facilitate a question-and-answer session for her. Jen cautiously walked to the front-and-center spot behind a small table, summoned all of her energy, and slowly began to address the group in Spanish. She explained to them the purpose of our course, the students' field research, and the information sought, slowly increasing the pace of her speech with each sentence. She answered their questions about the research (which they posed in equally slow and articulate Spanish, respectfully mimicking Jen's articulation) and then started asking the questions that her group had prepared. She readily took the mantle of leadership, established and maintained her presence, set the tone and pace, used her authenticity to gain the men's trust, and opened the door to establish a relationship and allow for information to come forth.

As she continued, other students overcame their initial fears and hesitancy, responded to her example of leadership, and joined her in the front of the room, handing her questions and recording answers. The meeting progressed well, the students got answers to all of their questions, and the meeting ended with the students conversing with the attendees in a friendly manner.

I sat back and beamed with great pride at the display of leadership.

↔

Jen's story allows us to clear away some of the clutter around the meaning of *twenty-first-century leadership*. Some think that leadership only comes from experience—that is, working your way up the ladder, taking on more powerful roles and increasing responsibility. But that leads to a chicken-or-egg conundrum (which comes first: being a leader or having the experience?) or to a vicious circle (how do I get leadership experience if I am not a leader?). Twenty-first-century leadership, though, does not implicate either question. Rather, it is more about how one steps into a role or position among others and leads. It is about paying attention with curiosity, humility, openness, and empathy and then meeting the moment with aligned behaviors. Jen would not have called herself a leader prior to the meeting in the church (and, mind you, she did not immediately see her actions as leadership until it was broken down for her), but she had tapped into her preexisting EI skills and led her classmates. Leadership is not just what someone does at the top of an organization. It is happening around you, all of the time. Jen was able to practice self-awareness of her fears and vulnerabilities, manage those anxieties in the moment, read the room appropriately to recognize what needed to be done to connect or resonate with the group of men, and then progress with culturally sensitive leadership.

Another misconception about leadership is that people learn to lead from examples or models, that is, that they watch others lead in their life, personally or professionally, and try to take on that approach. While you may think that this explains the students who watched Jen lead and then followed her example, their thought process was not "Wow, look at Jen lead" but rather "If she can do that, so can I. So, I am going to go out there with her." In other words, subconsciously, they saw someone *like them* doing something that they feared, and they were *inspired* to do the same. They recognized their emotional fear and were motivated by Jen's actions to use that emotion to power positive action. This is emotional intelligence at work.

3. Varied and Authentic Leadership Styles

Back in 2008, Cliff was creating videos on the law for incoming students. Basically, these videos recorded interviews with faculty as a way to introduce certain concepts about legal education and the legal profession to incoming law students. The desire to address the topic of leadership led to a conversation with a faculty colleague who firmly believed that leadership cannot be taught. Some people, he argued, are born with the charisma and other qualities that make a great leader—period. This colleague's sentiments highlight an outdated view of leadership training that focuses on the emulation of certain identified leadership styles or traits. Using "Jen's Story" above, none of Jen's classmates said to themselves, "Wow, Jen looks like [fill in a proven leader's name]. Therefore, she is now a leader!"

This view of leadership is limiting in several ways. First, it restricts who can be a leader by excluding anyone who does not adhere to a narrowly defined leadership type or style. This in itself may be self-replicating and help to "lock in" past leaders—not necessarily a very inclusive group. Second, if you are trying to be like someone else, then you are not being yourself; you are being inauthentic. The best leader you can be is to be your authentic self.

Focusing on leadership styles or leader role models necessarily excludes many from becoming leaders and misses key aspects of *why* certain leaders are viewed as great, inspirational, or successful. This approach correlates to our tendency to be blinded by traditional leadership displays of confidence, aggressiveness, and narcissism, while overlooking the underlying strengths that are accessible to all who seek to develop leadership skills in their own way.

Even the MBTI® recognizes leadership strength in all personality types:

- Logical decision-makers (TJs): ISTJ, INTJ, ESTJ, ENTJ
- Adaptable thinkers (TPs): ISTP, INTP, ESTP, ENTP
- Benevolent administrators (FJs): ISFJ, INFJ, ESFJ, ENFJ
- Gentle types (FPs): ISFP, INFP, ESFP, ENFP

All personality types can be effective leaders despite their differences in strengths and approach, and within each type, you can see aspects of high emotional intelligence. The logical decision-makers "are tough-minded[] executives ... analytical and instrumental" in their approach to leadership.[4] The adaptable thinkers "are objective, observant, and curious" in their leadership style.[5] The benevolent administrators are "[o]bservant about people and their needs[;] they spend energy making people happy and in bringing harmony into relationships."[6] The gentle types "are adaptable and seek affiliations and harmony"; they are "concerned with the human aspects of problems."[7] While you may strive to develop in ways that will make you more like those you admire, you must also strive to know yourself and understand how your natural tendencies are your leadership style.

↑↓↑

REFLECTIVE WRITING 22

1. Given that personality type is about defaults and aspirational change, what kind of leader is your type? Does that fit feel comfortable to you? If not, how can emotional intelligence enable you to readily move from one type to another?

2. Reflect on your type. What does it suggest about your default leadership style? What are the strengths and challenges inherent in your type?

[STOP and COMPLETE before reading further.]

□ □ □

CLIFF TAKING THE LEAD → I worked in a law firm with two partners. We did many trials together, and I learned a great deal from each. The one with whom I first did trials, and with whom I did more trials overall, was very much a "seat of the pants" attorney. He is the one who, in giving me an assignment early on in a case, would explain the importance of a point by segueing from there into a recitation of his closing argument to the jury (on that point). To him, the measure of a case was in that climactic moment (the closing argument), and he thought presenting that early on would help in understanding the merits of the case. As I said, I learned a great deal from him—particularly that I am not and would not for a long time be comfortable as a lawyer acting "in the moment" (but he did give me a wealth of knowledge and experience to draw on so that I could become more comfortable with my discomfort later in my career).

The first time I did a trial with the other partner, she wanted tabbed binders for every witness, including an outline of the needed testimony, a draft examination, the witness's deposition testimony, and all documents related to this witness, cross-referenced for ease of access and comparison. I was in heaven. This was my style—detailed and organized. In fact, having this style allowed me, at trial, to be effectively spontaneous with a witness. The rule of thumb at trial is that you never ask a question to which you do not know the answer; however, I was able to ask such questions because having the binder allowed me to see (in the moment) the two potential answers to the unasked question and know that both helped us and hurt the witness.

Learning from both attorneys allowed me to see my strengths and weaknesses, to try out each approach, and to ultimately find my own.

↔

B. The State of Leadership Theory: Lessons from One Hundred Years of Research

Leadership theory has come a long way over the past century, and this is a good point to highlight two theories, mentioned earlier in this book, that we encourage you to learn more about as they set the stage for the *Twenty-First-Century Leadership Profile.* Despite a hundred years and well over ten thousand studies, scholars' attempts to identify the definitive leadership styles and characteristics of great leaders have resulted in no single, clear, or definitive profile of an ideal leader. Instead, the research has identified key differentiating factors and styles, the best elements of which fit under the umbrella of emotional intelligence. Two theories, authentic leadership and resonant leadership, are noteworthy in showing how emotional intelligence is an integral and foundational component of leadership.* Let's take a closer look at each to reveal this connection.

1. Authentic Leadership Theory

The authentic leadership theory, created by Bill George, states that when you follow what is most important to you—your most cherished values, your passions and motivations, and your sources of satisfaction in your life—you are leading authentically. People naturally want to follow authentic people.

George has found, through his business career and research, that successful leaders are those who are authentic.[9] They know and follow their passion, apply their values, and find their purpose. Based on interviews with hundreds of the most successful executives in the world, George suggests that successful leadership takes conscious development and re-

* While we only address two models, we humbly assert that if you survey other leadership models, you will find elements of emotional intelligence acting as the glue holding the pieces together, the joint compound allowing pieces to fit and engage with each other, or the gap filler enabling one to get from point A to point B with ease. Some of this will be packaged in courage, transformation, etc., which are about the ability to manage one's feelings, have empathy for others, and inspire others to work with you.[8]

quires being and staying true to your life story. He utilizes the metaphor of a compass to highlight how successful leaders stay oriented to what matters most to them. His research acknowledges the importance of having a calling and pursuing it with passion, highlighting the significance of purpose.

The exercises and ideas in this book are intended to help you build your own emotional intelligence, part of which involves seeing and appreciating the connection between emotional intelligence and authenticity. Through passion mapping and writing out your life timeline, you have learned that key defining moments and influencers have helped to form the values and habits that you champion today. Along with this self-awareness comes awareness of what you are naturally good at doing and of your passions or mission statement. Practicing mindfulness, both formally and informally, will allow you to notice how you react to various day-to-day situations, and this in turn will allow you to stay connected to what matters most to you and maintain your true direction. Others will feel your authenticity and want to follow you.

As George noted and we discussed earlier, people respond to authenticity. We are all probably aware of this more in the political arena than in the business world (i.e., beyond the place where we work). For example, during every election season, candidates for office, especially presidential candidates, share their personal narratives in an effort to tap into voters' desire for authenticity and hopefully inspire these voters to cast ballots for them. As he considered running for president in the 2020 election, Howard Schultz, founder of Starbucks, shared his personal narrative of having to work to support his family at a young age after his father suffered a devastating accident and could no longer support the family. Schultz parlayed his authentic story into why he advocated certain health-care policy reforms.

Authenticity reflects aspects of strong self-awareness as well as self-management; these help you to stay focused on your calling, inspiration, and relationship building—all components of emotional intelligence. When your story and values authentically resonate with others, they become more open to your leadership. Developing your emotional intelligence is what allows you to take the skills you have learned and transform yourself into a leader.

2. Resonant Leadership Theory

The second current theoretical framework is resonant leadership theory, put forward by Richard Boyatzis and Annie McKee.[10] The core tenet of resonant leadership is that great leaders move us. They build resonant relationships with those around them by way of their emotional and social skills. By being tuned into others and what makes them tick, resonant leaders are able to inspire their organization.

Boyatzis and McKee highlight the role of emotional intelligence, mindfulness, and compassion in great leaders' ability to maintain resonance with the people they lead. Leaders with high levels of emotional intelligence are able to effectively manage their own responses and mood. As discussed in the preceding chapter on relationship management, these leaders are more likely to develop social intelligence, which informs how they understand and interact with others. "Leaders who develop[] emotional and social intelligence are effective because they act in ways that leave the people around them feeling stronger and more capable."[11]

3. Combination of Theories

Both George and Boyatzis/McKee have found there are crucial aspects of great leadership. Research shows that authenticity is linked to sustaining one's identity, building grit, experiencing happiness, and achieving workplace satisfaction.[12] And resonance theory builds directly on the strengths that flow from strong emotional intelligence.[13] We encourage you to dive deeper into both theories and see the overlap between them and the way strong emotional intelligence paves the path to being able to resonate effectively with others and to do so with authenticity.

C. Leading in the Law with Emotional Intelligence: The Twenty-First-Century Leadership Profile

In this section, we explain a model of leadership that we refer to as the *Twenty-First-Century Leadership Profile*, which is grounded in lessons that we have learned from our work with law students and lawyers over the past twenty-plus years and the empirical research on lawyer well-being and leadership, and which has at its center emotional intelligence and essential leadership outcomes found to differentiate the exceptional from the average.

Emotional intelligence culminates in the formation of a twenty-first-century leader. Indeed, our work with lawyers and law students has shown us time and again that the development of emotional intelligence brings about the necessary leadership outcomes to navigate current global challenges. Emotional intelligence manifests as leadership behaviors that bring out the best in others, produce highly effective teams, and nurture positive company cultures.

FIGURE 14
TWENTY-FIRST-CENTURY LEADERSHIP PROFILE

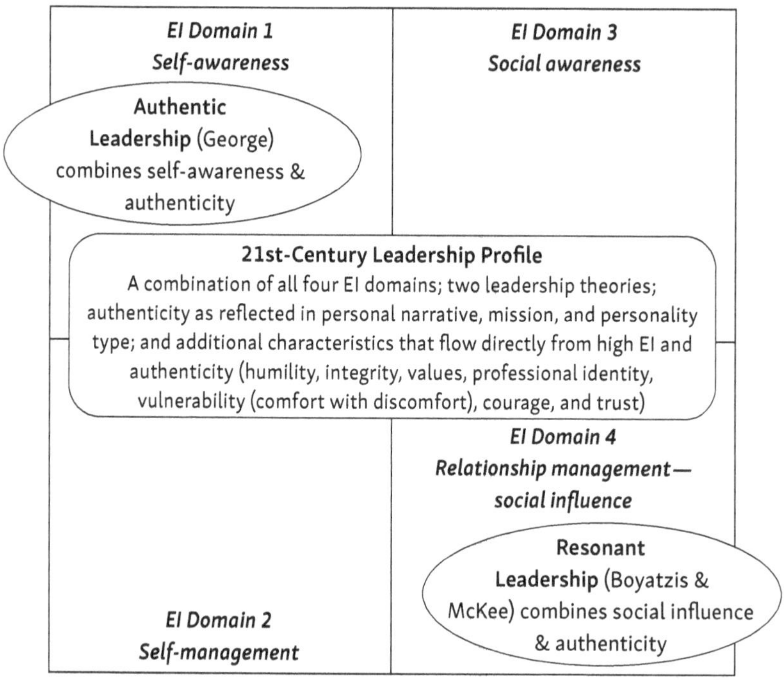

The *Twenty-First-Century Leadership Profile*, as shown in Figure 14 above, illustrates how the EI competencies play a foundational role in twenty-first-century leadership, as well as generally in the role, responsibilities, and work of lawyers. Furthermore, the *Leadership Profile* shows how a twenty-first-century leader needs both authenticity and resonance, borne of strong emotional intelligence. The *Leadership Profile* entails being able to present with authenticity as developed through identification and understanding of personal values, narrative, mission, and default settings (personality type), as well as related points discussed previously. And the *Leadership Profile* is also grounded in several key characteristics that flow from high emotional intelligence and authenticity: humility, integrity, values, professional identity, vulnerability (comfort with discomfort), courage, and trust.

These key characteristics, which often overlap, are all obvious core aspects of leadership, and all are profoundly strengthened by high emotional intelligence. Let's go through each as we drive home what leading in the law with emotional intelligence really looks like, and how it is not only the recipe for success and wellness for lawyers but also a recipe to successfully navigate the challenges before us as a global community.

1. Humility

Humility is, in essence, neither putting yourself ahead of nor behind others. It is closely related to empathy in terms of opening yourself to others' views, lives, and understanding; and it is about being comfortable sharing space with others.

This requires emotional intelligence on several levels. You first have to recognize when you do not know something—the essence of humility—which comes from in-the-moment self-awareness. You have to use self-management to tap the brakes on your default mode, whether that is grandiosity or withdrawal, and lean in with vulnerability.

Why do twenty-first-century leaders need humility? Because when leaders master humility, they have the courage and authenticity to say when they do not know something. This allows them to bring others into the fold and ultimately allows every team member to feel valued and invested in the mission. Humility is well acknowledged as a key differentiating factor among lawyers—separating those who are good from those who are great.[14] If you have ever worked for an arrogant leader, and chances are you have, you probably know why humility (and being humble) is so important.

Authoritarian leaders and lack of humility. We have to challenge the outdated notion that strong leaders must be arrogant or assertive. Many in the business world still rely far too heavily on authoritarian rule and organizational hierarchy. For some, being a humble leader might even sound like an oxymoron. (But of course, *you* are not now among these individuals because you have challenged these irrational and outdated beliefs!)

It is also important to point out that authoritarian leaders—those who focus more on aggressive and adversarial tactics and express grandiose and self-focused ideals—often lack self-confidence. Have you ever thought about the relationship between narcissism and self-esteem? We often assume that narcissists are "too confident," given that the appearance of overconfidence is inherent in the definition of narcissistic behaviors. But, in reality, overly confident behavior, not overconfidence itself, is the key characteristic of narcissists. In fact, narcissists are typically found to be the most fragile leaders in terms of self-esteem. Think about it for a minute: it takes confidence to be humble. If being humble is saying that you do not know something or admitting your errors and shortcomings—well, that takes confidence. Humility requires trust in yourself and acceptance of who you are; because narcissists do not have these traits, they rely on narcissistic tendencies—like dominance, thinking about themselves excessively, overestimating their importance and significance, and aggressive and adversarial rhetoric—in efforts to protect themselves and their fragility.[15]

These are defense mechanisms, and ones to watch out for in yourself and others. When you see them in yourself, tune in, check in with yourself, ask yourself what you are feeling insecure about, and see if you can practice some humility. If you see these practices in others, practice empathy. We often react strongly to narcissists because they are so off-putting, but highly emotionally intelligent leaders see these protective skills as just that—defenses—and react by validating and supporting in order to get the narcissists to lower their shield, and then they connect with the narcissists to help them grow.

Humility and leadership. Mounting empirical evidence supports the importance of humility in leadership. Researchers Brad Owens and David Heckman tested a theoretical framework of leader humility, based on over six hundred people across one hundred and sixty one teams, and found that when leaders behave humbly, followers emulate their behaviors; this creates a shared interpersonal team process that Owens and Heckman refer to as *collective humility*.[16] Their groundbreaking, gold-standard research suggests, first, that leader behavior can spread via social contagion and, second, that leadership humility positively influences team performance.

Leaders who practice humility create a culture of success. Social learning theory teaches us that employee behavior can be powerfully influenced by leaders consistently modeling the characteristics that they hope to see in their organization. In other words, practicing humility and having open dialogues are much more likely to become part of the workplace culture if you model these behaviors than if you simply write them in an employee handbook. Research by Amy Edmondson and Derrick Bransby highlights how leaders who openly share what they do not know as well as their limitations and mistakes create "psychological safety" in the workplace.[17] In an interview, Edmonson defined *psychological safety* as "a workplace where one feels that one's voice is welcome with bad news, questions, concerns, half-baked ideas, and even mistakes."[18] Leaders can *say* that they want to hear these ideas from their team, but it is what they actually *do*—their character as a leader—that determines the level of psychological safety in the workplace.

Ways to incorporate humility as a leader. We know for sure that we should not assume that others see us as humble or that we are already imbued with humility. In Rob's experience as an executive coach, it is common for leaders to feel that they are humble and assume that their colleagues see them as such, only to learn in a 360 assessment that such is not the case. This discrepancy between self- and other-ratings can be an uncomfortable reality to learn, but it is extremely important nonetheless. So what does humility look like in leadership, and how do you practice humility?

First (you guessed it!), humility comes from self-awareness—that is, knowing your strengths and weaknesses and default modes, and then giving the gift of sharing them with those around you. Remember, great leaders seek feedback, listen to it, open up to it, and then share with others their awareness of their limitations. Great leaders do not recognize only their strengths; they recognize areas they are lacking in as well, and then they surround themselves with people who balance their weaknesses. This is humility in action, and it will spread contagiously, forming the culture necessary to tackle the leadership challenges that we face today.

Gratitude and recognition programs are also key ways to demonstrate humility. It is easy to forget to pay attention to the efforts and gifts of those at all levels of the organization when you are so focused on getting the job done. Great leaders train their brain (remember, neuroscientists teach us about the negativity bias—the tendency to dwell on what is not going well) to focus on others' contributions and how they helped to achieve the firm's goals. You could even devise a recognition program to ensure that the culture is one that gives kudos, when warranted, on a regular basis. Such programs have been found to be a hallmark of positive workplace culture and a key predictor of retention and performance.

Furthermore, lawyers show humility in their legal work by taking a client-centered, not lawyer-centered, approach. The cornerstone of our profession is that our clients' interests come ahead of our own—every time. Thus, lawyers who cannot share space with their clients, who are unwilling to put their clients' interests ahead of their own, who do not allow their clients' needs and wants to drive their work, and who do not have their clients equally invested in the representation mission will struggle to have clients, will struggle to have job satisfaction, and may struggle to stay licensed.

↑↓↑

SELF-DISCOVERY EXERCISE 28: FIRM VALUES

1. Locate the websites for five law firms, and explore the sites for information about the firms, particularly what is most prominently displayed.
2. Do you find mission-driven information (a brand or logo that connects lawyers, clients, and work), client-based information (either how the lawyers work for clients or client testimonials to EI skills), or laudatory lawyer-based information (how great this lawyer is, suggesting that this is why you should hire the firm)?
3. Do you see a mission statement? The identification of firm values?

4. If you started your own firm, what would be your mission statement? How would you articulate your firm values?

[STOP and COMPLETE before reading further.]

□ □ □

The focus chosen tells you a great deal about the firm. More and more, firms are rebranding their virtual presence to display internal values, a client-centered practice, concern for the employee well-being, or some combination of these. The difference between firms regarding humility may rest in whether the advice the clients get will be more what the client needs or more what the attorney thinks the client needs. Think about which is better and why. While there may be some situational variance, the best client advice will always start with a focus on the client's needs. As is often said, no client comes into your office and says they want to spend a lot of money and have the case take years to resolve, with the result being that their name and case appear in some law school casebook. They want their issues to be in the foreground and your work to be focused on them—and anything that strays from that equation better not appear on their bill. Humility goes a long way toward achieving these client goals. How do your mission statement and firm values compare with what you found?

Humility will also demonstrate to a wide range of clients that you and your firm are open to their business, concerns, and perspectives—even when that business and those concerns are perspectives that do not necessarily reflect how you have seen the world. If the only people who will follow your leadership are people who look, act, think, and were brought up like you, then you unnecessarily limit the impact of your leadership and business. Extending humility through radical listening and narrative humility (truly setting aside your preconceived ideas and notions to listen to what is being said and why) will create an even wider resonance. This can only happen if you have the self-awareness to initially and repeatedly check whether your thoughts, emotions, and sensations are inhibiting your ability to focus on the client.

CLIFF TAKING THE LEAD → It was a difficult negotiation. We worked very hard to get the right people in the room, several of whom had traveled halfway around the world. All of the third parties were consulted and in agreement: the insurers, coinsurers, international insurers, independent risk managers, and prosecutors. We even employed an outside lawyer to broker the ancillary costs and travel to ensure that every interested person, lawyer or not, was present. We enlisted consultants on language and cultural norms, and our translator was apprised of concerns in that regard. We felt ready. Everyone gathered in the room together—lawyers, clients, and translators. This felt like a major achievement, especially because the other side's lawyer was pushy and controlling and squeezed for every potential drop of money and gain in construction of the language of the deal.

After consultation with experts, I thought I knew how to start the conversation and which topics to avoid. I was particularly nervous as the path through this part of the meeting was foundational and personal. Building this foundation required a healthy amount of "small talk," which is not a strength of mine. In addition, everyone was looking to me to talk through these informalities and then transition to the formal presentation. If we were to have the right dialogue in order to consummate the deal, then I had to talk more than others, both to start the dialogue and to answer questions. We had prepared what we knew to prepare, and I knew that meant there could be more.

The meeting started. I led some small talk for what seemed like a lengthy and healthy amount of time; then I made an overture, sharing the good news that we could give them something monetary, which they had been so adamant about getting and which we had been reserved in wanting to provide. With those words, I no longer needed to listen as I could feel the change in the air in the room. The conversation suddenly went cold. Their eye contact ended, and their body language said "I want to be anywhere but here." I turned to my translator and asked if she would ask them if they wanted to take a break. She said that would be a good idea, she translated, and they left the room quickly.

Knowing I had made a mistake, but not knowing where or what it was, I asked the translator what I had done wrong. She said simply that I did not engage in sufficient small talk. Despite my efforts, I was too abrupt and offended them by shifting to money before making them feel completely comfortable in the office.

A script and planning were only as good as my ability to read how the words and actions were received by others in the room. I am very glad that my ability to read the room caught this quickly. The cure was to humbly accept responsibility for my mistake and work hard to rebuild trust.

When everyone came back, I shifted my energy into humility, acknowledging my error, rekindling the conversation, and allowing the conversation to flow gently. I actively looked for a sign that we could move forward. Fifteen minutes later, viewing smiles on everyone, I got the nod from my translator that I had repaired the rapport through my exercise of humility. I was exhausted, a bit confounded, and grateful for a second chance—and now more keenly aware that my humility could repair the day and that my empathy has ever-expansive room for growth.

Later, I wondered why I had not had the same experience in prior telephone conversations. The answer was clear. I was not listening as carefully in person, perhaps due to having so many people in the room. I was too prepared and confident in my presentation to recognize that I might have missed something—until it was too late. In our phone conversations, I had been keen to pick up more than words, but in person I had turned my sensors off or down, tried to just talk through the topics as planned, and fallen back on habit without using any in-the-moment awareness.

↔

↑↓↑

SELF-DISCOVERY EXERCISE 29: FINDING HUMILITY

1. Think of a situation in your life, either presently or in the recent past, when you were unsure about something or did not have the knowledge or skills necessary to solve it on your own. Describe the situation.
2. How did you respond to the situation? Describe how you handled it.
3. Did you practice humility? If not, how could you have demonstrated humility? What would that have looked like? What would exercising humility have sounded like?

(If you are struggling to come up with an example, try to think of an example of a leader who has exercised humility with you. Describe a specific situation and make notes about how that leader acted and sounded.)

[STOP and COMPLETE before reading further.]

2. Integrity

Ralph Waldo Emerson is credited with saying, "What you do speaks so loudly, I cannot hear what you are saying." Indeed, actions speak louder than words. Great leaders act with strong moral character—that is, leadership integrity—and this has been well documented in the research.[19] Leadership integrity has been established as a key predictor of numerous important organizational, team, and employee outcomes.[20] The idea of a leader's character being central to exceptional leadership is nothing new and is essentially unquestioned by organizational behavior and leadership experts. We include leadership integrity, which is explicitly linked to emotional intelligence, in the *Twenty-First-Century Leadership Profile.*

Ask someone what *integrity* means, and you will get a range of answers: honesty, honor, virtuous, ethical, moral, decent, fair, trustworthy, and sincere. Even the experts have not exactly agreed on the definition.[21] But no matter the definition, a reputation for integrity attracts and keeps clients as well as top talent. People want to entrust their greatest concerns to lawyers and leaders who are honest, truthful, decent, ethical, moral, and virtuous. When people with integrity deliver bad news to us, we are comfortable knowing that is the best we can expect.

Bill George, in highlighting key skills for business leaders, discusses integrity in the context of sticking your neck out.[22] Businesses are not known for taking stances that could help the public and hurt their bottom line—and cynics might say that businesses that do something to help the public are hedging a bet that their principled stance will help their long-term bottom line. However, this business anomaly is the legal profession's mantra. Yes, law is a business, but our bottom-line duty is to our client, balanced with being an officer of the court sworn to abide by the law and the applicable ethical standards. While we are not quite to the medical profession's "do no harm" standard, we are plenty close in terms of elevating our clients' interests above our own. Such integrity implicates vulnerability, communicating the trust that lawyers and leaders need to convey, and is reflective of multiple domains of emotional intelligence.

Emotional intelligence and integrity. Chances are high that you want to lead with integrity in all facets of your life and recognize that integrity is central to exceptional leadership and legal practice. Emotional intelligence is the pathway to get there.

Emotional intelligence is about how you carry yourself and your actions. Just wanting to do something will only take you so far. Self-Discovery Exercises 9 ("Doing the ABCs") and 4 ("Passion Mapping") allowed you to connect with your values and bring that growth into your leadership. Our work has shown us time and again that leaders with high emotional intelligence lead with strong moral character. In guiding you to develop your emotional intelligence, we have focused on growing the psychological and social habits necessary for ethical leadership. Through helping you identify your values and what you firmly believe in, strategies to keep those front and center in your focus, and ways to manage your emotional reactions to prevent deviating from those (especially when emotions are running high), we have enabled you to act with moral character. As we noted at the beginning of this chapter, there is a serious shortage of leadership with integrity—but the research is clear that great leadership is about being honest and acting with integrity, regardless of the circumstances.

Self-awareness and integrity. Most ethical decision-making and conflict-management models highlight the importance of self-awareness. The emphasis is on that first step of navigating ethical dilemmas and conflict with the recognition that you are indeed in a situation involving a moral dilemma. This is the way that emotional intelligence boosts a leader's ability to practice high moral character. Without the ability to recognize that you are in a situation with a moral dilemma or some form of conflict, how you respond will simply be up to fate (a subconscious, default response). As you lead with emotional intelligence, you must continually watch for signs that you are in a situation requiring the exercise of leadership integrity. Maybe there is an uneasy feeling, a temptation, or an easier path that lures or baits you. With self-awareness of these red flags, you have an opportunity to exercise good judgment, a form of self-management. With self-awareness of the myriad emotions and beliefs at work, you have the power to choose your response and ground it in high moral standards.

Can you think of any leaders who have used their emotional intelligence to lead with integrity? Can you think of leaders who have lacked emotional intelligence and thus showed a lack of integrity in their leadership? How could emotional intelligence have helped them? Your leadership integrity will flourish naturally if you remain aware of the various emotional, financial, interpersonal, and team dynamics at work in your professional life and how they influence your decision-making and actions.

3. Values

Any discussion of integrity naturally leads to reiterating the importance of values.[23] Values are at your core individually and organizationally because values are fundamental to your individuality, your mission, and your culture.[24] Not knowing your values means that something else (something unseen, unshared, and inauthentic) is driving your work. It means that you are "flying blind," that is, you either do not know why you are doing what you are doing, or you are unknowingly following someone else's values (which may conflict with your own). This is why individuals have mantras, businesses have brands, and societies have cultures.

We have pressed you to understand your values, where they come from, and how you live by them. You were raised with values, good or bad, that stemmed from the influencers in your life (e.g., adults, religion, school, formative events). You then made choices about these values and, over time, held on to some and let go of others. Knowing your values is key to self-awareness.

Some forces in life, such as law school, will present you with new and different values that, intentionally or not, supplant some of your prior values. Again, research shows that law school replaces intrinsic values, such as self-worth and dedication to principles, with extrinsic values, such as monetary gain, grade-point achievement, and job status.[25] Extrinsic values such as these are not inherently bad; however, if they are inauthentic (i.e., not aligned with your values), then you are on a path that you did not choose, living a life you may not like (whether you realize that now or later), and suffering the emotional, social, and psychological toll that comes with a redirection of your narrative and values.

For twenty-first-century leaders, the challenges in maintaining one's values are ever-present. Again, this is why your personal narrative is so important: you must know it, live by it, and share it openly with others, even when that might be uncomfortable. Self-awareness plays a key role in all of this—you cannot ensure that your actions align with your values if you are not in tune with your personal narrative and values. The *Twenty-First-Century Leadership Profile* is all about keeping track of what is happening with you internally so that your outward actions match your internal values.

↑↓↑

SELF-DISCOVERY EXERCISE 30: FIND YOUR IDEAL SELF

1. What is your ideal self-image?
2. What is your dream vision for yourself and your life (recognizing that what you want now may not be what you want in five, seven, or ten years)? If it helps, break this up into parts—dream vision for work, dream vision for personal life and relationships, and dream vision for voluntarism and community—which will compel you to think about and address how these parts must fit together for you to feel that you are achieving success and happiness.
3. What changes do you need to make to be your *ideal self*?

[STOP and COMPLETE before reading further.]

↑↓↑

SELF-DISCOVERY EXERCISE 31: MY LEGACY

1. What would you wish to have as your legacy in life?
2. In other words, what will remain or continue as a result of your having lived and worked all of these years?

[STOP and COMPLETE before reading further.]

□ □ □

Sometimes the "My Legacy" self-discovery exercise is framed as "writing your own obituary." (We waited to mention this because of the inherently morbid quality to it.)

4. Professional Identity

You and everyone else in the legal profession have a professional identity, the keys to which are how you maintain authenticity and agency over your values and narrative. Either your professional identity will be of your own making, or it will be determined for you by mentors, superiors, or perhaps even those who pressed you to go to law school.

Ideally, you will create your own professional identity. To do this, you must examine your personal values vis-à-vis organizational and societal ones and then determine which to follow in the profession. Then you need work that is consistent with those values, or else you will be forever moving from one dissatisfying job experience to another. Remember that you control your own story—whether in the personal or professional context—and that you control the connection between your values and those of your employment. The sure way to be authentic is to exercise your agency over both from the start.[26]

5. Vulnerability (Comfort with Discomfort)

As just noted, formation of professional identity happens in a socialization process, one that pressures you to give up both authenticity and agency and in this way can change your values.[27] Reckoning with these institutional forces that challenge your values and trying to steady the course of your journey in the law and as a leader reveal a path that can be marked by discomfort.

We all want to be comfortable in our lives, in our work, and in our decisions. Comfort eases stress, and we know that too much stress is bad. However, comfort can also breed complacency, lack of initiative, lack of creativity, and failure to take reasonable chances.

Furthering your personal comfort can also keep you from considering "otherness." As discussed earlier, seeing another perspective and valuing it are key to empathy, and empathy is key to being a twenty-first-century leader. Thus, you must also become comfortable with your discomfort; otherwise, you will just keep doing things the way they always have been done—because it's comfortable.

CLIFF TAKING THE LEAD → I was talking with a friend about how to reenergize his teaching (at his request). He thought his years of teaching had refined and honed his courses to their perfect configuration. But he had told me about an inspirational session on syllabus revision, so I suggested he do that—try revising his syllabus, even though he thought that his current syllabus was perfectly configured after his many years of teaching. He agreed to try and eventually sent me his updated syllabus for some feedback. When I told him that his revised syllabus just presented the same content as the original but in a framing meant to appeal to the millennial generation, he balked.* I suggested that he rebuild the class from scratch. He balked again, falling back on his years of experience in creating great courses.

So, I told him two stories. One was about my Torts teacher, who used a terrible book—it was full of little case squibs (heavily edited paragraphs), six to a page and devoid of reasoning. When we asked him why he used this unreadable and incomprehensible casebook, he was visibly taken aback and said, "This is the book I learned Torts from at [fill in the name of a Top 3 law school]." The second story was about a fire that burned down the economics building when I was an undergrad. At the time, no one was using laptops or desktop computers, and data analysis relied on computers so large that they filled rooms—in other words, people wrote things down on tangible pieces of paper. As a result, most faculty lost all of their lecture notes in this fire, and rather than re-create their teaching from scratch, many just retired.

I pointed out to my friend that the moral of these stories is that sometimes we just need to rebuild something to learn if and how we can do it better. The starting point, though, is to be vulnerable to change and get comfortable with that discomfort. He smiled and added it to his summer projects list.

↔

* *Balk* means to hesitate or be unwilling to accept an idea or take an action. If you are familiar with baseball, then you know that the term also describes an occurrence where a pitcher in baseball makes an impermissible move intended to deceive a base runner, resulting in the umpire's call to allow all base runners to advance one base. I do not mean to suggest that my friend was being deceptive, feigning, or doing anything other than declining to take an action.

These vignettes became particularly salient when the COVID-19 pandemic forced courses to move online. Would teachers approach the challenge by thinking about how to make their existing material and classroom delivery fit into the virtual space? Or, alternatively, would they think about how students engage in the new space and adjust the material and their teaching accordingly? Taking the latter path required a great deal of discomfort, vulnerability, and courage.

Indeed, another way to describe becoming comfortable with discomfort is making ourselves vulnerable. George discussed vulnerability as key to authentic leadership; Brené Brown discussed vulnerability in terms of being yourself.[28] Being willing to make yourself vulnerable is how you show others who you truly are and can be. When you become comfortable with your discomfort, you enable yourself to see and feel things as others do, and you let others see you in a way that is both revealing and inspiring. That combination bolsters your integrity, values, and resilience and helps you to define yourself in ways others cannot help but notice. You will step up and into roles as never before, exhibiting twenty-first-century leadership (as Jen did).

6. Courage

Vulnerability also leads directly to releasing your inner courage, a key attribute (virtue) of every lawyer and leader.[29]

Our first thoughts about courage may well start with heroic images of armed struggle, risk-taking, and rescue of others. "Courage ... requires judgment, and involves acts undertaken in the presence of some form of danger, risk, or personal cost."[30] Erik Larson described Churchill standing on a London rooftop and watching the German bombing of London, literally daring the Germans to come after him.[31] While often conjuring predominantly masculine images, courage is also a decidedly feminine strength. The word *courage* stems from the Latin *cor*, meaning "heart." We all have one, so it is truly a universal trait.

Courage is brought on by the harnessing of emotion (fire!). We may not realize it, but our courage is challenged constantly, whether it is subconsciously driven every time we step into a street shared with vehicles or onto an airplane. Our courage was also challenged at an early age: as children struggle for their identity, the processing of where they fit with others can build courage or tear it down.[32]

Brené Brown has written at length about how courage is a key aspect of being yourself. How many of you in high school tried out for a team or tried to join a group (the jocks, the cheerleaders, the cool kids, the brains, or the burnouts) purely in an attempt to fit in? Or did you have the courage to be yourself? It takes courage to be yourself, to be comfortable with being unique, and to avoid feeling inadequate when peers seek different things than you do.

Law school and the legal profession can be quite similar to high school in these respects. While all law students have excelled (or they would not be where they are), many still struggle to fit in now that they are (most likely) a small fish in a new, bigger pond. If you think about the first year of law school and the wildfire of grades, interviews, and jobs, it epitomizes the idea of getting caught up in the crowd—wanting to and trying to fit in with others or getting caught up in the flow of the crowd. "Braving the wilderness" takes courage.[33] However, being authentic yields untold rewards.[34]

Law students and lawyers have to be courageous. Moral courage means that sometimes you do not go along with the majority or consensus when you have a principled reason not to. In law, this can come up when the deal is close to done, when the appeal is pending, or when the wealthy client really needs advice counter to the firm's financial interest.[35]

How does this relate to being a twenty-first-century leader? Acts of courage inspire others to do the same; thus, when twenty-first-century leaders show courage, they encourage others to act likewise when the circumstances call for it.[36]

7. Trust

The twenty-first-century leader knows how to build trust and share space. Often, leaders focus too much on loyalty without realizing that the best loyalty starts with trust. Loyalty is usually seen as a one-way street: the worker is loyal to the company, the staffer is loyal to the supervisor, the mentee is loyal to the mentor. However, effective leaders and team members need trust, which is inherently two-way. To work together effectively, to be an effective team, and to be an effective leader, trust must flow both ways.

Trust comes from—no surprises here!—personal contact, interpersonal connection (yes, that means empathy and humility), mutual respect, and shared mission, among other things. Looking at this list, you can readily see why virtual teams, which abound in our age of telecommuting, outsourcing, multilocation work, and online courses, might be additionally challenged.[37] The combination of characteristics from which trust emanates reveals a powerful tool for the twenty-first-century leader: building trust by being vulnerable, having courage, knowing your biases, expanding your cultural competence, and being willing to engage with others.[38]

For lawyers, trust is essential. Our clients entrust their greatest concerns to us and expect not only that we will never violate that trust but also that we will lead them to a good resolution. Be mindful that their trust is not blind; as discussed in the previous chapter, trust is built through hard work and earned through vulnerability. What can you do or say to show clients that you understand why they are seeking your help? The answer lies in our prior discussion about listening and empathy, with a healthy dose of honesty and transparency.

CLIFF TAKING THE LEAD → When you cannot give the clients what they want most, be honest. Most clients in my Section 1983 practice came to me because they had been arrested or injured by the police (or both) in violation of a constitutional right. They wanted the police officer fired for what he did (most were men). The law does not provide this form of relief. Most clients became more trusting when I was honest with them from the start, that is, that getting the police officer fired was not something that we could ask for in court. We could ask for money and, in limited circumstances, ask to change policies. In many cases, we had to hope that we would win enough money to convince the city that it was no longer economically feasible to employ the officer. Explaining candidly what we could and could not do helped to establish trust.

↔

Take time to explain. The processes of law can be complex. Clients have some points of reference for the practice of law, like television shows and movies, but these are not always accurate or complete. Clients deserve to know more than we might imagine (the outer boundary being something that must be kept secret per court order). Obviously, not sharing information runs the risk that the client will later learn the information and that you did not share it, thus eroding trust. How you share the information, bringing the law to your client and your client to the law (as opposed to an explanation that makes the client feel like the law is something that only lawyers can comprehend), is key to building this trust and your relationship at the same time.

CLIFF TAKING THE LEAD → As a twenty-first-century leader, you can go further to show your clients that you trust them. In one police brutality trial, we were doing *voir dire* on the jury (the process of asking potential jurors questions to determine if there is any bias that would support excusing the juror). Counsel has a limited number of "strikes"—a tool used that allows counsel to exclude potential jurors without having to give a reason (as long as counsel does not do so based on a protected classification, like striking all women or striking people on the basis of race). We sat at the counsel table with our clients. We had one strike left and two potential jurors to use it on—one had a friend who was a police officer, and the other had a close relative who was a police officer. Who should we use the strike to excuse from the panel? We turned to our clients and explained the situation. One client immediately said, "You pick your friends, not your relatives." We excused the juror with the police officer friend.

In this example, we read the situation and people carefully and built trust with our clients by including them in what easily could have been an attorneys-only decision. Other lawyers might have made the decision themselves (based on the same saying), without consult or sharing reasons. Instead, we readily engaged our clients, brought them into the conversation, and posed the question without judgment on the answer. Had we told them what we thought first or just made the same decision and confirmed with them later, they might have been hesitant to express disagreement and certainly would have thought that we did not appreciate or trust (or value) their judgment.

↔

Recognizing opportunities like this can also be drilled down further—revealing a close connection between trust and empathy and connecting self-awareness and relationship awareness.

It is easy to read obvious signs, like when someone is talking too much or when someone is making no eye contact or is rolling their eyes. But signs are not always obvious, and that is when you need to be able to sense or be more sensitive that something unspoken is happening. Will you notice that one person is not speaking? Or that when one person talks, another person always follows the comment with criticism or by changing the subject? Will you notice that certain speakers of comments, including yourself, limit the ability of others to contribute? Whether these speakers are clients, coworkers, or people who report to you, recognizing these situations and making space for all to contribute builds trust as a two-way street.

Twenty-first-century leaders can read the room when they are speaking and help to change the direction of the conversation to ensure that everyone's voice and perspective are included. Two prior stories in this text exemplify reading the room: one to stop talking (see Chapter VII, "Cliff Taking the Lead," page 255) and the other to ask a question that totally changes the course of the conversation (Chapter III, "Sinead's Story," page 45). This skill will grow with your empathy, trust, and humility because you are necessarily elevating the importance of the thoughts and voices of others—in other words, you are actually putting those thoughts and voices on a level with your own.

D. The Path Forward as a Twenty-First-Century Leader

Today's emerging leaders will bring about a new culture of personal and professional ethos and integrity. Failures of the previous generations of leaders give us insight into twenty-first-century leadership in terms of what is needed and expected in the future. Progressive, grassroots movements have illuminated the failures of this outdated leadership, and the key competencies and skills of twenty-first-century leadership have emerged to address these failures. Twenty-first-century leadership is marked by bringing together self-awareness, social awareness, cultural awareness, openness, compassion, mindfulness, unity, empathy, passion, and authenticity.

The final self-discovery exercise gives you the opportunity to pull together all of the different parts of emotional intelligence to create a personal path for you to follow as a twenty-first-century leader. By completing this final exercise, you will be able to gauge where you are, where you want to go, and what you need to do to get there.

↑↓↑

SELF-DISCOVERY EXERCISE 32: WRITING A GROWTH CONTRACT FOR YOURSELF

Each of the following questions asks you to revisit earlier responses and think deeply about yourself as a twenty-first-century leader.

1. What does it mean to be a twenty-first-century leader?
   a. What do you see as the essential leadership qualities necessary for highly effective twenty-first-century leadership?
   b. How would you measure your emotional intelligence at this point? What are your core EI strengths and areas of growth?
   c. What have you learned about your personality type? What key strengths in your personality are you able to capitalize on, and are there any over-strengths you should monitor?
   d. What do you need to work on, in terms of competencies and skills, to build upon this base?
   e. Choose three to five specific EI habits or skills you have learned in this book and make an action plan to put them in place. When will you practice them?
2. What are your values and personal narrative? Can you translate them into a personal mission statement?
   a. What personal values drive your leadership and career? How will they fit into your professional identity?
   b. What key formative experiences and influencers led you to these values and who you are today?
   c. What is your personal mission statement? Try to write it out, and be specific.
   d. What emotional intelligence skills will you need to achieve that mission?
3. How is leadership important in the area of work that you plan to go into?
   a. How will your EI skills fit within your specific area of law?
   b. Where do you anticipate leadership to arise in your work and roles?

   c. What types of teams will be involved in these leadership situations?
   d. What are your strengths and weaknesses on those teams?
   e. In these professional roles, how will you exercise and develop your leadership?
4. How do you define success?
   a. How, if at all, has your definition of or perspective on success changed in your journey through law school? In your legal career? Through this book?
   b. With some detail, describe yourself and your work five years from now.
5. Now set goals for yourself for what else you need to do with respect to each of the four parts and subparts of emotional intelligence.

Consider your answers to this exercise to constitute a personal growth contract. You have identified your foundation—now build on it with ambition, specificity, and consideration of your ultimate goals. Consider this contract subject to your authenticity and agency, and revisit and revise it from time to time.

□ □ □

You have the power to make positive waves in the organizations, groups, and institutions you work in or with. The call for great leadership is widespread, and the competencies and skills identified in this book pave the path for you as a twenty-first-century leader. How will you use emotional intelligence to become that kind of leader?

We can't wait to see the leader you become! Thank you for letting us be part of your leadership journey!

Endnotes

PREFACE

1. Geetu Bharwaney, Reuven Bar-On, & Adele MacKinlay. (2011). EQ and the Bottom Line: Emotional Intelligence Increases Individual Occupational Performance, Leadership and Organisational Productivity. https://www.eiconsortium.org/pdf/Bharwaney_BarOn_MacKinlay_EQ_and_Bottom_Line.pdf; Patrick Grehan, Rosemary Flanagan, & Robert Malgady. (2011). Successful Graduate Students: The Roles of Personality Traits and Emotional Intelligence: Successful Students. *Psychology in the Schools*, *48*(4), 317–331. https://doi.org/10.1002/pits.20556; Michael Sony & Nandakumar Mekoth. (2016). The Relationship between Emotional Intelligence, Frontline Employee Adaptability, Job Satisfaction, and Job Performance. *Journal of Retailing and Consumer Services*, *30*, 20–32. https://doi.org/10.1016/j.jretconser.2015.12.003.

INTRODUCTION

1. American Bar Association. (Oct. 2017). How Emotional Intelligence Makes You a Better Lawyer. https://www.americanbar.org/news/abanews/publications/youraba/2017/october-2017/how-successful-lawyers-use-emotional-intelligence-to-their-advan/.

2. Some medical school admissions processes assess emotional intelligence through the use of multiple mini interviews:

> The multiple mini interview involves a series of short conversations between you and several different interviewers—instead of the traditional one-on-one or panel interview....
>
> Research shows that having applicants interact with many interviewers, instead of one or two, reduces the chance that interviewer bias affects scoring. Studies have also shown that an applicant's scores on the multiple mini interview are predictive of their performance on clinical clerkships, measures of professionalism, and future scores on clinical exams.

The format can help you convey your cultural sensitivity, maturity, empathy, and reliability—all important physician characteristics that aren't necessarily reflected by Medical College Admission Test® (MCAT) scores and undergraduate grades. Although you may feel nervous about participating in the multiple mini interview, applicants often tell us they enjoyed the process once they've completed it.

NYU Langone Health. (n.d.). What to Expect from the MD Multiple Mini Interview. https://med.nyu.edu/education/md-degree/md-admissions/multiple-mini-interview. *See also* Janine C. Edwards, Eugene K. Johnson, & John B. Molidor. (1990). The Interview in the Admission Process. *Academic Medicine*, *65*(3), 167–177. https://doi.org/10.1097/00001888-199003000-00008; Kevin W. Eva, Jack Rosenfeld, Harold I. Reiter, & Geoffrey R. Norman. (2004). An Admissions OSCE: the multiple mini-interview. *Medical Education*, *38*(3), 314–326. https://doi.org/10.1046/j.1365-2923.2004.01776.x.

3. Dana Joseph, Jing Jin, Daniel Newman, & Ernest O'Boyle. (2015). Why Does Self-Reported Emotional Intelligence Predict Job Performance? A Meta-Analytic Investigation of Mixed EI. *Journal of Applied Psychology*, *100*(2), 298–342. https://doi.org/10.1037/a0037681; Ernest H. O'Boyle, Ronald H. Humphrey, Jeffrey M. Pollack, Thomas H. Hawver, & Paul A. Story. (2011). The Relation between Emotional Intelligence and Job Performance: A meta-analysis. *Journal of Organizational Behavior*, *32*(5), 788–818. https://doi.org/10.1002/job.714.

4. National Soft Skills Association. (2015, Feb. 13). *The Soft Skills Disconnect*. https://www.nationalsoftskills.org/the-soft-skills-disconnect/.

5. Lawrence S. Krieger & Kennon M. Sheldon. (2015). What Makes Lawyers Happy: Data-driven prescription to redefine professional success. *George Washington Law Review*, *83*(2), 554–627. https://heinonline.org/HOL/Page?public=true&handle=hein.journals/gwlr83&div=17&start_page=554&collection=journals; Jerome M. Organ, David B. Jaffe, & Katherine M. Bender. (2016). Suffering in Silence: The survey of law student well-being and the reluctance of law students to seek help for substance use and mental health concerns. *Journal of Legal Education*, *66*(1), 116–156.

6. Patrick R. Krill, Ryan Johnson, & Linda Albert. (2016). The Prevalence of Substance Use and Other Mental Health Concerns among American Attorneys. *Journal of Addiction Medicine*, *10*(1), 46–52. https://doi.org/10.1097/ADM.0000000000000182.

7. Edward L. Deci & Richard M. Ryan. (2012). *Self-Determination Theory*. In Paul A. M. Van Lange, Arie W. Kruglanski, & E. Tory Higgins (Eds.), Handbook of Theories of Social Psychology (pp. 416–436). Sage Publications Ltd. https://doi.org/10.4135/9781446249215.n21; Richard Ryan & Edward Deci. (2000). Self-Determination Theory and the Facilitation of Intrinsic Motivation, Social Development, and Well-Being. *The American Psychologist*, *55*(1), 68–78. https://doi.org/10.1037//0003-066X.55.1.68.

8. Kennon M. Sheldon & Lawrence S. Krieger. (2007). Understanding the Negative Effects of Legal Education on Law Students: A longitudinal test of self-determination theory. *Personality & Social Psychology Bulletin*, *33*(6), 883–897. https://doi.org/10.1177/0146167207301014.

9. Gosta Carlsson & Katarina Karlsson. (1970). Age, Cohorts and the Generation of Generations. *American Sociological Review*, *35*(4), 710–718. https://doi.org/10.2307/2093946.

10. MLA Staff, Major, Lindsey & Africa. (2023, Mar. 27). Gen-Z: Now influencing today's law firm culture. Major, Lindsey & Africa. https://www.mlaglobal.com/en/insights/research/genz-now-influencing-todays-law-firm-culture.

CHAPTER I

1. Shawn Achor. (2018). Big Potential: How transforming the pursuit of success raises our achievement, happiness, and well-being. Crown Currency Publishing Group. (overall success); Emily Amdurer, Richard Boyatzis, Argun Saatcioglu, Melvin Smith, & Scott N. Taylor. (2014). Long Term Impact of Emotional, Social, and Cognitive Intelligence Competencies and GMAT on Career and Life Satisfaction and Career Success. *Frontiers in Psychology*, *5*, 1447–1447. https://doi.org/10.3389/fpsyg.2014.01447 (overall success); Dana Joseph, Jing Jin, Daniel Newman, & Ernest O'Boyle. (2015). Why Does Self-Reported Emotional Intelligence Predict Job Performance? A Meta-Analytic Investigation of Mixed EI. *Journal of Applied Psychology*, *100*(2), 298–342. https://doi.org/10.1037/a0037681 (performance); Nicola Schutte, John M. Malouff, Einar Thorsteinsson, Navjot Bhullar, & Sally Rooke. (2007). A Meta-Analytic Investigation of the Relationship between Emotional Intelligence and Health. *Personality and Individual Differences*, *42*(6), 921–933. https://doi.org/10.1016/j.paid.2006.09.003 (health); Ana Soto-Rubio, Maria del Carmen Giménez-Espert, & Vicente Prado-Gascó. (2020). Effect of Emotional Intelligence and Psychosocial Risks on Burnout, Job Satisfaction, and Nurses' Health during the COVID-19 Pandemic. *International Journal of Environmental Research and Public Health*, *17*(21), 79–98. https://doi.org/10.3390/ijerph17217998 (health).

2. Ki Kim, Nicole L. Cundiff, & Suk B. Choi. (2014). The Influence of Emotional Intelligence on Negotiation Outcomes and the Mediating Effect of Rapport: A structural equation modeling approach. *Negotiation Journal*, *30*(1), 49–68. https://doi.org//10.1111/nejo.12045.

3. Michael Andreychik. (2019). Feeling Your Joy Helps Me to Bear Feeling Your Pain: Examining associations between empathy for others' positive versus negative emotions and burnout. *Personality and Individual Differences*, 137, 147–156. https://doi.org/10.1016/j.paid.2018.08.028; Emma Jones. (2018). Making Practice More Affective: Emotional intelligence as a legal meta-competency. *European Journal of Current Legal Issues*, *24*(1). http://webjcli.org/article/view/565; Richard D. Lane, Eric M. Reiman, Beatrice Axelrod, Lang-Shen Yun, Andrew Holmes, & Gary E. Schwartz. (1998). Neural Correlates of Levels of Emotional Awareness: Evidence of an interaction between emotion and attention in the anterior cingulate cortex. *Journal of Cognitive Neuroscience*, *10*(4), 525–535. https://doi.org/10.1162/089892998562924; Kristen Konrad Tiscione. (2019). Feelthinking Like a Lawyer: The role of emotion in legal reasoning and decision-making. *Wake Forest Law Review*, *54*(4), 1159–1196.

4. Goizueta Business School, Emory University. (n.d.). Goizueta Business Principle No. 76: Lead with your head and your heart. https://goizueta.emory.edu/about/principled-leadership; Melissa Korn. (2013, May 1). B-Schools Know How You Think, but How Do You Feel?. Wall Street Journal. http://www.wsj.com/articles/SB10001424127887324582004578456770420379666 (citing other business schools as well); Brittany Wisniewski. (2022, Aug. 10). Kellogg Application Tips: Written and video essays. Northwestern Kellogg School of Management. https://www.kellogg.northwestern.edu/news/blog/2022/08/10/application-tips-essays-2022-2023.aspx (current questions include "Provide a recent example where you have demonstrated leadership and created value. What challenges did you face and what did you learn?" and "Values are what guide us in our life and work. What values are important to you and how have they influenced you?")

5. Michelle Merlin. (2017, Mar. 20). With a Few Graduates So Far, Valley Medical Schools Edge toward Making New Doctors. The Morning Call. https://www.mcall.com

/business/mc-outlook-medical-school-research-20170318-story.html; Alicia D. Monroe & Allesa English. (2013). Fostering Emotional Intelligence in Medical Training: The SELECT program. *AMA Journal of Ethics, 13*(6), 509–513; Kira Zwygart & Amy B. Smith. (2016). OSSE—A SELECT Medical Student Competency Assessment. *Medical Science Educator, 26*(2), 199–202. https://doi.org/10.1007/s40670-016-0232-0.

6. Jack Silverstein. (2015, Apr. 26). Law School Clinics Matter, but How Much?. Chicago Daily Law Bulletin. https://www.chicagolawbulletin.com/law-day/2015/law-school-clinics-ld2015.aspx.

7. William Blatt. (2015). Teaching Emotional Intelligence to Law Students: Three keys to mastery. *Nevada Law Journal, 15*, 464–447; Eduardo R.C. Capulong. (2016). Client as Subject: Humanizing the legal curriculum. *Clinical Law Review, 23*(1), 37–52. https://dx.doi.org/10.2139/ssrn.2864582; Susan Swaim Daicoff. (2012). Expanding the Lawyer's Toolkit of Skills and Competencies: Synthesizing leadership, professionalism, emotional intelligence, conflict resolution, and comprehensive law. *Santa Clara Law Review, 52*(3), 795–874; Gretchen Duhaime. (2012). Practicing on Purpose: Promoting personal wellness and professional values in legal education. *Touro Law Review, 28*(4), 1207–1238. https://digitalcommons.tourolaw.edu/cgi/viewcontent.cgi?referer=&httpsredir=1&article=1174&context=lawreview; Justine Dunlap. (2008). "I'd Just as Soon Flunk You as Look at You?" The Evolution to Humanizing in a Large Classroom. *Washburn Law Journal, 47*(2), 389–418; Barbara Glesner Fines. (2008). Fundamental Principles and Challenges of Humanizing Legal Education. *Washburn Law Journal, 47*(2), 313–326.

8. Cabello Rosario & Pablo Fernández-Berrocal. (2015). Implicit Theories and Ability Emotional Intelligence. *Frontiers in Psychology, 6*. https://psycnet.apa.org/doi/10.3389/fpsyg.2015.00700.

9. Susan Sturm & Lani Guinier. (2007). The Law School Matrix: Reforming legal education in a culture of competition and conformity. *Vanderbilt Law Review, 60*(2), 515–554, 524.

10. Sturm & Guinier, 2007, p. 520.

11. Sturm & Guinier, 2007, pp. 519–20.

12. Lawrence S. Krieger. (2002). Institutional Denial about the Dark Side of Law School, and Fresh Empirical Guidance for Constructively Breaking the Silence. *Journal of Legal Education, 52*(1–2), 112–129. https://heinonline.org/HOL/Page?public=true&handle=hein.journals/jled52&div=17&start_page=112&collection=journals; Lawrence S. Krieger & Kennon M. Sheldon. (2015). What Makes Lawyers Happy: Data-driven prescription to redefine professional success. *George Washington Law Review, 83*(2), 554–627. https://heinonline.org/HOL/Page?public=true&handle=hein.journals/gwlr83&div=17&start_page=554&collection=journals; Patrick R. Krill, Johnson, Ryan, & Albert, Linda. (2016). The Prevalence of Substance Use and Other Mental Health Concerns among American Attorneys. *Journal of Addiction Medicine, 10*(1), 46–52. https://doi.org/10.1097/ADM.0000000000000182; Jerome M. Organ, David B. Jaffe, & Katherine M. Bender. (2016). Suffering in Silence: The survey of law student well-being and the reluctance of law students to seek help for substance use and mental health concerns. *Journal of Legal Education, 66*(1), 116–156.

13. Krieger, 2002; Krieger & Sheldon, 2015; Krill et al., 2016 n. 30; Lizzy McLellan. (2020, Feb. 19). Lawyers Reveal True Depth of Mental Health Struggles. Law.com. https://www.law.com/2020/02/19/lawyers-reveal-true-depth-of-the-mental-health-struggles/?slreturn=20210222193544 (more than one in six); Organ et al., 2016 n. 29.

14. Mike Spivey. (2019, Mar. 24). How to Choose between a Higher Ranked School at Sticker Price and a Lower Ranked School with a Scholarship. Spivey Consulting. https://blog.spiveyconsulting.com/how-to-choose-between-a-higher-ranked-school-at-sticker-price-and-a-lower-ranked-school-with-a-scholarship/.

15. American Bar Association, Young Lawyers Division. (2020). 2020 Law School Student Loan Debt Survey Report. https://www.americanbar.org/content/dam/aba/administrative/young_lawyers/2020-student-loan-survey.pdf.

16. Jill Howieson & Shane L. Rogers. (2019). Rethinking the Lawyer-Client Interview: Taking a relational approach. *Psychiatry, Psychology, and Law*, *26*(4), 659–668. https://doi.org/10.1080/13218719.2019.1618749.

17. Christopher Campbell, Janet Moore, Wesley Maier, & Mike Gaffney. (2015). Unnoticed, Untapped, and Underappreciated: Clients' perceptions of their public defenders. *Behavioral Sciences & the Law*, *33*(6), 751–770. https://doi.org/10.1002/bsl.2182; Jean Sternlight & Jennifer Robbennolt. (2008). Good Lawyers Should be Good Psychologists: Insights for interviewing and counseling clients. *Ohio State Journal on Dispute Resolution*, *23*(3), 437–548.

18. Sternlight & Robbennolt, 2008.

19. Campbell et al., 2015, p. 751.

20. Krieger, 2002; Krieger & Sheldon, 2015; Krill et al., 2016; Organ et al., 2016.

CHAPTER II

1. Daniel Goleman. (1998). Working with Emotional Intelligence, p. 317. Bantam. (italics original).

2. Ernest H. O'Boyle, Ronald H. Humphrey, Jeffrey M. Pollack, Thomas H. Hawver, & Paul A. Story. (2011). The Relation between Emotional Intelligence and Job Performance: A meta-analysis. *Journal of Organizational Behavior*, *32*(5), 788–818. https://doi.org/10.1002/job.714.

3. Reuven Bar-On. (2006). The Bar On Model of Social and Emotional Intelligence (ESI). *Psicothema*, *18*(1), 13–25, 14. https://www.psicothema.com/pdf/3271.pdf.

4. O'Boyle et al., 2011; Michael Sony & Nandakumar Mekoth. (2016). The Relationship between Emotional Intelligence, Frontline Employee Adaptability, Job Satisfaction and Job Performance. *Journal of Retailing and Consumer Services*, *30*, 20–32. https://doi.org/10.1016/j.jretconser.2015.12.003; David L. Van Rooy & Chockalingam Viswesvaran. (2004). Emotional Intelligence: A meta-analytic investigation of predictive validity and nomological net. *Journal of Vocational Behavior*, *65*(1), 71–95. https://doi.org/10.1016/S0001-8791(03)00076-9.

5. Nicholas Clarke. (2010). Emotional Intelligence and Learning in Teams. *Journal of Workplace Learning*, *22*(3), 125–145. https://doi.org/10.1108/13665621011028594.

6. Kihwan Kim, Nicole L. Cundiff, & Suk B. Choi. (2015). Emotional Intelligence and Negotiation Outcomes: Mediating effects of rapport, negotiation strategy, and judgment accuracy. *Group Decision and Negotiation*, *24*(3), 495. https://doi.org/10.1007/s10726-015-9435-9; Kimberlyn Leary, Julianna Pillemer, & Michael Wheeler. (2013). Negotiating with Emotion. *Harvard Business Review*, *91*(1), 2. https://hbr.org/2013/01/negotiating-with-emotion.

7. Sarah K. Davis & Neil Humphrey. (2014). Ability versus Trait Emotional Intelligence. *Journal of Individual Differences*, *35*(1), 54–62. https://doi.org/10.1027/1614-0001/a000127.

8. Reuven Bar-On. (2005). The Impact of Emotional Intelligence on Subjective Well-Being. *Perspectives in Education*, *23*(1), 41–62. https://eric.ed.gov/?id=EJ692494.

9. Jose Manuel De Haro, Juan Luis Castejon, & Raquel Gilar. (2020). Personality and Salary at Early Career: The mediating effect of emotional intelligence. *The International Journal of Human Resource Management*, *31*(14), 1844–1862. https://doi.org/10.1080/09585192.2017.1423365; Victoria Mattingly & Kurt Kraiger. (2019). Can Emotional Intelligence Be Trained? A meta-analytical investigation. *Human Resource Management Review*, *29*(2), 140–155. https://doi.org/10.1016/j.hrmr.2018.03.002; Kathryn Thory. (2013). Teaching Managers to Regulate Their Emotions Better: Insights from emotional intelligence training and work-based application. *Human Resource Development International*, *16*(1), 4–21. https://doi.org/10.1080/13678868.2012.738473; Kathryn Thory. (2016). Developing Meaningfulness at Work through Emotional Intelligence Training: Developing meaningfulness at work. *International Journal of Training and Development*, *20*(1), 58–77. https://doi.org/10.1111/ijtd.12069; Van Rooy & Viswesvaran, 2004.

10. Rosario Cabello, Miguel A. Sorrel, Irene Fernández-Pinto, Natalio Extremera, & Pablo Fernández-Berrocal. (2016). Age and Gender Differences in Ability Emotional Intelligence in Adults: A cross-sectional study. *Developmental Psychology*, *52*(9), 1486–1492. https://doi.org/10.1037/dev0000191; John E. Hunter & Ronda F. Hunter. (1984). Validity and Utility of Alternative Predictors of Job Performance. *Psychological Bulletin*, *96*(1), 72–98. https://doi.org/10.1037/0033-2909.96.1.72; Esther Lopez-Zafra & Leire Gartzia. (2014). Perceptions of Gender Differences in Self-Report Measures of Emotional Intelligence. *Sex Roles*, *70*(11), 479–495. https://doi.org/10.1007/s11199-014-0368-6; Ioannis Tsaousis & Smaragda Kazi. (2013). Factorial Invariance and Latent Mean Differences of Scores on Trait Emotional Intelligence across Gender and Age. *Personality and Individual Differences*, *54*(2), 169–173. https://psycnet.apa.org/doi/10.1016/j.paid.2012.08.016.

11. Howard E. Gardner. (2011). Frames of Mind: The theory of multiple intelligences. Hachette UK; David Wechsler. (1943). Non-Intellective Factors in General Intelligence. *The Journal of Abnormal and Social Psychology*, *38*(1), 101–103. https://doi.org/10.1037/h0060613.

12. Wechsler, 1943.

13. Joseph D. Matarazzo, Wechsler's Measurement and Appraisal of Adult Intelligence (5th and enlarged ed. 1972). p. 79. Williams & Wilkins Co. (italics original).

14. Wechsler, 1943, pp. 101–103.

15. Gardner, 2011.

16. Gardner, 2011, p. 9.

17. Gardner, 2011, p. 9.

18. Gardner, 2011, p. 9.

19. Peter Livesey. (2017). Goleman-Boyatzis Model of Emotional Intelligence for Dealing with Problems in Project Management. *Construction Economics and Building*, *17*(1), 20–45. https://doi.org/10.5130/AJCEB.v17i1.5101.

20. John D. Mayer, Peter Salovey, & David R. Caruso. (2008). Emotional Intelligence: New ability or eclectic traits? *American Psychologist*, *63*(6), 503–517. https://doi.org/10.1037/0003-066X.63.6.503; John D. Mayer, Peter Salovey, & David R. Caruso. (2008). *What Is Emotional Intelligence and What Does It Predict?*. In Patrick Kyllonen, Richard Roberts, & Lazar Stankov (Eds.), Extending Intelligence: Enhancement and new constructs (pp. 319–348). Lawrence Erlbaum Associates. https://unhlibrary.on.worldcat.org/oclc/61865183.

21. Consortium for Research on Emotional Intelligence in Organizations. The Emotional Quotient Inventory (EQ-i 2.0). (n.d.).http://www.eiconsortium.org/measures/eqi.html; Daniel Goleman. (2001). *An EI-Based Theory of Performance.* In Cary Cherniss & Daniel Goleman (Eds.), The Emotionally Intelligent Workplace: How to select for, measure, and improve emotional intelligence in individuals, groups, and organizations (pp. 27–45). Jossey-Bass; John D. Mayer & Peter Salovey. (1997). *What Is Emotional Intelligence?.* In Peter D. Salovey & David Sluyter (Eds.), Emotional Development and Emotional Intelligence: Educational implications (pp. 3–31). Basic Books; Charles Spielberger. (2004). Encyclopedia of Applied Psychology. Elsevier Academic.

22. Goleman, 2001.

23. Goleman, 1998.

24. Mayer et al., 2008.

25. Reuven Bar-On. (2006). The Bar On Model of Social and Emotional Intelligence (ESI). *Psicothema, 18*(1), 13–25. https://www.psicothema.com/pdf/3271.pdf

26. Konstantinos Petrides & Adrian Furnham. (2000). On the Dimensional Structure of Emotional Intelligence. *Personality and Individual Differences, 29*(2), 313–320. https://doi.org/10.1016/S0191-8869(99)00195-6.

27. Parvesh. K. Chopra & Gopal K. Kanji. (2010). Emotional Intelligence: A catalyst for inspirational leadership and management excellence. *Total Quality Management & Business Excellence, 21*(10), 971–1004, 976.

28. Brené Brown. (2019). Braving the Wilderness: The quest for true belonging and the courage to stand alone. Penguin Random House.

CHAPTER III

1. Carl G. Jung. (1973). Letters, Vol.1:1906–1950 (R.F.C. Hull, trans.; G. Adler & A. Jaffe, eds.). Routledge.

2. Dan P. McAdams. (2008). *Personal Narratives and the Life Story.* In O. John, R. Robins, L. Pervin (Eds.), Handbook of Personality: Theory and research (pp. 242–262). Guilford Publications.

3. Brené Brown. (2010). The Gifts of Imperfection: Let go of who you think you're supposed to be and embrace who you are, p. 6. Hazelden.

4. Herminia Ibarra & Roxana Barbulescu. (2010). Identity as Narrative: Prevalence, effectiveness, and consequences of narrative identity work in macro work role transitions. *Academy of Management Review, 35*(1), 135–154. https://doi.org/10.5465/AMR.2010.45577925; Kate McLean, Moin Syed, Monisha Pasupathi, Jonathan Adler, William Dunlop, David Drustrup, Robyn Fivush, Matthew Graci, Jennifer Lilgendahl, Jennifer Lodi-Smith, Dan McAdams, & Tara McCoy. (2020). The Empirical Structure of Narrative Identity: The initial big three. *Journal of Personality and Social Psychology, 119*(4), 920–944. https://doi.org/10.1037/pspp0000247.

5. Susan Sturm & Lani Guinier. (2007). The Law School Matrix: Reforming legal education in a culture of competition and conformity. *Vanderbilt Law Review, 60*(2), 515–554.

6. Francesca Gino & Gary P. Pisano. (Apr. 2011). Why Leaders Don't Learn from Success. Harvard Business Review. https://hbr.org/2011/04/why-leaders-dont-learn-from-success.

7. Karen Dillon. (Apr. 2011). I Think of My Failures as a Gift. Harvard Business Review. https://hbr.org/2011/04/i-think-of-my-failures-as-a-gift.

8. Tom Robbins. (1976). Even Cowgirls Get the Blues, p.198. Bantam Dell.

9. Monisha Pasupathi & Timothy Hoyt. (2009). The Development of Narrative Identity in Late Adolescence and Emergent Adulthood: The continued importance of listeners. *Developmental Psychology*, *45*(2), 558–574. https://doi.org/10.1037/a0014431.

10. McAdams, 2008.

11. William L. Dunlop & Lawrence J. Walker. (2013). The Life Story: Its development and relation to narration and personal identity. *International Journal of Behavioral Development*, *37*(3), 235–247. https://doi.org/10.1177/0165025413479475; Dan P. McAdams, & Kate McLean. (2013). Narrative Identity. *Current Directions in Psychological Science: A Journal of the American Psychological Society*, *22*(3), 233–238. https://doi.org/10.1177/0963721413475622.

12. Lawrence S. Krieger. (2002). Institutional Denial about the Dark Side of Law School, and Fresh Empirical Guidance for Constructively Breaking the Silence. *Journal of Legal Education*, *52*(1–2), 112–129. https://heinonline.org/HOL/Page?public=true&handle=hein.journals/jled52&div=17&start_page=112&collection=journals; Kennon Sheldon & Lawrence Krieger. (2007). Understanding the Negative Effects of Legal Education on Law Students: A longitudinal test of self-determination theory. *Personality & Social Psychology Bulletin*, *33*(6), 883–897. https://doi.org/10.1177/0146167207301014.

13. Jen Guo, Miriam Klevan, & Dan P. McAdams. (2016). Personality Traits, Ego Development, and the Redemptive Self. *Personality & Social Psychology Bulletin*, 42(11), 1552–1553. https://doi.org/10.1177/0146167216665093; Dan P. McAdams. (2006). The Redemptive Self: Stories Americans live by. Oxford University Press. https://doi.org/10.1093/acprof:oso/9780195176933.001.0001.

14. Patrick Longan, Daisy Floyd, & Timothy Floyd. (2020). The Formation of Professional Identity: The path from student to lawyer. Routledge; David I. C. Thomson, The Way Forward for Legal Education (2023).

15. Jeremy Hogeveen, Carola Salvi & Jordan Grafman. (2016). 'Emotional Intelligence': Lessons from Lesions. Trends in Neurosciences, 39(10), 694–705. http://dx.doi.org/10.1016/j.tins.2016.08.007.

16. Daniel Goleman. (2006). Emotional Intelligence: Why it can matter more than IQ, pp. 8–9. Bantam Books. (Original work published 1995).

17. Goleman, 2006, p. 9.

18. Chade-Meng Tan. (2012). Search Inside Yourself: The unexpected path to achieving success, happiness (and world peace). HarperOne.

19. Jon Kabat-Zinn. (2013). Full Catastrophe Living: Using the wisdom of your body and mind to face stress, pain, and illness (Rev. ed.). Bantam Books.

20. Tan, 2012.

21. Amanda Ruggieri. (2018, Feb. 20). The Dangerous Downsides of Perfectionism. BBC Future. https://www.bbc.com/future/article/20180219-toxic-perfectionism-is-on-the-rise.

22. Daniel Goleman. (2001). *An EI-Based Theory of Performance*. In Cary Cherniss & Daniel Goleman (Eds.), The Emotionally Intelligent Workplace: How to select for, measure, and improve emotional intelligence in individuals, groups, and organizations (pp. 27–45). Jossey-Bass.

23. Goleman, 2006, 46.

24. Debra Austin & Rob Durr. (2016). Emotion Regulation for Lawyers. *Wyoming Law Review*, *16*(2), 387–411. https://doi.org/10.59643/1942-9916.1367.

25. Viktor E. Frankl. (2006). Man's Search for Meaning. Beacon Press.

26. Austin & Durr, 2016, p. 407.

27. Hay Group. (n.d.). [Infographic]. https://perma.cc/Y2R6-AFKS.

28. Austin & Durr, 2016.

29. Northwestern Pritzker School of Law. Student Wellness. https://www.law.northwestern.edu/student-life/student-services/wellness/.

30. Eileen A. Scallen, Sophie Sparrow, & Cliff Zimmerman. (2014). Working Together in Law: Teamwork and small group skills for legal professionals, p. 16. Carolina Academic Press.

31. Scallen et al., 2014, pp. 18–20.

CHAPTER IV

1. *Christian v. Mattel*, 286 F.3d 1118, 1124–1125 (9th Cir. 2002).

2. Daniel Goleman. (2001). *An EI-Based Theory of Performance.* In Cary Cherniss & Daniel Goleman (Eds.), The Emotionally Intelligent Workplace: How to select for, measure, and improve emotional intelligence in individuals, groups, and organizations (pp. 27–45). Jossey-Bass.

3. *Boulder Falcon v. Brown*, 2:22-cv-00042-JNP-JCB (D. Utah, March 8, 2023), p. 5.

4. *Boulder Falcon*, 2023, p. 6.

5. *Boulder Falcon*, 2023, pp. 16–17.

6. Goran Simic, Mladenka Tkalcic, Vana Vukic, Damir Mulc, Ena Spanic, Marinsa Sagud, Francisco E. Olucha-Bordonau, Mario Vuksic, & Patrick R. Hof. (2021). Understanding Emotions: Origins and roles of the amygdala. *Biomolecules*, *11*(6), 823. https://doi.org/10.3390/biom11060823.

7. Ad J. J. M. Vingerhoets, Ivan Nyklíček, Johan Denollett. (2008). Emotion Regulation: Conceptual and clinical issues. Springer.

8. Elaine Fox. (2008). Emotion Science Cognitive and Neuroscientific Approaches to Understanding Human Emotions. Red Globe Press.

9. Charles Darwin. (1872). The Expression of the Emotions in Man and Animals. Murray.

10. Paul Ekman. (1992). An Argument for Basic Emotions. *Cognition and Emotion*, 6(3–4), 169–200. https://psycnet.apa.org/doi/10.1080/02699939208411068.

11. Daniel Goleman. (2006), Working with Emotional Intelligence. Bantam.

12. Guido Alessani, Enrico Perinelli, Evelina De Longis, Wilmar Schaufeli, Annalisa Theodorou, Laura Borgogni, Gian Vittorio Caprara, & Luigi Cinque. (2018). Job Burnout: The contribution of emotional stability and emotional self-efficacy beliefs. *Journal of Occupational and Organizational Psychology*, *91*(4), 823–851. https://doi.org/10.1111/joop.12225; Gill Hasson. (2014). Emotional Intelligence: Managing *emotions to make a positive impact on your life and car*eer. Wiley.

13. Hasson, 2014.

14. Christian Von Scheve. (2012). Emotion Regulation and Emotion Work: Two sides of the same coin? *Frontiers in Psychology*, *3*, 496. https://doi.org/10.3389/fpsyg.2012.00496.

15. Ainize Peña-Sarrionandia, Moïra Mikolajczak, & James Gross. (2015). Integrating Emotion Regulation and Emotional Intelligence Traditions: A meta-analysis. *Frontiers in Psychology*, *6*, 160–160. https://doi.org/10.3389/fpsyg.2015.00160.

16. Klaus R. Scherer. (1999). *Appraisal Theory.* In Tim Dagleish & Mick Power (Eds.), Handbook of Cognition and Emotion (pp. 637–663, 637). Wiley. https://doi.org/10.1002/0470013494.ch30.

17. Richard S. Lazarus. (1966). Psychological Stress and the Coping Process. McGraw-Hill.

18. Commission for Lawyer Discipline. (2017–2018). State Bar of Texas Commission for Lawyer Discipline Annual Report, June 1, 2017–May 31, 2018. https://www.texasbar.com/AM/Template.cfm?Section=Home&Template=/CM/ContentDisplay.cfm&Con tentID=41986; Robert, Amanda. (2020, Feb. 28). Ethical Dilemmas Emerge when Attorneys Keep Mental Health Struggles Private. ABA Journal. https://www.abajournal.com/news/article/Ethical-dilemmas-emerge-when-attorneys-keep-mental-health-struggles-private.

19. Rebecca Burwell. (2015). Self-Evaluative and Emotion Processes Linked with Brooding Rumination among Adolescents. *Journal of Adolescence*, *41*, 162–174. https://doi.org/10.1016/j.adolescence.2015.03.007; Alice Lo & Maree Abbott. (2013). The Impact of Manipulating Expected Standards of Performance for Adaptive, Maladaptive, and Non-perfectionists. *Cognitive Therapy and Research*, *37*(4), 762–778. https://doi.org/10.1007/s10608-013-9528-1; Alice Lo & Maree Abbott. (2019). Affective and Cognitive Responses to Repeated Performance Feedback across Adaptive and Maladaptive Dimensions of Perfectionism. *Journal of Experimental Psychopathology*, *10*(4), 204380871988070–. https://doi.org/10.1177/2043808719880702.

20. Kenneth Rice & Clarissa Richardson. (2014). Classification Challenges in Perfectionism. *Journal of Counseling Psychology*, *61*(4), 641–648. https://doi.org/10.1037/cou0000040; Lisa Tran & Katharine Rimes. (2017). Unhealthy Perfectionism, Negative Beliefs about Emotions, Emotional Suppression, and Depression in Students: A mediational analysis. *Personality and Individual Differences*, *110*, 144–147. https://doi.org/10.1016/j.paid.2017.01.042.

21. Niki Hayatbini, Katherine Knauft, & Vrinda Kalia. (2021). Cognitive Reappraisal Moderates the Relationship between Perfectionism and Cognitive Flexibility. *Journal of Clinical Psychology*, *77*(7), 1685–1696, p. 1696. https://doi.org/10.1002/jclp.23124.

22. Lyn Y. Abramson, Martin E. Seligman, & John D. Teasdale. (1978). Learned Helplessness in Humans: Critique and reformulation. *Journal of Abnormal Psychology*, *87*(1), 49–74. https://psycnet.apa.org/doi/10.1037/0021-843X.87.1.49.

23. Amy C. Edmondson. (2011). Strategies of Learning from Failure. *Harvard Business Review*, *89*(4), 48–55. https://hbr.org/2011/04/strategies-for-learning-from-failure.

24. Craig Impelman. (2008, June 30). Words of Wisdom: UCLA legend John Wooden. Success.com. https://www.thewoodeneffect.com/words-of-wisdom/.

25. Jessica Cohen. (2021). Perfectionism, Goal Pursuit, and Work-Related Outcomes: A self-determination theory perspective [Doctoral dissertation, Carleton University]. https://doi.org/10.22215/etd/2021-14329; Lo & Abbott, 2013; Lo & Abbott, 2019.

26. Daniel Goleman. (2006). Emotional Intelligence: Why it can matter more than IQ. Bantam Books. (Original work published 1995).

27. Albert Ellis & Debbie Joffe Ellis. (2019). Rational Emotive Behavior Therapy. American Psychological Association.

28. David D. Burns. (1980). Feeling Good: The new mood therapy. William Morrow & Company.

29. Goleman, 2006.

30. Goleman, 2006.

31. Shawn Achor. (2010). The Happiness Advantage: How a Positive Brain Fuels Success in Work and Life. Currency.

32. Christopher N. Cascio, Matthew Brook O'Donnell, Francis J. Tinney, Matthew D.Lieberman, Shelley E. Taylor, Victor J. Strecher, & Emily B. Falk. (2016). Self-affirmation activates brain systems associated with self-related processing and reward and is

reinforced by future orientation. Social Cognitive and Affective Neuroscience, 11(4), 621-629. doi:10.1093/scan/nsv136; Geoffrey L. Cohen & David K. Sherman. (2014). The Psychology of Change: Self-Affirmation and Social Psychological Intervention. Annual Review of Psychology, 645, 333–371. https://doi.org/10.1146/annurev-psych-010213-115137.

33. Sonia K. Kang, Adam D. Galinsky, Laura J. Kray, & Aiwa Shirako. (2015). Power Affects Performance when the Pressure Is on: Evidence for low-power threat and high-power lift. *Personality and Social Psychology Bulletin*, *41*(5), 726–735. https://doi.org/10.1177/0146167215577365.

34. MindTools. (n.d.). Using Affirmations. https://www.mindtools.com/air49f4/using-affirmations.

35. MindTools.

36. William W. Eaton, James C. Anthony, Wallace Mandel, & Roberta Garrison. (1990). Occupations and the Prevalence of Major Depressive Disorder. *Journal of Occupational Medicine: Official publication of the Industrial Medical Association*, *32*(11), 1079–1087. https://doi.org/10.1097/00043764-199011000-00006; Patrick R. Krill, Ryan Johnson & Linda Albert. (2016). The Prevalence of Substance Use and Other Mental Health Concerns among American Attorneys. *Journal of Addiction Medicine*, *10*(1), 46–52. https://doi.org/10.1097/ADM.0000000000000182.

37. Shawn Achor. (2010). The Happiness Advantage: The seven principles of positive psychology that fuel success and performance at work. Crown Business.

38. Achor, 2010.

39. Achor, 2010.

40. Lisa C. Walsh, Julia K. Boehm, & Sonja Lyubomirsky. (2018). Does Happiness Promote Career Success? Revisiting the evidence. *Journal of Career Assessment*, *26*(2), 199–219.

41. Christina N. Armenta, Peter M. Ruberton, and Sonja Lyubomirsky. (2015). *Subjective Wellbeing, Psychology of.* In James D. Wright (Ed.), International Encyclopedia of Social & Behavioral Sciences (2nd ed., vol. 23, pp. 648–653). Elsevier.

42. Achor, 2018.

CHAPTER V

1. Brené Brown. (2008). I Thought It Was Just Me (but It Isn't): Making the journey from "What will people think?" to "I am enough." Penguin Random House.

2. Twenty One Toys. (n.d.). Dr Brené Brown: Empathy vs Sympathy. https://twentyonetoys.com/blogs/teaching-empathy/brene-brown-empathy-vs-sympathy.

3. Twenty One Toys, n.d.

4. Chade-Meng Tan. (2012). Search Inside Yourself: The unexpected path to achieving success, happiness (and world peace). HarperOne.

5. Roman Krznaric. (2015). Empathy: Why It Matters, and How to Get It. Perigree.

6. Daniel Goleman. (2006). Working with Emotional Intelligence. Bantam.

7. Richard Boyatzis & M. Burckle. (1999). Psychometric Properties of the ECI. Hay/McBer Group.

8. Douglas Linder & Nancy Levit. (2014). The Good Lawyer: Seeking quality in the practice of law, p. 1. Oxford University Press, USA.

9. Linder & Levit, 2014, p. 2.

10. Linder & Levit, 2014, p. 3.

11. Linder & Levit, 2014, p. 3.

12. Daniel Goleman. (2006). Emotional Intelligence: Why it can matter more than IQ. Bantam Books. (Original work published 1995).

13. Jorge A. Barraza, & Paul J. Zak. (2009). Empathy Toward Strangers Triggers Oxytocin Release and Subsequent Generosity. *Annals of the New York Academy of Sciences, 1167*, 182–189. https://doi.org/10.1111/j.1749-6632.2009.04504.x; Phil Cowan, Carolyn P. Cowan, & Neera Mehta. (2005, Sept. 1). Feeling Like Partners. Greater Good Magazine. https://greatergood.berkeley.edu/article/item/feeling_like_partners; Helen Riess. (2017). The Science of Empathy. *Journal of Patient Experience*, *4*(2), 74–77. https://doi.org/10.1177/2374373517699267; Meifen Wei, Kelly Y. H. Liao, Tsun-Yao Ku, & Phillip A. Shaffer. (2011). Attachment, Self-Compassion, Empathy, and Subjective Well-Being among College Students and Community Adults. *Journal of Personality*, *79*(1), 191–221. https://www.ncbi.nlm.nih.gov/pubmed/21223269.

14. Graham B. Bell & Harry E. Hall (1954). The Relationship Between Leadership and Empathy. *Journal of Abnormal and Social Psychology*, *49*(1), 156–157. https://doi.org/10.1037/h0053927; Krznaric, Roman. (2012, Nov. 7). Six Habits of Highly Empathic People. Greater Good: The science of a meaningful life. https://greatergood.berkeley.edu/article/item/six_habits_of_highly_empathic_people1.

15. Linder & Levit, 2014.

16. John C. Coffee, Jr. (2020, Jan. 6). The Future of the Large Law Firm: Growth, mergers, and inequality. CLS Blue Sky Blog. https://clsbluesky.law.columbia.edu/2020/01/06/the-future-of-the-large-law-firm-growth-mergers-and-inequality/.

17. Legal Practice Intelligence. (2023, May 30). Legal Market Consolidation: Recent trends. https://www.legalpracticeintelligence.com/blogs/practice-intelligence/legal-market-consolidation-recent-trends; Staci Zaretsky. (2023, Apr. 3). Biglaw Mergers Off to a Hot Start in 2023. Above the Law. https://abovethelaw.com/2023/04/biglaw-mergers-off-to-a-hot-start-in-2023/.

18. Zaretsky, 2023.

19. Businessolver.com, Inc. (2020). *The State of Workplace Empathy*. https://f.hubspotusercontent40.net/hubfs/378546/Empathy-2020/2020%20State%20of%20Workplace%20Empathy%20Executive%20Summary/businessolver-2020-state-of-workplace-empathy-executive-summary.pdf.

20. Kendra Brodin. (2021). What Is Empathy? Why Does It Matter in the Practice of Law? American Bar Association, https://www.americanbar.org/groups/young_lawyers/resources/after-the-bar/professional-development/what-is-empathy-why-does-it-matter/.

21. Riess, 2017.

22. Krznaric, 2012.

23. Chade-Meng Tan. (2012). Search Inside Yourself: The Unexpected Path to Achieving Success, Happiness (and World Peace). HarperOne.

24. Marshall B. Rosenberg & Deepak Chopra. (2015). Nonviolent Communication: A language of life: Life-changing tools for healthy relationships, p. 148. PuddleDancer Press.

25. Tan, 2012, pp. 234–235.

26. Quotefancy. Top Ten Daniel Amen Quotes (2024 Update). https://quotefancy.com/daniel-amen-quotes.

27. Rosenberg & Chopra, 2015.

28. Jean Sternlight, & Jennifer Robbennolt. (2008). Good Lawyers Should Be Good Psychologists: Insights for interviewing and counseling clients. *Ohio State Journal on Dispute Resolution*, *23*(3), 437–548.

29. TEDx Talks. (2013). Narrative Humility: Sayantani DasGupta at TEDxSLC [Video]. YouTube. https://www.youtube.com/watch?v=gZ3ucjmcZwY.

30. Sayantani DasGupta. (2008, Mar. 22). The Art of Medicine: Narrative Humility. *The Lancet*, *371*, 980, 980–981. https://www.thelancet.com/action/showPdf?pii=S0140-6736%2808%2960440-7.

31. Karen B. LeFevre. (1986). Invention as a Social Act. SIU Press.

32. Ronald B. Adler & Russell F. Proctor II. (2011). Looking Out, Looking In (13th ed.). Cengage Learning.

33. Tan, 2012, p. 180.

CHAPTER VI

1. Goodreads. (n.d.) Maya Angelou quotes. https://www.goodreads.com/quotes/663523-at-the-end-of-the-day-people-won-t-remember-what.

2. Robert Waldinger & Marc Schulz. (2023). The Good Life: Lessons from the world's longest scientific study of happiness. Simon & Schuster.

3. Cynthia Roberts. (2013). Building Social Capital through Leadership Development. *Journal of Leadership Education*, *12*(1), 54–73. https://doi.org/10.12806/V12/I1/54.

4. Judith K. Hellerstein & David Neumark. (June 2020). Social Capital, Networks, and Economic Wellbeing, p. 1. IZA Institute of Labor Economics. https://docs.iza.org/dp13413.pdf.

5. Robert D. Putnam. (1995). Bowling Alone: America's declining social capital. *Journal of Democracy*, *6*(1), 65–78. Project MUSE, https://doi.org/10.1353/jod.1995.0002; Robert D. Putnam. (2000). Bowling Alone: The collapse and revival of American community. Simon & Schuster.

6. Waldinger & Schulz, 2023.

7. Damian F. Santomauro, . . . Alize J. Ferrari. (2021). Global Prevalence and Burden of Depressive and Anxiety Disorders in 204 Countries and Territories in 2020 Due to the COVID-19 Pandemic. *The Lancet*, *398*(10312), 1700–1712. https://doi.org/10.1016/S0140-6736(21)02143-7.

8. Gregory Thwaites, Pawal Smietanka, Philip Bunn, Paul Mizen, & Nicholas Bloom. (2020). The Impact of Covid-19 on Productivity. NBER Working Paper Series. https://doi.org/10.3386/w28233

9. Liana DesHarnais Bruce, Joshua S. Wu, Stuart L. Lustig, Daniel W. Russell, & Douglas A. Nemecek. (2019) Loneliness in the United States: A 2018 national panel survey of demographic, structural, cognitive, and behavioral characteristics. *American Journal of Health Promotion*, 33(8), 1123–1133, https://doi.org/10.1177/0890117119856551; Bianca DiJulio, Liz Hamel, Cailey Muñana, & Mollyann Brodie. (August 30, 2018) Loneliness and Social Isolation in the United States, the United Kingdom, and Japan: An international survey. Research Report of Henry J. Kaiser Family Foundation. https://files.kff.org/attachment/Report-Loneliness-and-Social-Isolation-in-the-United-States-the-United-Kingdom-and-Japan-An-International-Survey; Health Resources & Service Administration. Henry J. Kaiser Family Foundation.

10. Robert D. Putnam. (2020). The Upswing: How America came together a century ago and how we can do it again. Simon & Schuster.

11. Michael Davern, Rene Bautista, Jeremy Freese, Stephen Morgan, Tom Smith. (2021). General Social Survey 2021 Cross-Section. NORC. https://gss.norc.org/Documents/codebook/GSS%202021%20Codebook.pdf.

12. Viji Kannan & Peter J. Veazie. (2021). US Trends in Social Isolation, Social Engagement, and Companionship—nationally and by age, sex, race/ethnicity, family income, and work hours, 2003–2020. *SSM—Population Health*, *21*, 1–11. https://doi.org/10.1016/j.ssmph.2022.101331.

13. Yalda T. Uhls, Nicole B. Ellison, & Kaveri Subrahmanyam. (2017). Benefits and Costs of Social Media in Adolescence. *Pediatrics*, *140*(Supp. 2), S67–S70. https://doi.org/10.1542/peds.2016-1758E.

14. Putnam, 2020.

15. Cigna Corporation. (2021). The Loneliness Epidemic Persists: A post-pandemic look at the state of loneliness among U.S. Adults. https://newsroom.thecignagroup.com/loneliness-epidemic-persists-post-pandemic-look.

16. Jaana Juvonen, Leah Lessard, Naomie G. Kline, & Sandra Graham. (2022). Young Adult Adaptability to the Social Challenges of the COVID-19 Pandemic: The protective role of friendships. *Journal of Youth and Adolescence*, *51*, 585–597. https://doi.org/10.1007/s10964-022-01573-w.

17. Emily Long, Susan Patterson, Karen Maxwell, Carolyn Blake, Raquel Boso Perez, Ruth Lewis, Mark McCann, Julie Riddell, Kathryn Skivington, Rachel Wilson-Lowe, & Kirstin R. Mitchell. (2022). COVID-19 Pandemic and Its Impact on Social Relationships and Health. *Journal of Epidemiology and Community Health*, *76*(2), 128–132. https://doi.org/10.1136/jech-2021-216690.

18. Long et al., 2022, p. 130.

19. Long et al., 2022, p. 131.

20. Juvonen et al., 2022.

21. Long et al., 2022.

22. Ilham Nur Hanifan Maulana, & Tasya Fiane Wardah. (2023). Fostering Community Resilience through Social Capital. *Journal of Transformative Governance and Social Justice*, *1*(1–2), 1–10. https://lppm.unmer.ac.id/webmin/assets/uploads/lj/LJ202305241684934432973.pdf.

23. Erik Snel, Godfried Engbersen, Jan de Boom, & Marianne van Bochove. (2022). Social Capital as Protection against the Mental Health Impact of the COVID-19 Pandemic. *Frontiers in Sociology*, *7*. https://doi.org/10.3389/fsoc.2022.728541.

24. Maulana & Wardah, 2023.

25. Waldinger and Schulz, 2023.

26. Yang C. Yang, Courtney Boen, Karen Gerken, Ting Li, Kristen Schorpp, and Kathleen Mullan Harris. (2016). Social relationships and physiological determinants of longevity across the human lifespan. *Proceedings of the National Academy of Sciences USA*, 2016, *113*(3): 578–583. doi: 10.1073/pnas.1511085112.

27. Laura Alejandro Rico-Uribe, Francisco Félix Caballero, Natalia Martín-María, María Cabello, José Luis Ayuso-Mateos, & Marta Miret. (2018). Association of Loneliness with All-Cause Mortality: A meta-analysis. *PloS one*, *13*(1), e0190033. https://doi.org/10.1371/journal.pone.0190033.

28. Waldinger and Schulz, 2023, pp. 36–37

29. Waldinger and Schulz, 2023, pp. 36–37

30. TEDx Talks. (2010, Oct. 6). The Power of Vulnerability: Brené Brown [Video]. YouTube. https://www.youtube.com/watch?v=X4Qm9cGRub0.

31. Paul J. Zak. (2017). The Neuroscience of Trust. *Harvard Business Review*, Jan.–Feb., pp. 85–90.

32. Jon Kabat-Zinn. (2013). Full Catastrophe Living: Using the wisdom of your body and mind to face stress, pain, and illness (Rev. ed.). Bantam Books.

33. Maurice J. Elias, Linda Buene-Butler, Lisa Blum, and Thomas Schuyler. (1997). How to Launch a Social & Emotional Learning Program. *Journal of the Department of Supervision and Curriculum Development, N.E.A.*, *54*(8), 15–19. https://eric.ed.gov/?id=EJ545858; Roger P. Weissberg, & Mary Utne O'Brien. (2004). What Works in School-Based Social and Emotional Learning Programs for Positive Youth Development. *The ANNALS of the American Academy of Political and Social Science*, *591*(1), 86–97. https://doi.org/10.1177/0002716203260093.

34. Bill George. (2003). Authentic Leadership: Rediscovering the secrets to creating lasting value. Jossey-Bass.

35. Zak, 2017, p. 89.

36. Deloitte Finds Trust and Ethics in the Workplace Battered by the Recession: Asset-based financial services industry. (2010). *The Secured Lender*, *66*(7), 15. http://turing.library.northwestern.edu/login?url=https://www.proquest.com/trade-journals/deloitte-finds-trust-ethics-workplace-battered/docview/762437351/se-2.

37. Ken Blanchard, Cynthia Olmstead, & Martha Lawrence. (2013). Trust Works!: Four keys to building lasting relationships. William Morrow.

38. American Bar Association (2016). Resolution 113. https://www.americanbar.org/groups/diversity/DiversityCommission/model-diversity-survey/.

39. Shilpa Coorg, & David Ramirez-Galvez. (2021). Retention Is Key to Meaningful Diversity at Law Firms. Law360. https://www.law360.com/articles/1411047/retention-is-key-to-meaningful-diversity-at-law-firms; Karen Sloan. (2022, Oct. 19). Report Finds "Huge Gaps" in New US Lawyer Employment by Race. Reuters. https://www.reuters.com/legal/legalindustry/report-finds-huge-gaps-new-us-lawyer-employment-by-race-2022-10-19/.

40. McKinsey & Company. (2020). Diversity wins: How inclusion matters. https://www.mckinsey.com/~/media/mckinsey/featured%20insights/diversity%20and%20inclusion/diversity%20wins%20how%20inclusion%20matters/diversity-wins-how-inclusion-matters-vf.pdf; Deirdre O'Donovan. (2017). *Diversity and Inclusion in the Workplace*. In C. Machado & J. P. Davim (Eds.), Organizational Behaviour and Human Resource Management: A Guide to a Specialized MBA Course (pp. 73–109). Springer.

41. Andreas Hundschell, Stefan Razinskas, Julia Backmann, & Martin Hoegl. (2022). The Effects of Diversity on Creativity: A literature review and synthesis. *Applied Psychology*, *71*(4), 1598–1634. https://doi.org/10.1111/apps.12365; Yang Yang & Alison M. Konrad. (2011). Diversity and Organizational Innovation: The role of employee involvement. *Journal of Organizational Behavior*, *32*, 1062–1083. http://doi.org/10.1002/job.724.

42. Matt Krentz, Ashley Dartness, Dinesh Khanna, & Susanne Locklair. (2021). Inclusive Cultures Have Healthier and Happier Workers. Boston Consulting Group. http://mkt-bcg-com-public-pdfs.s3.amazonaws.com/prod/building-an-inclusive-culture-leads-to-happier-healthier-workers.pdf.

43. Stephanie Downey, Lisa van der Werff, Kecia M.Thomas, & Victoria C. Plaut. (2015). The Role of Diversity Practices and Inclusion in Promoting Trust and Employee Engagement. https://psycnet.apa.org/doi/10.1111/jasp.12273.

44. Michael W. Kraus, Brittany Torrez, & LaStarr Hollie. (2022). How Narratives of Racial Progress Create Barriers to Diversity, Equity, and Inclusion in Organizations. *Current Opinion in Psychology*, *43*, 108–113. https://doi.org/10.1016/j.copsyc.2021.06.022.

45. Brittany Long. (2023, July 28). Analysis: Partner Diversity Lags Despite Firms' DEI Efforts. Bloomberg Law. https://news.bloomberglaw.com/bloomberg-law-analysis/analysis-partner-diversity-lags-despite-law-firms-dei-efforts.

46. Spencer Stuart. (2023). Fortune 500 C-Suite Snapshot: Profiles in functional leadership. https://www.spencerstuart.com/-/media/2023/december/f500-profiles/fortune-500-c-suite-snapshot-profiles-in-functional-leadership.pdf.

47. Tina Alemao. (2022). A Critical Discourse Analysis of Online DEI Curriculum in One Corporation. [Doctoral dissertation, University of Oklahoma]. SHAREOK Repository. https://shareok.org/bitstream/handle/11244/335556/2022_Alemao_Tina_Dissertation.pdf?sequence=1&isAllowed=y; Zachary Kalinoski, Debra Steele-Johnson, Elizabeth Peyton, Keith Leas, Julie Steinke, & Nathan Bowling. (2013). A Meta-Analytic Evaluation of Diversity Training Outcomes. *Journal of Organizational Behavior, 34*(8), 1076–1104. https://psycnet.apa.org/doi/10.1037/a0037681; Carey K. Morewedge, Haewon Yoon, Irene Scopelliti, Carl W. Symborski, James H. Korris, & Karim S. Kassam. (2015). Debiasing Decisions: Improved decision making with a single training intervention. *Policy Insights from the Behavioral and Brain Sciences, 2*(1), 129–140.

48. *Burlington Industries v. Ellerth*, 524 U.S. 742 (1998); *Faragher v. City of Boca Raton*, 524 U.S. 775 (1998).

49. Annaliese A. Singh, Sylvia C. Nassar, Patricia Arredondo, & Rebecca Toporek. (2020). The Past Guides the Future: Implementing the multicultural and social justice counseling competencies. *Journal of Counseling & Development, 98*(3), 238–252. https://psycnet.apa.org/record/2020-41481-002.

50. Jessie Wilson, Colleen Ward, & Ronald Fischer. (2013). Beyond Culture Learning Theory: What can personality tell us about cultural competence?. *Journal of Cross-Cultural Psychology, 44*(6), 900–927, 900. https://psycnet.apa.org/doi/10.1177/0022022113492889.

51. Darla K. Deardorff. (2004). The Identification and Assessment of Intercultural Competence as a Student Outcome of International Education at Institutions of Higher Education in the United States, p. 184 [Unpublished dissertation]. North Carolina State University, Raleigh.

52. Derald Wing Sue, Patricia Arredondo, & Roderick J. McDavis, (1992). Multicultural Counseling Competencies and Standards: A call to the profession. *Journal of Multicultural Counseling and Development, 20*(2), 64–88. https://doi.org/10.1002/j.2161-1912.1992.tb00563.x.

53. Alexander J. Hilert & Camila Tirado. (2019). Teaching Multicultural Counseling with Mindfulness: A contemplative pedagogy approach. *International Journal for the Advancement of Counselling*, 41(4), 469–480. https://psycnet.apa.org/doi/10.1007/s10447-018-9363-x.

54. Hilert & Tirado, 2019.

55. Rhonda Magee. (2021). The Inner Work of Racial Justice: Healing ourselves and transforming our communities through mindfulness. TarcherPrigee.

56. Najmeh Sharifi, Mohsen Adib-Hajbaghery, & Maryam Najafi. (2019). Cultural Competence in Nursing: A concept analysis. *International Journal of Nursing Studies, 99*, 103386–103386. https://doi.org/10.1016/j.ijnurstu.2019.103386.

57. Alexis Hoag. (2021). Black on Black Representation. New York University Law Review, 96(5), 1493–1548.

58. Patricia Arredondo, Rebecca Toporek, Sherlon Pack Brown, Janet Jones, Don C. Locke, Joe Sanchez, & Holly Stadler. (1996). Operationalization of the Multicultural Counseling Competencies. AMCD. https://doi.org/10.1002/j.2161-1912.1996.tb00288.x.

59. Arredondo et al., 1996.

60. Arredondo et al., 1996 (built from the counseling process).

61. Patrice Gordon. (2022). Reverse Mentoring: Removing barriers and building belonging in the workplace. Hachette Books.

62. Gordon, 2022.

63. Gordon, 2022.

64. Eileen A. Scallen, Sophie Sparrow & Cliff Zimmerman. (2014). Working Together in Law: Teamwork and small group skills for legal professionals. Carolina Academic Press.

65. Scallen et al. 2014.

66. Scallen et al. 2014.

67. Victor Garro-Abarca, Pedro Palos-Sanchez, & Mariano Aguayo-Camacho. (2021). Virtual Teams in Times of Pandemic: Factors that influence performance. *Frontiers in Psychology*, *12*, 1–14. https://doi.org/10.3389/fpsyg.2021.624637.

68. Sylvaine Castellano, Komes Chandavimol, Insaf Khelladi, & Mehmet A. Orhan. (2021). Impact of Self-Leadership and Shared Leadership on the Performance of Virtual R&D Teams. *Journal of Business Research*, 128, 578–586, 583. https://doi.org/10.1016/j.jbusres.2020.12.030

69. Sarah Morrison-Smith & Jaime Ruiz. (2020). Challenges and Barriers in Virtual Teams: A literature review. *SN Applied Sciences*, *2*, art. 1096. https://doi.org/10.1007/s42452-020-2801-5.

70. Morrison-Smith & Ruiz, 2020.

71. Morrison-Smith & Ruiz, 2020.

72. Namita Mangla. (2021). Working in a Pandemic and Post-Pandemic Period—Cultural intelligence is the key. *International Journal of Cross Cultural Management*, *21*(1), 53–69. https://doi.org/10.1177/14705958211002877.

73. Sean A. Newman & Robert C. Ford. (2021). Five Steps to Leading Your Team in the Virtual COVID-19 Workplace. *Organizational Dynamics*, *50*(1), 1–11. https://www.ncbi.nlm.nih.gov/pmc/articles/PMC9753911/.

74. Newman & Ford, 2021.

75. Mangla, 2021.

76. Morrison-Smith & Ruiz, 2020.

77. Morrison-Smith & Ruiz, 2020.

78. Morrison-Smith & Ruiz, 2020, p. 7.

79. Castellano et al., 2021.

80. Morrison-Smith & Ruiz, 2020.

81. Morrison-Smith & Ruiz, 2020.

82. Lena Waizenegger, Brad McKenna, Wenjie Cai, & Taino Bendz. (2020). An Affordance Perspective of Team Collaboration and Enforced Working from Home during COVID-19. *European Journal of Information Systems*, *29*(4), 429–442. https://doi.org/10.1080/0960085X.2020.1800417.

83. Newman & Ford, 2021.

84. Sternlight & Robbenolt, 2008, p. 497.

85. Cliff Zimmerman. (1999). "Thinking beyond My Own Interpretation": Teflections on collaborative and cooperative learning theory in the law school curriculum. *Arizona State Law Journal*, *31*(3), 957–1020.

86. Scallen et al., 2014.

87. Karen B. LeFevre. (1986). Invention as a Social Act. SIU Press.

88. David Chavkin. (2001). Clinical Legal Education: A textbook for law school clinical programs. Carolina Academic Press.

89. Elizabeth L. Inglehart, Kathleen Narko, & Cliff S. Zimmerman. (2003). From Cooperative Learning to Collaborative Writing in the Legal Writing Classroom. *Legal Writing: The Journal of the Legal Writing Institute*, *9*, 185–226. https://dx.doi.org/10.2139/ssrn.3192134.

90. Inglehart et al., 2003.

91. Inglehart et al., 2003.

92. Inglehart et al., 2003.

93. Inglehart et al., 2003, p. 214.

94. Inglehart et al., 2003, p. 214.

95. Inglehart et al., 2003, p. 215.

96. Inglehart et al., 2003, pp. 185–186 (* footnote original, two other footnotes omitted).

97. Gordon D. Lawrence. (2009). People Types and Tiger Stripes: Using psychological type to help students discover their unique potential. Center for Applications of Psychological Type. (Original work published 1979).

98. Brené Brown. (2019). Braving the Wilderness: The quest for true belonging and the courage to stand alone. Penguin Random House; Daniel Goleman. (1998). Working with emotional intelligence. Bantam Books. (italics original); Scallen et al., 2014.

99. Anne M. Nicotera. & Laura K. Dorsey. (2006). *Individual and Interactive Processes in Organizational Conflict*. In John G. Oetzel & Stella Ting-Toomey (Eds.), The SAGE Handbook of Conflict Communication (pp. 293–326). Sage Publications, Inc.

100. Goleman, 1998.

101. Brown, 2019.

102. Scallen et al., 2014.

103. Xuan Yu, Luxiaohe Zhang, Meilin Liu, & Bin He. (2023). The Effect of Empathy on Team Members' Moqi in Virtual Teams: A moderated mediation model. *Psychological Research and Behavior Management*, *16*, 2619–2633. https://doi.org/10.2147/PRBM.S414860.

104. Yu et al., 2023.

105. Deniz Bedir, Fatih Agduman, Fatih Bedir, & Suleyman Erim Erhan. (2023). The Mediator Role of Communication Skill in the Relationship Between Empathy, Team Cohesion, and Competition Performance in Curlers. *Frontiers in Psychology*, *14*, 1–10. https://doi.org/10.3389/fpsyg.2023.1115402.

106. Bedir et al., 2023.

CHAPTER VII

1. Daulatram B. Lund. (2003). Organizational Culture and Job Satisfaction. *Journal of Business & Industrial Marketing*, *18*(3), 219–236. https://doi.org/10.1108/0885862031047313; Muzainah Mansoor & Mahamad Tayib. (2010). An Empirical Examination of Organizational Culture, Job Stress, Job Satisfaction within the Indirect Tax Administration in Malaysia. *International journal of Business and Social Sciences*, *1*(1), 81–95.

2. Lund, 2003; Mansoor & Tayib, 2010.

3. Isabel Coronado-Maldonado & Maria-Dolores Benítez-Márquez. (2023). Emotional Intelligence, Leadership, and Work Teams: A hybrid literature review. *Heliyon*, *9*, 1–19. https://doi.org/10.1016/j.heliyon.2023.e20356; Mukmin Jufrizen, Dinda Nurmala, & Hanifah Jasin. (2021). Effect of Moderation of Work Motivation on the Influence of

Organizational Culture on Organizational Commitment and Employee Performance. *International Journal of Business Economics (IJBE)*, *2*(2), Article 2.

4. Gerald P. Macdaid, M. U. Fields & J. B. Reid (n.d.). Building a Living Type Table (p. 9). [Table]. https://www.capt.org/catalog/MBTI-Book-20040.htm; Isabel Briggs Myers & Mary H. McCaulley. (1985). Manual: A Guide to the Development and Use of the Myers-Briggs Type Indicator, p. 36. Consulting Psychologists Press.

5. MacDaid (n.d.); Myers & McCaulley, 1985, p. 36.

6. MacDaid (n.d.); Myers & McCaulley, 1985, p. 37.

7. MacDaid (n.d.); Myers & McCaulley, 1985, p. 37.

8. Tom Rath. (2007). Strengths Finder 2.0. Gallup Press; Daniel J. Siegel. (2010). Mindsight: The new science of personal transformation. Bantam. (Original work published 2009).

9. Bill George. (2003). Authentic Leadership: Rediscovering the secrets to creating lasting value. Jossey-Bass; Bill George. (2015). Discover Your True North (1st ed.). Wiley.

10. Richard Boyatzis & Annie McKee. (2005). Resonant Leadership: Renewing yourself and connecting with others through mindfulness, hope, and compassion. Harvard Business School Press; Annie McKee, Richard Boyatzis, & Fran Johnston. (2008). Becoming a Resonant Leader: Develop your emotional intelligence, renew your relationships, sustain your effectiveness. Harvard Business Review Press.

11. McKee et al., 2008, p. 25.

12. Rom Brafman. (2008, Aug. 18). Does Authenticity Lead to Happiness?. Psychology Today. https://www.psychologytoday.com/us/blog/dont-be-swayed/200808/does-authenticity-lead-happiness; Astrid Emmerich & Thomas Rigotti. (2017). Reciprocal Relations between Work-Related Authenticity and Intrinsic Motivation, Work Ability and Depressivity: A two-wave study. *Frontiers in Psychology*, *8*, 307–307. https://doi.org/10.3389/fpsyg.2017.00307; Susan R. Jones, Yoolee Choe Kim, & Kristan Cilente Skendall. (2012). (Re-)Framing Authenticity: Considering multiple social identities using autoethnographic and intersectional approaches. *Journal of Higher Education*, *83*, 698–724. https://www.tandfonline.com/doi/pdf/10.1080/00221546.2012.11777263?-casa_token=ASuHmS98YbwAAAAA:iynHAzwZ333H27OjPshBuol3Z853lpthecEhzVmk4xR9URIp5F7loU0qNj5EGFLS0qyD_VWHob6C; Scott. B. Kaufman. (2016, June 21). Grit and Authenticity. Scientific American Blog Network. https://blogs.scientificamerican.com/beautiful-minds/grit-and-authenticity/; Julie Ménard & Luc Brunet. (2011). Authenticity and Well-Being in the Workplace: A mediation model. *Journal of Managerial Psychology*, *26*(4), 331–346. https://doi.org/10.1108/02683941111124854.

13. Daniel Goleman, Richard Boyatzis, & Annie McKee. (2002). Primal Leadership: Realizing the power of emotional intelligence. Harvard Business Review Press.

14. Douglas Linder & Nancy Levit. (2014). The Good Lawyer: Seeking quality in the practice of law. Oxford University Press, USA.

15. Tomas Chamorro-Premuzic. (2019). Why Do So Many Incompetent Men Become Leaders? (and how to fix it), p. 41–55. Havard Business Review Press.

16. Bradley Owens & David Heckman. (2016). How Does Leader Humility Influence Team Performance? Exploring the mechanisms of contagion and collective promotion focus. *Academy of Management Journal*, *59*, 1088–1111, 1089. https://doi.org/10.5465/amj.2013.0660.

17. Amy C. Edmonson & Derrick P. Bransby (2023). Psychological Safety Comes of Age: Observed themes in an established literature. *Annual Review of Organizational Psychology and Organizational Behavior*, *10*, 55–78.

18. Cory Stieg. (2020, Oct. 5). "Psychological safety" at Work Improves Productivity—Here are 4 ways to get it, according to a Harvard expert, para. 2. CNBC Make It. https://www.cnbc.com/2020/10/05/why-psychological-safety-is-important-at-work-and-how-to-create-it.html.

19. David C. Bauman. (2013). Leadership and the Three Faces of Integrity. *The Leadership Quarterly*, *24*(3), 414–426. https://doi.org/10.1016/j.leaqua.2013.01.005.

20. Amos S. Engelbrecht, Gardielle Heine, & Bright Mahembe. (2017). Integrity, Ethical Leadership, Trust, and Work Engagement. *Leadership & Organization Development Journal*, *38*(3), 368–379; Mehdi Yazdanshenas & Mehdi Mirzaei. (2023). Leadership Integrity and Employees' Success: Role of ethical leadership, psychological capital, and psychological empowerment. *International Journal of Ethics and Systems*, *39*(4), 761–780. https://psycnet.apa.org/doi/10.1108/LODJ-11-2015-0237.

21. Steven L. Grover & Robert H. Moorman. (2007). Grasping the Meaning and Interpretation of Integrity in Business Leadership. *European Management Journal*, *25*(3), 167–170; Manjit Monga. (2016). Meaning of Integrity from the Upper Echelons' Perspective. *The Journal of Developing Areas*, *50*(6), 333–340. https://doi.org/10.1353/jda.2016.0126.

22. Bill George. (2003). Authentic Leadership: Rediscovering the secrets to creating lasting value. Jossey-Bass.

23. Bil George. (2015). Discover Your True North (1st ed.). Wiley.

24. George, 2015; Dan P. McAdams. (2006). The Redemptive Self: Stories Americans live by. Oxford University Press. https://doi.org/10.1093/acprof:oso/9780195176933.001.0001.

25. Lawrence S. Krieger & Kennon M. Sheldon. (2015). What Makes Lawyers Happy: Data-driven prescription to redefine professional success. *George Washington Law Review*, *83*(2), 554–627. https://heinonline.org/HOL/Page?public=true&handle=hein.journals/gwlr83&div=17&start_page=554&collection=journals.

26. Many people have written about the formation of professional identity in legal education and connected that formation to leadership. See, for example: Susan Swaim Daicoff. (2015). Lawyer, Form Thyself: Professional identity formation strategies in legal education, professional responsibility, and experiential courses. *Regent University Law Review*, *27*(2), 205–224; Larry O. Natt Gantt, II, & Benjamin V. Madison III. (2015). *Teaching Knowledge, Skills, and Values of Professional Identity Formation*. In Deborah Maranville, Lisa Radtke Bliss, Carolyn Wilkes Kaas, Antoinette Sedillo Lopez (Eds.), Building on Best Practices: Transforming legal education in a changing world. Carolina Academic Press; Benjamin V. Madison III. (2017). Professional Identity and Professionalism. *ABA's Professional Lawyer*, *24*(3), https://ssrn.com/abstract=3033314; Donald C. Peters & Martha M. Peters. (2014). Using Psychological Type Theory to Help Law Students Develop Professional Identity. *Regent University Law Review*, *27*, 255; David I. C. Thomson. (2015). "Teaching" Formation of Professional Identity. *Regent University Law Review*, *27*, 303–337; Cliff Zimmerman. (2025) [Forthcoming]. The Hidden Curriculum and the Discounting of Students' Identity: The sources of disaffection and the challenge in formation of professional identity; Mary Walsh Fitzpatrick & Rosemary Queenan. (2020). Professional Identity Formation, Leadership, and Exploration of Self. *University of Missouri-Kansas City Law Review*. https://dx.doi.org/10.2139/ssrn.3719354.

27. Cliff Zimmerman. (2025) [Forthcoming].

28. Brené Brown. (2019). Braving the Wilderness: The quest for true belonging and the courage to stand alone. Penguin Random House; George, 2003.

29. Linder & Levit, 2014.
30. Linder & Levit, 2014, p. 52.
31. Larson, 2020.
32. Brown, 2019; Erik H. Erikson. (1994). Identity and the Life Cycle (Rev. ed.). W.W. Norton & Co.
33. Brown, 2019, p. 46.
34. George, 2003; George, 2013.
35. Linder & Levit, 2014.
36. Linder & Levit, 2014.
37. Eileen A. Scallen, Sophie Sparrow, & Cliff Zimmerman. (2014). Working Together in Law: Teamwork and small group skills for legal professionals. Carolina Academic Press.
38. Derald Wing Sue, Christina M. Capodilupo, Gina C. Torino, Jennifer M. Bucceri, Aisha Holder, Kevin L. Nadal, & Marta Esquilin. (2007). Racial Microaggressions in Everyday Life: Implications for clinical practice. *American Psychologist*, *62*(4), 271–286. https://psycnet.apa.org/doi/10.1037/0003-066X.62.4.271.

Index

A

ABC Model of Human Functioning, 98
Achievement orientation, 23, 27, 28, 77, 78, 108–110, 127, 158, 208
Achor, Shawn, 115
Adaptability/Adaptive leadership, 23, 27, 77, 78, 106–108, 127, 158, 177
Arredondo, Patricia, 206
Attentional deployment, 62, 89
Authentic Leadership, 237, 244, 247, 250, 264

B

Boyatzis, Richard, xv, 21, 23, 78, 127, 158, 249
Brown, Brené, 44, 125, 128, 194, 264, 265

C

Cognitive appraisal, 62
Cognitive fusion, 64
Courage, xxix, 37, 138, 196, 237, 247, 250, 251, 264–266
Cultural competency, 140
Cultural relativity, 205

D

DasGupta, Sayantani, 156
Defining moments, 23, 24, 42–44, 53–58, 63, 190, 248
Diversity, Equity, Inclusion, and Engagement (DEIE); See cultural competency

E

Ellis, Albert, 98
Emotional and Social Competency Inventory (ESCI), 22, 27
Emotional Intelligence (EI); See relationship management; See self-awareness; See self-management; See social awareness
- Frameworks
  - Salovey-Mayer model, 21
  - Goleman model, 21–23, 77
  - the Bar-On model, 21
- And work performance, 199

Empathy; See social awareness
Explanatory Style, 92–94, 105
Extrinsic Values/intrinsic values; See Values

F

Five Dysfunctions of a Team, 199, 200
Five Practices of Empathy, 137, 138, 146, 162, 164–167

G

Gardner, Howard, 20
George, Bill, xv, 247, 258
Goleman, Daniel
  Goleman Model, 21–23, 77
  Emotional Self-Control, 23, 27, 78, 84, 127, 158

H

Happiness Advantage, 114, 115
Heckman, David, 252
Humility, xix, xxiii, 36, 155–157, 173, 204, 205, 207, 226, 237, 239, 240, 243, 250–255, 257, 258, 265, 268

I

Influencers, 42, 43, 53, 54, 57, 63, 190, 236, 248, 260, 269
"Inside-Out" Leadership, 128
IQ, xxiii, 19, 20, 36, 58, 60, 136

K

Krznaric, Roman, 137

L

Lencioni, Patrick, 199, 200
Listening; See social awareness
Loneliness, 37, 173, 174, 176–179

M

Mantra, 105, 106, 112, 258
McKee, Annie, xv, 249
Meditation, 25, 61, 64, 163, 209
Mental health
  and law school, 124
  and lawyers, xxii, xxvii, xxviii, xxx, xxxii, xxxiii, 3, 8, 14, 50, 64, 84, 108, 109, 130, 135, 145, 157, 195, 197, 203, 216, 218, 219, 249, 265
Metacognition, 64, 98
Mindfulness, xxii, xxiii, 26, 28, 36, 40, 58, 61, 64–66, 72, 77, 117, 137, 146, 150, 163, 186, 198, 206, 234, 239, 248, 249, 268
Modus operandi (MO), 85
Mood boost, 92
Multicultural leadership, three competencies of, 206–07
Myers-Briggs Type Indicator (MBTI)
  Benefits, xxv, 19, 118, 145, 168, 174, 177, 178, 191, 203, 212, 216–218, 226

N

Narrative humility, 155–157, 204, 205, 255
Neuroplasticity, 58, 77

O

Owens, Brad, 252

P

Personal narrative, xxiii, 24, 41–47, 49, 50, 52, 53, 56–58, 204, 237, 248, 250, 260, 261, 269
Polarized Thinking, 100
Positive affirmations, 112
Professional identity, 24, 52, 57, 80, 237, 250, 251, 262, 269

R

Radical Listening, 137, 138, 150, 152, 153, 255
Relationship management
  Four-stage model of relationship management, 188
  Loneliness, 37, 173, 174, 176–179
  Managing conflict, 173, 226
  MBTI, xvii, 40, 52, 66–72, 184, 216, 217, 224, 236, 245
  Trust
    And leadership, xxi, xxiii, xxv, 10, 35, 36, 44, 121, 133, 179, 195, 212, 250, 252, 258
    And virtual teams, 199, 212, 216

Building, xix, 10, 31, 37, 39, 50, 67, 77, 134–137, 140, 141, 144, 145, 148, 149, 153, 157, 171–173, 175, 178, 180, 181, 183, 184, 189, 192, 194, 197, 199–201, 204, 206, 212, 213, 215, 217–220, 230, 238, 248, 249, 256, 263, 266, 267
Teamwork, xv, 23, 30, 69, 78, 122, 127, 133, 158, 160, 178, 198, 199, 216, 217, 219–223, 226, 227, 229, 234, 236, 240
Resilience, 94, 95, 178, 234, 264
Resonant Leadership, 237, 247, 249, 250
Response flexibility, 64

S

Self-awareness
Deep insight, 23, 24, 27, 40–43
Mindfulness, xxii, xxiii, 26, 28, 36, 40, 58, 61, 64–66, 72, 77, 117, 137, 146, 150, 163, 186, 198, 206, 234, 239, 248, 249, 268
Present moment awareness, 42
Relation to psychological assessment, xxiv, 40, 66
Two branches, 27, 40, 121, 132
Self-Determination Theory, xxx
Self-management
Fire and brakes, 28, 76, 77, 80–82, 119, 121, 122, 201, 251, 263, 264
Re-appraisal, 90
Regulating attention, 83
Suppression, 90, 91
Seligman, Martin, 92
Social awareness
Application of, xxix, 216, 228
Empathy
Building/Five practices, xix, 10, 31, 37, 39, 50, 67, 77, 134 et seq.
Defined, xx, xxiii, xxiv, xxvii, 20, 39, 57, 64, 174, 203, 240–242, 244, 253
Listening, 11, 29, 30, 35, 106, 124, 137, 138, 150–153, 155, 158, 168, 255, 257, 266
Radical, 137, 138, 150, 152, 153, 255
Social Capital, 174, 178, 215
Social Learning Theory, 253
Socially responsible culture, 203

T

Tan, Chade-Meng, 126, 137, 159
Teamwork Benefits of, xxv, 145, 168, 177, 178, 217
Twenty-first century leadership
Meaning, xxi, xxxvii, 24–26, 65, 71, 83, 86, 87, 101, 105, 117, 195, 214, 217, 224, 243, 264
And authenticity, 11, 12, 237, 248, 250, 251, 268
And resonance, 249, 251
And humility, 205, 207, 265, 268
And integrity, 259, 268
And identity, xxi
And trust, 90, 226, 237, 239, 250, 251
And values, xxix, xxxii, 24, 41, 42, 44, 46, 49, 72, 73, 113, 122, 178, 189, 210, 248, 260, 261

V

Values; See twenty-first century leadership
Extrinsic, xix, xxiv, xxx, xxxii, 8, 39, 51, 53, 110, 260
Intrinsic, xix, xxv, xxx, xxxii, 8, 51, 109, 110, 260
Vulnerability, 11, 12, 107, 141, 150, 153–155, 193, 194, 196, 199, 203, 207, 226, 228, 237, 250, 251, 259, 262, 264, 266

W

Wechsler, David, 21

About the Authors

ROB DURR, Ph.D., is a Licensed Psychologist and Founder of Carolina Psychological Assessment Center (CPAC), a psychological services practice based in Asheville, NC. He is an Executive Coach and Adjunct Professor, Northwestern University Pritzker School of Law. Dr. Durr specializes in executive coaching and leadership assessment based in psychological science and emotional intelligence. He has consulted closely with C-Suite executives across a range of industries on a variety of leadership development initiates and is a trusted advisor. Prior to starting the CPAC, Dr. Durr was a full-time Psychologist at Northwestern University where he held an appointment in both the Health Center and the Law School. He has taught multiple undergraduate and graduate-level courses at Northwestern University and worked closely with the Schools of Medicine, Engineering, and Law to develop evidence-based emotional intelligence, wellness, and leadership programs. He has published in both law and psychology journals and presented nationally on various leadership and well-being topics. Dr. Durr lives in the southern Appalachian mountains in Asheville with his wife and three daughters where he enjoys coaching youth sports, having backyard bonfires, and soaking up the expansive arts and natural beauty of the region.

CLIFF ZIMMERMAN is a Professor of Practice at Northwestern University Pritzker School of Law. Prior to teaching, he was a civil litigator in Chicago focused primarily on police misconduct, free expression, and anti-discrimination cases. He teaches across a wide range of subjects, all of which connect the substance of practice to personal and professional development in identity and leadership. He served for more than a dozen years as Associate Dean and Dean of Students at Northwestern, developing innovative programming to support students and develop essential skills for success in the profession and life. He is co-author of *Working Together in the Law: Teamwork and Small Group Skills for Legal Professionals* and numerous articles on legal education and has presented nationally and internationally in many areas including formation of professional identity in the law. He facilitates regular mindfulness and running sessions with the students, both of which are intrinsically related to complementing their legal and life skills. He has run races in nearly every state and completed ten marathons to date.